Studies in
Salvation History

PRENTICE-HALL INTERNATIONAL, INC., *London*
PRENTICE-HALL OF AUSTRALIA, PTY., LTD., *Sydney*
PRENTICE-HALL OF CANADA, LTD., *Toronto*
PRENTICE-HALL OF INDIA (PRIVATE) LTD., *New Delhi*
PRENTICE-HALL OF JAPAN, INC., *Tokyo*

C. LUKE SALM, F.S.C.

Chairman, Department of Theology, Manhattan College

Studies in Salvation History

Prentice-Hall, Inc. *Englewood Cliffs, New Jersey*

Nihil obstat:
James F. Rigney, S.T.D.
CENSOR LIBRORUM

Imprimatur:
✠ Francis Cardinal Spellman
ARCHBISHOP OF NEW YORK

February 27, 1964

Current printing (last digit):
13 12 11 10 9 8 7 6 5 4

LIBRARY OF CONGRESS CATALOG CARD NO.: 64-18184
PRINTED IN THE UNITED STATES OF AMERICA: C-85849

Preface

In the years since the publication by Pius XII of the Encyclical *Divino afflante Spiritu* in 1943, Catholic biblical studies have advanced so far as to constitute one of the most progressive and creative scholarly movements in the Church today. American scholars, trained in the great centers at Rome and Jerusalem, have made significant contributions to this advance, and many of them have willingly sacrificed time and convenience to make the results of their research generally known. This they have done during summers, vacation periods, and over weekends at conferences, conventions, and workshops sponsored by a variety of learned and educational societies whose members have occasion to come into vital contact with the word of God. The excellent papers delivered at these sessions have remained buried in "Proceedings" too long; it is the purpose of this volume to bring them to light and to make them available to a wider audience capable of profiting from the riches they contain.

The choice of articles for this collection was limited to those that originated in such circumstances. Thus, no attempt was made to include articles from publications, for example, such as *The Catholic Biblical Quarterly*. Although some of the articles here have since found publication in learned journals, all of them were originally prepared to bring the problems and findings of contemporary scripture studies to an interested, educated, but not technically minded audience. Some are survey articles; others are more detailed and provocative. Some are fully developed and documented; others are brief but incisive statements of a scriptural theme. All of them reflect in one way or another the best of contemporary American biblical scholarship.

This collection is not intended primarily for the professional or research scholar. Accordingly, the footnotes of the original papers have in most cases been considerably reduced, especially where references are made to very technical or foreign works not usually available to the general reader or student. Footnotes have been retained, however, where they would serve as a source of useful bibliography, where they further explain or elaborate some point made by the author, or where the sense of a passage or scholarly integrity obviously demands the citation of a source. Editing, likewise, has been limited to necessary cuts, some title changes, and deletion of remarks intended only for the original audience.

The biblical movement has gone forward, but not without misunderstanding. Too often problems arise from an unwise and irresponsible popularization of detailed conclusions espoused by this or that scholar without sufficient preparation of the audience in question to understand the background and principles upon which such conclusions are based. It is hoped that the carefully reasoned and richly documented articles in this collection will help the nonprofessional in this field to appreciate the integrity and responsible scholarship of the authors, their deep devotion to Christ and His Church, and the very positive tone of the conclusions they propose. In this way, the unwise and unfortunate popularization against which the Holy See warns will have been obviated; in the present anthology the work of popularization is in the hands of those most qualified to achieve it, the biblical scholars themselves.

The editor wishes to acknowledge his deep gratitude to the many persons and organizations whose help and support have made this project possible: to the Catholic Theological Society of America (St. John's University, Jamaica 32, N.Y.), to the Society of Catholic College Teachers of Sacred Doctrine (Regis College, Weston 93, Mass.), to the Liturgical Conference (3428 Ninth St., N.E., Washington 17, D.C.) for wholesale permissions to reproduce their copyrighted materials; to Fides Publishers and the editor of *Apostolic Perspectives* for permission to use two articles from their September-October 1960 issue; to the Basilian Fathers of Toronto and the editor of *The Basilian Teacher* for permission to use three articles from their February 1961 issue; to the editor of *Thought* for permission to include the significant paper of Monsignor Myles Bourke as revised for publication in the Spring 1964 issue of that distinguished voice of Fordham University; and, most of all, to the authors themselves who, without exception, manifested willingness and enthusiasm for this wider diffusion of their valuable work.

C. Luke Salm, F.S.C.
Manhattan College

Contents

C. LUKE SALM, F.S.C.

Introduction to Salvation History

Salvation history has become the unifying theme that dominates biblical studies today. Sacred scripture, in fact, is itself sacred history or salvation history. In the articles that comprise this collection the expression occurs often, sometimes in connection with the German *Heilsgeschichte* which it translates. Salvation history is a special sort of history; it records the "mighty works of God" rather than of men. Some general introduction into this specialized history and its principal themes is necessary if the more detailed studies that follow are to be properly understood. The wear and tear on theological terminology is such that the reader already familiar with this theme will find that fresh approaches are always necessary to rescue even the best expressions from the meaninglessness of cliché.

The Problem. Before we can hope to understand the answer to anything, the solution to any difficulty, we must first understand what the problem or the question is. The meaning of salvation cannot be grasped apart from the problem of evil—physical and moral evil—for it is evil or failure that poses the question to which salvation is the answer.

The problem of evil is not an exclusively religious problem. It is a human problem; we might even say that it is *the* human problem. Sooner or later all men experience failure in their lives: the physical failures that go with disease, catastrophe, suffering, and death most obviously. More subtly but no less forcefully men come to recognize that they also fail precisely as men: by ignorance and error, by animal behavior, through betrayal of others and of themselves, by resistance or *hybris* against the divine. Strangely enough some men argue against the very existence of God because they cannot explain the existence of evil in men.

The Bible knows not only the solution, which is salvation, but also the problem, which is failure. In its theology of origins, Genesis makes clear that the cosmos, the earth, and everything in it, man included, all come from God and are therefore good. Whatever evil there is in the world, whether it be the moral evil of sin or the physical evils of toil, suffering, and death, these have their origin in man's disobedience to God. Evil is not God's invention, but man's. The Old Testament especially is preoccupied with this problem. Job and Qoheleth (Ecclesiastes) and many of the Psalms develop the complexities: if suffering comes from sin, why do the wicked seem to prosper while the just fail? Before it supplies an answer, the Bible faces up realistically to the question.

Human Solutions. The problem of evil and failure is so completely a part of the human condition that it is probably true to say that every thinking man subscribes to some theory or plan of salvation. Men very often have quite explicit notions, not only of what they want to be saved *from*—failure as structures, as men, and as persons—but also what they would be saved *for*—self-fulfillment in one form or another.

The hedonist discovers that he can alleviate the problem of evil through pleasure and may even entertain the idea, for a while at least, that ultimate salvation can be found along these lines. The secular humanist bases his hopes on the spread of culture and a sense of human dignity; the political optimist looks more to world federations and international cooperation; the Buddhist tries to escape from his materiality and seeks to attune himself to the divine; the existentialist despairs of the problem and embraces, for all it is worth, the experience of the here and now.

God's Solution. What sacred scripture tells us is that this problem, human in its origin, is incapable of human solution. The loving God, giver of life and Father of all men, so wills to save man from his self-inflicted dilemma that He lovingly breaks into human history to achieve for man what man cannot effect for himself. God has a plan for man's salvation, a plan that He works for man in man's way —through human mediators—in man's time—through human history —respecting man's dignity—leaving human free choice intact.

Yet the plan remains God's and must be accepted on God's terms. Man is led gradually by God's revealing love to recognize that the solution cannot be conceived in merely human terms, described in human categories, or achieved in this world alone. God's plan remains

God's—supernatural, therefore as the theologians say—and looks for its final solution in a consummation and fulfillment that is literally "out of this world."

God's Word. God instructs man in the details of His plan little by little. He uses men in this process—intermediaries or mediators as they are called—who bring the word of God's salvation to their fellow men. God's word as it is in God is timeless and infinite, but it speaks its living and effectual message to men in human accents: through the patriarchs, the prophets, and the inspired authors of God's sacred book. But finally God speaks in time His own personal and eternal Word who becomes "mortal man and pitches His tent among us." Through His incarnate Word, God reveals and effects the plan of our salvation.

Man's Response. God invites men to attend to His word and to respond. That response is called faith. Faith means belief, but it also means surrender, commitment, sacrifice, trust. It means that man says a total and personal "yes" to God's word. Abraham in faith responded to God's word to the point of sacrificing his only son; that faith was his covenant response to God's promise and choice. God made a covenant with Moses, also, that was celebrated in the sprinkling of the blood of life and ratified by the Israelites who replied in faith: "Everything the Lord has said, we will do." God in love renewed the covenant with David and his house; the Israelites, over a rocky history of alternate fidelity and infidelity, could seek salvation in their covenant faith. The Word incarnate sheds His blood "for the remission of sins" in the "new and eternal covenant" to which the Christian responds in faith, hope, and love.

The Plan Succeeds. There is no evidence that any human plan of salvation has ever worked: not generally, at any rate, and not for long. The hedonist becomes jaded, the Buddhist loses contact, the secular humanist and political optimist are disillusioned, and the existentialist talks of suicide. But God's plan has worked. The man, Jesus, grappled on Calvary with the forces of evil, physical and moral. Incapable Himself of sin, He was yet victimized by sin: betrayed, beaten, abandoned, lied about, spat upon, and mocked; He suffered intensely, died, and was buried. Evil, physical and moral, that day seemed to enjoy another in a long and seemingly endless series of triumphs over a man.

But that was the last time, really. The man Jesus, much perhaps to everyone's surprise, arose from the experience of death transformed in body and soul. Death and sin at last had met their match and would "no longer have dominion over Him." In His risen glory and ascension to the Father, Jesus as much as says "It happened once; it can happen again." (The assumption of Mary, body and soul, shows that.) Here, then, is humanity saved, saved *from* any possibility of being victimized by sin or death, saved *for* the fulfillment and consummation of glorified union with God. God's plan for salvation works, and it works because the man Jesus who works it is personally God.

Here is the root of Christian hope and the object of Christian faith. The Christian freely associates himself with Christ in Christ's suffering and death convinced, as St. Paul says, that he will be associated in the likeness of His resurrection also.

A "Group" Plan. How is God's plan of salvation communicated to men? From the beginning, God's plan operated through men brought together in association—the assembly called out, the *qahal*, the *ekklesia*, or the church. Although applicable to the individual and always explicitly personal, God's plan works through the community. The Jewish nation was a chosen and priestly people of God, the salvation community, and every mediator—the prophet, the priest, the king, the servant, the son of man—each of them had a community dimension and impact. Jesus Himself, as the Gospels make clear, is personally the New Israel.

Christ brings the salvation of His risen life precisely in His role as the New Israel. God who became man, now, so to speak, becomes incorporated in His body which is the Church. In this mystical salvation community, in this visibly organized but invisibly united and living body of Head and members, the loving action of God's salvation descends to us through the Son and in the Holy Spirit; in this same body, the committed response of our common faith and worship ascends with the Son and in the Spirit back to the Father.

The characteristic act of this salvation community, where all these facets of God's plan are joined together, is the celebration of the Eucharist sacrifice-banquet. The active, communal, and intelligent participation in the Church's liturgy is our day-to-day act of faith in the Christian mystery. It is the divinely instituted way we have of bearing witness to the world that we know where we are going and we know where we stand at this particular moment in the history of salvation. This moment of communal action incorporates all the others—those past and those to come. We turn or are "converted" to the Lord by actually going to the church building, the physical, sanctified place where we meet God's saving presence. We hear His word and respond in faith and adoration. We participate in the renewal of Christ's self-offering to the Father and join with mind and will in the sacramental re-presentation of His passage from death to life. We feast on heavenly food and so show together the heavenly banquet of the kingdom yet to come.

The Plan Completed. Although God's plan is essentially complete in the salvation events accomplished in Christ, there are "details" that must still be worked out. We yet pray, "Thy kingdom come," by which we express our hope for the ultimate consummation in transformed glory when all creation will be made new in God. Meanwhile, despite Christ's victory, the forces of sin and death have a reprieve. Moral and physical failure is still very much part of the human condition. The Christian knows that this is only temporary, yet he is caught in the strange situation of fighting a war that has already been won. Possessing the life of Christ in grace, the Christian has in one sense already risen; but the possibility of failure is always there, even to the danger of ultimate loss.

Hope, then, is the characteristic virtue of the Christian: hope that the triumph he already possesses in grace will be actuated in glory; hope that the resurrection of Christ will be personally experienced as his own; hope that the body of Christ of which he is a member will be filled with the fulness of its Head; hope, that is, for salvation, when the man-originated problem of evil will have its final solution in God's saving love, when sin and death and failure of every kind will be no more.

This, in its broadest outline, is the scope and essence of the salvation history recorded in the sacred scripture. Direct contact with that inspired word is the first and best way to encounter the saving message. But there is a place, too, for the serious and penetrating scholarship in the articles that follow. The principles and details of interpretation they contain can serve, as their authors undoubtedly hope, to prepare us better to receive and to respond to God's word in its authentic voice.

Studies in
Salvation History

I. INTRODUCTORY STUDIES

"From thy infancy thou hast known the Sacred Writings, which are able to instruct thee unto salvation. . . ." (2 Timothy 3:15)

THOMAS BARROSSE, C.S.C.

How to Approach the Bible

The alert reader will find in this introductory article a discussion of questions such as these: What is meant by saying that Judaism and Christianity are historical religions? How is the Bible a record of God's intervention in human history? How is this record traced through the various books of the Old and the New Testaments? How does the history of a people become a record of the gradual formation of a Church? How should we read the Bible? How different is that from reading other books? Is it possible to keep track of the literary forms? Can we learn to recognize the main ideas in the Bible?

Father Barrosse is professor of Sacred Scripture at Holy Cross College in Washington, D.C., and the author of *God Speaks to Men.*

The Contents of the Bible

An altogether unique property of Judaism and Christianity setting them off among the world's great religions is their *historical* character. The other religions are sets of beliefs and practices that have no essential connection with any particular time or person. Even if we were to hold that no one but Gautama Buddha could have formulated primitive Buddhism's tenets and practices, the person of the Buddha and the time he proposed his teaching are inci-

In its original form this article was part of a paper entitled "Aims and Methods in Teaching Scripture in the High School and College" that was delivered at the 1960 Christmas Conference of the Basilian Fathers in Toronto and was published originally in *The Basilian Teacher.* It is reprinted here with permission.

dental to the teaching itself. Perhaps only Mohammed with his particular background and his peculiar temperament could have conceived primitive Islam's creed and code. But the person of the prophet is accidental to his teaching. It would still be the same had it been proclaimed by another in altogether different circumstances. Israelite religion, however, rested on the Exodus from Egypt and the Sinai convenant as historical facts. If the God of Israel had never made the covenant with the ancestors, then there would no longer have been any meaning to Israel's observing the Ten Commandments, which were simply the terms of the covenant (or at least the meaning of such an observance would have been essentially altered). Israelite hopes rested on David's dynasty and the divine promise made to it as historical realities: through that line Israel hoped for salvation. As regards Christianity, unless Jesus of Nazareth was God incarnate, unless He died and rose, "your faith is vain," as St. Paul remarks, "and you are still in your sins" (1 Cor 15:17). These and other historical facts are altogether essential to the Judaeo-Christian religion.[1] God's successive interventions in the history of man pertain to the very fiber of Old Testament and New Testament religion.

The Bible is for the most part the record of these divine interventions. The accounts of God's interventions in Israel's early days were surely the nucleus of the Old Testament around which the rest was assembled. Originally recited at the various Israelite shrines on the occasion of religious festivities, they date from the earliest days in Canaan.[2] They were probably also the first parts of the Bible to be set down in writing. When other types of literature such as laws and chants became an official part of Mosaic religion, they were incorporated into the story of the beginnings. Thus, though the laws occupy a larger part of the Pentateuch than the narratives, they are so completely woven into these latter that the first five books of the Old Testament still retain the over-all appearance of a narrative rather than a collection of laws.

The story of Israel's beginnings is continued through the books of Joshua, Judges, Samuel, Kings, Chronicles, Ezra, and Nehemia. These books form the axis around which the prophetic books must be assembled. Most of these books come substantially from the period of the Exile and the century or two immediately preceding or following it. They are not abstract treatises on religion or detached predictions about the future but the collected preachings of men sent by God to change the course of His people's history. The ministry, the writings, and the oracles of these men cannot be understood independently of the concrete situation in which they lived, worked, and preached.

The sapiential literature, consisting in general of the latest Old Testament books, is more timeless or less "dated" than the rest of the Old Testament. But it makes up a relatively small portion of the Bible, and even it finds God's wisdom best illustrated in His successive interventions in the earlier history of His people.

The New Testament is no less a record of divine intervention than the Old. Christianity was first preached by the apostles (the Book of Acts is our source)[3] as a proclamation that God had made His definitive intervention in man's history through and in Jesus of Nazareth. That proclamation took the form of a narrative: it alluded to the preaching and miracles of Jesus, recalled His passion and death, and announced His Resurrection, concluding to His Messiahship. Our written Gospels are simply expansions of this basic proclamation, or kerygma. The epistles not only presuppose a knowledge of the Gospel—at least the preached Gospel—by their readers, but generally purpose merely to deepen one or another facet of the understanding of Christ's doctrine, work, or person which they already have from the Gospel itself. The remaining New Testament books, the Acts and the Apocalypse, show the Church Christ launched continuing His work in the world, or better, they show the later believer that the faith he has accepted goes back by unbroken historical succession to Jesus Himself. The Apocalypse looks to the future consummation when God's final intervention in man's history will achieve its full scope.

The Bible, then, is substantially a record of successive divine interventions that gradually formed Old Testament Judaism and Christianity. It is history, sacred history, or—to use a term that has become more or less technical—salvation history. If we are to present what the Bible has to say—the Bible's message, if you will—how else can we do it than historically?

To some, an historical approach means rehearsing event after isolated event and perhaps even getting lost in a maze of only loosely connected happenings. Whatever may be said about the interconnection of the events of profane history, be it political, economic, military, or cultural, sacred history is not a succession of more or less unrelated divine deeds. "God's gifts . . . are without repentance," says St. Paul (Rom 11:29). The Lord does not change His mind.

Each successive divine intervention in man's history brings that history closer and closer to the realization of the one same unchanging divine goal. Salvation history has all the continuity of the growth of a child into adulthood, and for the Christian who sees the term toward which the whole process is moving, the final goal toward which each of the earlier steps is directed is clear.

In the patriarchal period Israel was a family—a family with a faith in their God and confidence in His designs on their future. With Moses Israel has grown into a people whose faith and trust fix or concretize themselves in a covenant with their God and who receive a moral code to live by. With David they become a single united society, a kingdom, and in him possess an ideal. Through the efforts of the prophets the catastrophe of the Exile turns them into a Church, a society in which the religious element comes to the foreground and the material (political and economic) slips into the background without, however, wholly disappearing as yet. Finally, with Christ they become a Church in the full sense of the term or, even more, an organism, and the creed and code and cult of God's people are transformed into the faith and charity and sacraments of God's sons.

Presenting the Bible as history, then, means presenting it as a record of the gradual fashioning and growth of Abraham's offspring into the Church—or, rather, the Mystical Body—of Christ. And this is precisely what the Bible is. Can any other presentation offer the Bible's contents as the Bible itself offers them? Can any other approach so effectively present the Bible for what it really is? Perhaps, too, no other presentation will so fully bring out the relevancy of the Old Testament for the Christian. "The Law" says St. Paul, "was the pedagogue that brought us to Christ" (Gal 3:24). When the Christian sees it as God's preparation of mankind for Christ, it comes to have as much meaning for him as the events of his own childhood and adolescence have for his later life. Perhaps, finally, no other presentation will so lead us to a sense of Christ as the central reality of all creation, in particular of history, and especially of our own individual lives.

Is this approach tested and tried? Yes. It is really no different from what used to be the usual way of presenting Scripture: so-called "Bible history." [4] It is the Church's own way, used through the whole patristic period: in her catechesis of candidates for baptism, she regularly took them through the Old Testament first, and then the New.[5] It was the apostles' way and that of the Church's first missionaries. Open the Acts of the Apostles and read how Peter, Paul, Stephen, and the others recount the Old Testament salvation history, climaxing it with their proclamation of Christ. . . .

How to Read the Bible

A Scripture course should teach the student what is found in the Bible; it should also teach him how to read it. The Bible is different. It cannot, therefore, be read like other books. First of all, it is inspired. This, of course, presents no problem. Though the attempts of theologians to elucidate the notion of inspiration may be many, the idea that the Scriptures in their entirety are God's word is quite simply accepted by a believer as a matter of faith, and he accordingly reads and handles them with reverence. But the Bible is also the word of men, and it is from this aspect of the sacred text that our difficulties with reading it stem. These men employed a wide variety of *literary forms* or genres, most or all of them noticeably different from those with which we are familiar. Even more basic is the difference of the *notions* with which they worked—covenant, torah, prophet, spirit, and the like—unfamiliar to our modern mind. Most basic of all is the difference of their *mentality and thought processes:* their use of hyperbole, of symbolism, of sources. . . . (Evidently, to read the Bible intelligently a person needs some appreciation of all these points.) To convey such an appreciation . . . may seem an all but impossible task. But is this really the case?

The Bible is not a hopeless hodgepodge of literary forms. They succeed one another with a fair degree of order. The chapters on the beginnings (Gen 1-11) are a collection of folk stories or, if we take the word in the sense it seems to be acquiring in modern anthropology, myths. The patriarchal accounts (Gen 12-50) are for the most part legends—and I use the word in the dictionary's sense: ostensibly historical accounts whose factuality cannot be proved or disproved but which doubtless go back, in large part at least, to the times and places of which they treat. The books from Exodus through Joshua (excepting the legislative texts and the statistics) recount the national epic: as in all epics, everything moves on the heroic plane.

From Deuteronomy or Joshua through the books of Kings we have the Deuteronomist history of pre-Exilic Israel, a collection made up largely of accounts that antedated the author, that are substantially factual, and that become more and more strictly historical as we move from the Judges through Samuel to the books of Kings: a collection composed to show from pre-Exilic Israel's history the validity of Deuteronomy's great principle that fidelity to the God of the covenant brings well-being and infidelity certain disaster. 1 and 2 Chronicles and Ezra-Nehemia are the Chronicler's presentation of the Judaean community, pre- and post-Exilic, organized around the Temple worship and under Davidic rule as the ideal realization of God's designs for men—it is an example of what we might call selective history, omitting much of the darker side of life in Judah as we know it, for example, from the books of Samuel and Kings and emphasizing the brighter in order to present this community as an ideal to later Judaism. The prophetic literature dates almost wholly from the Exile and the one or two centuries immediately preceding and following it. The Wisdom books, at least in the form in which we have them in the Old Testament, are all late.

In the New Testament the gospel-form, so different from modern biography, is found only in the books that concern themselves with recounting the ministry and glorification of Christ. The somewhat more historical Acts is the only writing concerned with directly recounting events of the Church's early years, and the highly imaginative Apocalypse is the only New Testament book concerned with a detailed discussion of the Church's future. In brief, since the various literary forms succeed one another in rather orderly fashion, a new form will be encountered practically only as Scripture study moves into the examination of a new period of sacred history. The student can be introduced to the new genre simply by way of preface to consideration of the book or books in which he finds recounted the next segment of salvation history.

If the Bible's various literary forms appear in ordered succession, so do its chief ideas. The notion of covenant is ancient, going all the way back to Sinai. It is perhaps the first key notion met with. The concepts of kingship and Messiah (in the broad sense of God's chosen king) occur only later. The notion of prophet comes to the fore still later. . . .

Probably the mentality, outlook, and style of the biblical authors are the greatest obstacle to intelligent reading of the Scriptures—even more than the key Old Testament (and New Testament) concepts, about which most readers of the Bible already have some ideas, and more than the literary forms, which can be explained and handled and studied more easily and directly than the author's mentality and style. An appreciation of Semitic love for hyperbole, of favorite biblical metaphors and symbolism, of the scriptural authors' very unmodern use of sources will probably be acquired . . . only through . . . having these things repeatedly pointed out. . . .

In short, the repeated indication of recurring manifestations of the mentality of the biblical authors and repeated references to key concepts as they occur will impress these on the student's mind and should enable him to recognize them when he reads the Bible without a teacher's help. A brief consideration of the various literary forms of biblical books as he examines each of them should at least leave him with the conviction that he cannot read them as he would read modern writing, especially modern history-writing. In this way, within limits, his study of the Bible will teach him not only what it contains but also how to read it.

These proposals may seem somewhat ambitious or complex. Really they are not. Evidently they can be implemented in only a rudimentary way on the high school level and in only a somewhat less rudimentary way at the college level, at least in a survey course that must cover the whole Bible in a single semester or year. But in substance they are merely a matter of guiding the student intelligently through the history of salvation, the story of God's salvific interventions in mankind's history culminating in Christ. They are merely a matter of helping him through the Bible, Old Testament and New, in abridged form in such a way as to enable him to see what is there and to teach him to discover what is there for himself.

References

[1] So far was this true already in Old Testament times that it gave ancient Israel a notion of history unique in the Near East. For other peoples history described a great circle, forever returning to its point of origin only to begin the cycle all over again; for Israel history had a rectilinear movement: God had made a covenant with His people, and history was the working out of that covenant.

[2] Cf. C. Stuhlmueller, "Interdependence of Old Testament Liturgy and the Bible" in *The Church Year—Proceedings of 19th North American Liturgical Week* (The Liturgical Conference, 1959), pp. 139-55 for suggestions on this liturgical origin of large parts of the Old Testament, and cf. D. Stanley, "Liturgical Influences on the Formation of the Four Gospels," *ibid.*, pp. 159-67 for the same background to our Gospels. On the origin of the Pentateuch, see the good presentation in N. McEleney, *The Law Given Through Moses—Intro-*

duction to the Pentateuch (New York: Paulist Press, 1959), or see my own *God Speaks to Men—Understanding the Bible* (Notre Dame: Fides Publishers, 1960), pp. 29-36.

[3] See Acts 2:14-41, esp. vss. 22ff.; 3:12-26; 4:8-12; 5:29-32; 7:2-60; 10:34-43; 12:16-41; and so forth. See also 2 Timothy 2:8

[4] J. Jungmann, *Handing on the Faith* (St. Louis: B. Herder Book Company, 1959), pp. 103-14.

[5] *Ibid.*, pp. 103ff.

DAVID M. STANLEY, S.J.

The Concept of Biblical Inspiration

The beginning student of theology will find in this somewhat technical but rewarding article a discussion of questions such as these: What is of faith concerning the divine inspiration of Scripture? What were the faults of the critical approach to the Bible that characterized the nineteenth century? What is outmoded in the Catholic apologetic reaction to this challenge? What are the characteristics of the newer and more psychological approach to the theology of inspiration? Why is the concept of authorship central to this problem? What are the differences between the Semitic and the Western approach to truth? What new insights into the process of inspiration are supplied by Benoit? by Coppens? by Rahner? by Brinkmann? What problems still remain for the future?

Father Stanley is Associate Professor of New Testament theology in the School of Religion at the State University of Iowa. He is the author of *The Gospel of St. Matthew* in the *New Testament Reading Guide* series.

Christianity's traditional attitude toward its sacred books, both those received as a legacy from Israel and those produced by its own apostolic writers, has always been reverently maintained by the Catholic Church as part of the deposit of faith. It is the belief that these sacred books were written under a peculiar divine influence, so that God is rightly regarded as their Author, and in consequence,

This article was originally published in the *Proceedings of the Thirteenth Annual Convention* of the Catholic Theological Society of America and is reproduced here with permission.

the Christian Bible is a normative record of those truths which God has deigned in His mercy to reveal to us.

All this, of course, is axiomatic in Catholic theology; and such a statement has the air of a truism. Yet . . . such a simple seeming statement involves not a few difficult problems. Indeed, before we can discuss these questions fruitfully, it will help to determine more accurately three notions which this statement contains: namely, What view should be taken of the Bible itself, considered as a whole? What does the word, author, signify, particularly when applied to the divine source of this written revelation? What is meant by truth from the biblical viewpoint?

The Nature of the Bible

What then is the nature of the Bible? What approach will best reveal to us the meaning of our sacred literature? There are, broadly speaking, two attitudes which have been taken, historically, to the Scriptures: the critical method, which enjoyed such a vogue in the nineteenth and early twentieth centuries; and that which Dom Célestin Charlier has called the psychological method,[1] which might also be termed the theological method.

The critical method, practiced by rationalist liberals like Wellhausen, Gunkel, Loisy, was essentially an intellectual approach in the narrow sense. Its inventors were engrossed in comparing the Bible with other forms of literature, and, often enough, intoxicated with the heady discovery that the Scriptures were very human documents. These men belonged to an age obsessed with the search for scientific objectivity, with the making of factual inventories, with the recovery and criticism of documentary sources; and they were imbued with a crusading iconoclasm bent on destroying the old-fashioned view held by so many earnest Christians that the Bible had somehow dropped ready-made from its celestial home, a kind of divine oracle without any necessary relation to time, human culture, or history.

While it would be unjust to slight the contributions made by these scholars to biblical science, it must be admitted that they were children of an age notorious as a low point in religious thought, both philosophically and theologically. It was an age blissfully unaware of the profound differences separating the culture and genius of the Semitic peoples from the thought-forms and civilization of the Greek-formed West. It suffered most of all from the fact that, in its anxiety to acquire what it considered a detached, purely scientific view of the essentially religious, personal Semitic viewpoint, it had unconsciously adopted the basically irreligious *Weltanschauung* of ancient Greece.[2]

The pernicious effects of this rationalist approach to the Bible are well known: a disdainful neglect of the divine origin of the Scriptures, an ever-increasing skepticism and infidelity manifested toward the Judaeo-Christian revelation, based on the denial of its historical character. In such circumstances, it is not surprising that biblical inspiration should become confused with that "inspiration" exhibited by the world's great literary artists who had created the classics, while inerrancy, conceived in the image and likeness of nineteenth-century liberalism, was categorically denied to the Bible.

In the face of such a destructive onslaught, the Catholic theologian bent every effort to devise an apologetic that could save the eternal values of the ancient Christian faith. Not ill-equipped, in many instances, with the scientific methods and erudition of his opponents, the Catholic scholar endeavored to turn these very weapons against their unbelieving inventors. This meant, inevitably, that the Catholic critic was forced to meet his adversary on the adversary's ground; and it need surprise no one that today many of his arguments appear as outmoded as the opinions he was trying to refute. He tended to accept the excessively idealistic view of historical and scientific truth, the quite modern concept of authorship, and, more generally, the almost exclusively intellectual approach to the Bible, characteristic of his own Greek education. I mention all this merely because it forms part of the picture of the Catholic attitude to the study of biblical inspiration prior to Pius XII's *Divino afflante Spiritu*, and not in any spirit of criticism, which would be as unfair to pioneers like Franzelin and Lagrange as it would be disrespectful to the affirmations of the Church found in encyclicals like *Providentissimus*.

What is the theological or psychological approach to the Scriptures, the newer and more comprehensive view of the Bible's meaning? It is a method that was born, partly of a generally felt dissatisfaction with the old, purely literary Higher Criticism, partly of a growing desire to recover the religious values which Christian tradition had always found in the Bible, and partly of the widening of scientific horizons by fresh discoveries in archeology, ethnology, and psychology. Scholars began to realize the necessity of attending not merely to the literary context, immediate or remote, of the inspired books, but also to the historical, cultural, racial milieux in which the Bible had been produced. They became conscious of the singular nature of Semitic thought-patterns, dominated by an existentialist interest in living reality. Where the Greek mind was haunted by the problem of the one and the many, Semitic dialectic was fascinated by the spiritual mystery of the unity of all things. It found in the symbol, rather than the abstract concept, a natural vehicle of expression.[3] The religion of the Hebrews had begun, not with a metaphysical deduction of God's existence, but with a vital, supernatural experience of the living God veiled in awful mystery upon cloud-wrapt Sinai.

This new awareness of the character of the Semitic religious genius produced in modern biblical scholarship the realization that "none of the human factors which have influenced the birth, formation, and final shape of the sacred Book can be withdrawn from the productive and formative activity of the Holy Spirit."[4] These words of Dom Charlier suggest that for a comprehensive understanding of divine inspiration we must consider the effects of this charism not only upon the written or oral sources, the various redactors and glossators of the sacred books, but upon the entire ambient culture in which God's activity had worked for generations as an energizing leaven. As Charlier remarks, "Inspiration is then infinitely more than the communication by God of a kind of mechanical influx which subordinates to it the literary activity of certain free instruments: it is the productive, all-embracing penetration, by the Holy Spirit's vivifying action, of the whole history and life of the people of God."[5]

Permit me to cite but one consequence of this new attitude which has a bearing upon the doctrine of biblical inspiration: the recently renewed interest in the spiritual sense of the Scriptures as understood and exploited by the Fathers of the Church and by the modern creation of biblical theology. This viewpoint is important for a proper study of the Bible's inspiration because it rests ultimately upon what we might call an "incarnational" conception of our sacred literature. Scripture is not the mere projection of divine ideas upon human events or human formulations, providing God's word with some sort of figurative connection with time and space. The divine scriptural word is, like the Incarnation of the personal divine Word, a profoundly real entry of God into human existence. "Just as the second person of the Trinity, the Word of God, became in every way like man, sin excepted, so the words of God (His revelation) expressed in human language are completely like human language, error apart. That is what John Chrysostom meant by his magnificent praise of the divine condescension found, as he repeatedly affirms, in the sacred books." [6] This familiar doctrine of Pius XII is a faithful echo of the patristic teaching regarding scriptural inspiration. We shall refer to it again in a moment in discussing our next point, the concept of author as applied to the Bible.

The Concept of Author in Biblical Inspiration

One of the most elusive ideas in the treatise on biblical inspiration is the notion of author, both as applied to God and to the sacred writer. Clearly, of course, it is an analogous concept, since there is question of the collaboration of God and man.

To characterize the inspired writers, the modern doctrinal affirmations of the Church have applied the very precise, modern concept of literary authorship to them. The idea of authorship entertained by the ancient world comes much closer . . . to the notion of patron—witness the Jewish custom of placing under the egis of Moses, David, and Solomon, the Law, the psalter, and the Wisdom literature.[7] Today we have perhaps a better grasp of the complexity of the process by which many of our sacred books were composed and so can solve more satisfactorily than was possible fifty years ago the questions created by modern criticism's denial of immediate literary authorship, to certain Old Testament and New Testament figures, of books traditionally regarded as their work.

As regards the divine authorship, we must re-examine the meaning of the Church's age-old assertion that "God is Author of Sacred Scripture." The expression, it appears, was first employed in the doctrinal battle waged by the fourth- and fifth-century African Church against Manichean dualism. Just as the existence of the two "authors" of the universe was denied by the councils of the period, so the one God was acknowledged as unique "author" of the new and old Covenants.[8] *Auctor* in these decrees is probably employed in its primary meaning, "producer," "originator." This seems clear from the second Council of Lyons' use of *archēgos* in the Greek text in which it simply reproduces the earlier formula.[9]

Moreover, there is need of careful investigation into the precise sense in which, in many patristic writings, Scripture is said to be divinely inspired. It may well be that these texts affirm prophetic inspiration, which does not necessarily provide a basis for God's literary authorship. In any event, we have to examine the grounds for attributing such literary authorship to God. As applied to human writers, the notion involves certain stylistic individualities which bear a close relation to a man's character, temperament, and background, qualities which cannot be applied to the divine author of Holy Writ. Accordingly, it is very much a question whether the insistence of theologians since Franzelin's day that God is literary Author of the Bible is an explanation of the dogma of inspiration, or whether this is simply a matter which was not defined.

Again, there is a very real problem connected with the assertion of the double authorship, human and divine, of Scripture. God's literary authorship in no way impairs that of the inspired writer, who cannot be reduced to the status of a secretary. In fact, God's authorship does not merely tolerate the co-operation of men: it demands it. Yet the attribution of literary authorship to God must somehow put Him in the same category as the human author. Any vague comparison seeking to describe God's activity as a kind of concursus, in which the divine causality remains transcendental, provides no basis for the kind of predication we are speaking of. We must be able to show precisely how God and man can be truly called authors of any biblical book. Nor . . . can we sufficiently explain the individual literary qualities of each hagiographer by simply stating that God permits him to work "in a free and personal manner."

How, then, describe the divine literary authorship of the Bible? How can we justify the attribution to God of authorship of books written by men? Can it be done without prejudice to the real, yet subordinate, authorship of the sacred writers?

We might attempt an answer to these questions by beginning with the notion that the Scriptures are the record of God's personal dealings with men. God's purpose in entering human history is twofold: to save men and to reveal Himself to them. This purpose was accomplished by God's giving of His Son as redeemer of men and revealer of the Father. The written record of this *Heilsgeschichte*, the Bible, is God's self-revelation. However, it is obvious that God cannot reveal Himself to men except in human language, which is only to say that God cannot reveal Himself except in terms of man's reaction to His self-revelation. In other words, God's will to have the Bible written as He intended necessarily involves the hagiographer's personal reaction, personal testimony, to God's manifestation of Himself.

Indeed, since any author always puts something of himself into his book, I think it is safe to say that the notion of self-revelation provides the basis for the analogous concept of authorship we are seeking. Since the Bible as salvation history is *primarily* God's self-revelation, God must be regarded as principal Author of Scripture. At the same time, and of necessity, the Bible, written by men, is an epiphany of those men's response of loving obedience and faith to God's message. It is also a self-revelation on the hagiographer's part, in which he records his personal reply in the dialogue between God and man which is *Heilsgeschichte*. For the human author is not a mere secretary; nor can he be, if God's aim is to be achieved. In consequence, the hagiographer must contribute something of his own: not merely his individual way of expressing the divine word (his *genus litterarium*), but also his own faith's response to God's message. The Bible is accordingly, *at one and the same time*, God's self-revelation and that of the inspired writer. While these two are to be distinguished, they must not be divided up materially, as if, for instance, Jesus' words in the Gospels are the divine element and the evangelist's remarks, the human. The entire narrative is necessarily a divine-human word. Failure to appreciate this incarnational character of Scripture has sometimes led to a wrong emphasis upon the *ipsissima verba Christi* [the literal words of Christ] as employed in theological proofs. Of course, the text contains Christ's words, but it reproduces those words as already interpreted, to a greater or lesser degree, by the evangelist. He is author no less of these logia than of the rest of his Gospel. Still these (and all the other words of Scripture) are, in the first place, God's words also, even those containing the writer's own reflections, because they constitute, in their entirety, God's chosen way of revealing Himself to men. This remains true even of those scriptural books, like the epistle to the Romans, where, it might appear, we have merely Paul's reaction to God's self-revelation. The apostle's stated aim corrects such an impression. He writes to expose "the Good News" as "God's dynamic force effecting salvation" (Rom 1:16).

Here it might help to employ the analogy provided by *Divino afflante*, to which we have already referred. God is *personally* present in history through the Incarnation of the Son, who assumed a human nature without diminshing its human spontaneity or other human perfections. On the contrary, these were immeasurably enhanced by the hypostatic union. Moreover, the only way God could enter humanity personally was by assuming a human nature without becoming a human person. Similarly, God could only be Author of Scripture through the exercise of a uniquely divine prerogative, the employment of men as real authors, not secretaries. God cannot reveal Himself, as He has willed to do, without causing the sacred writer to reveal himself, giving his individual response and expression to this divine-human work which is the Bible.

The Semitic Conception of Truth

We must now recall briefly the difference which separates the Semitic concept of truth from the Greek. Greek philosophy considers truth as the perfect conformity of the mind to reality, found properly in the speculative judgment.[10] Yet it was not through minds formed by Hellenistic culture (a rare exception might be made for the book of Wisdom and possibly Hebrews) but through the Semitic mentality that God gave us His revelation. Hence, if we wish to understand the charism of inspiration and God's purpose in bestowing it, we must appreciate Israel's attitude to truth.[11]

To the Semite, truth is essentially something which is lived. It is a matter not of speculation but of experience, and—in its deepest sense—experience of God. Knowing is basically a personal encounter. Adam "knew his wife" by having intercourse with her—one of the most personal and intimate experiences possible for a human being. Adam knew God by encountering Him personally. In the Fourth Gospel, we are urged to "live the Truth" because it pertains to the existential order of Christian living. Conversely, faith belongs to the order of doing: in fact, it is the only thing Christ commands us to "do," if we wish "to perform the works of God" (Jn 6:28-29).

It was to communicate their love of Truth (to the Semitic mind, loving and knowing are correlatives) that the inspired writers undertook their task. Their primary purpose was not the propagation of truths, the composition of a body of doctrines, but the attraction and conversion of men by exhortation, consolation, reprimand, and encouragement, so that they might "live the Truth." The Bible contains truth (one need hardly add, and nothing but truth) in our western, intellectual sense. But the value of the Scriptures, on the view of its Semitic authors, far surpassed any merely negative quality of inerrancy. It was the dialogue between God and man: a written dialogue, containing divine testimony to the living God, which sought primarily to involve men personally by eliciting their proper response in this dialogue, the whole-hearted self-commitment of man in his total being through faith, an engagement "person-to-person" with the God who acts to reveal Himself.

Recent Contributions to Inspiration Theology

The Work of Pierre Benoit

The theological thought of Pierre Benoit on scriptural inspiration is conditioned by thomistic principles and may be characterized by its emphasis upon scholastic method rather than upon the historical context in which the Bible was produced.[12]

He begins with a discussion of the instrumentality of the sacred writer, a subject to which he has made a significant contribution. He situates this instrumentality between the instrumental activity such as that of the waters of baptism, which would exclude real authorship, and that instrumental activity proper to the soul under the influence of God's natural concursus. The sacred writer is an instrument because he does not act on his initiative, nor does he receive complete knowledge of the supernatural message he expresses.[13] Yet his individuality is not suppressed: he is moved to compose his book "in a free and personal manner."[14]

There are three main points in Benoit's presentation of the nature of inspiration: (1) his distinction between prophetic and scriptural inspiration; (2) the varying effects of the charism upon the speculative and practical judgment of the human author; (3) the consequently analogous nature of scriptural inspiration.

Following St. Thomas' treatment of prophecy, we must distinguish between revelation, in which God gives both the means of representation (sensations, phantasms, ideas) and also the "light" to make a true judgment; and scriptural inspiration, where only the "light" is God-given, the inspired writer employing his own ideas and phantasms. However, to avoid the difficulties of Franzelin's system, we must again distinguish between the divine effect on the speculative and that on the practical judgment. The illumination of the speculative judgment which provides divine certitude is prophetic inspiration. On the other hand, scriptural inspiration which affects the practical judgment is primarily an impulse of the will. It directs the practical reason of the writer to carry out his purpose of writing a book. Normally, both practical and speculative intellects are inspired in varying degrees, accordingly as there is question of teaching truth. This is the first illustration of the analogous nature of the concept of inspiration. It permits Benoit to assert that while the whole Bible is inspired in every part, there can be question of the "negative privilege" of inerrancy only when there is some teaching.

The analogous nature of the concept of inspiration may be further illustrated by the way it extends proportionally to all the faculties which come into play in composing a book, as well as to the entire contents of Scripture, to all the authors and redactors who produced any given book, and to all the real senses of Scripture.[15]

Biblical inerrancy is not the final cause of inspiration, nor its sole consequence, since God did not have the Bible written merely to teach doctrine but for the spiritual guidance of its readers. How explain the so-called "errors" in the Bible? In the past, failure to distinguish inspiration clearly from revelation led to unsatisfactory solutions like the restriction of inspiration to matters of faith and morals, an exaggerated appeal to "implicit citations," or to the theory of "historical appearances." To define the limits of biblical inerrancy, formal instead of material criteria must be used. These come down to three questions: What attitude does the author adopt toward his subject? What degree of affirmation does he employ in speaking of it? How far does he demand acceptance of his views?

Only at the end of his study does Benoit refer to the study of *genera litteraria* as a solution for the problem of inerrancy. Quite frankly, one might wish he had begun with this method adopted officially by the *magisterium* which enables us to maintain the absolutely fundamental principle that the Bible contains no error. Pedagogically speaking, it has always seemed to me that this point of departure produces upon the inquirer a much healthier psychological effect.

The Contribution of Joseph Coppens

In reviewing Benoit's exposition in *Initiation Biblique*, Joseph Coppens, the celebrated Louvain scholar, criticized several points, of which three have relevance here: (1) The Bible can contain false "affirmations," provided they are not "taught";[16] (2) The "teaching" of the sacred writers is restricted to "objectively religious and supernatural truths" and to natural and profane truths which the author considers "in their religious and supernatural significance"; (3) The only kind of error excluded by inspiration is that which would compromise the objectively religious and supernatural truths of its teaching.[17]

In a subsequent article, Coppens takes issue with the three principles which we pointed out earlier as fundamental to Benoit's view of inspiration: the theory of the two-fold inspiration of the Bible (namely, the distinction between scriptural and prophetic inspiration), the distinction between judgments as speculative and practical, and the rejection of material criteria in ascertaining the author's meaning. He questions whether Benoit's subdividing of inspiration into purely scriptural and prophetic is really useful or founded in reality. He prefers to restrict prophetic inspiration to passages where there is also question of some revelation. As regards Benoit's categories of judgment, he finds the terms "speculative" and "practical" vague and inadequate: it is not evident that practical judgments never include a speculative aspect. Terminologically, Coppens would prefer to call them judgments of *apprêt* and *arrêt:* the first connoting an approximative, provisory judgment; the second, a definitive affirmation which the writer intends to teach, engaging his (and God's) authority, and demanding the reader's assent. Finally, while Coppens admits that material criteria alone are insufficient for judging the author's mind, he insists they are necessary because they include "the classical means of evaluating the doctrinal signification of a scripture text." [18]

The Thought of Karl Rahner

With the brilliant essay of Karl Rahner, a new element is introduced into the recent discussion of the nature of biblical inspiration: the historical process in which the divine influence actually operated.[19]

Rahner's thesis may be expressed as follows: The formal, predefining act of the divine Will by which God founded the Church of the apostolic age (the *Urkirche*) includes the inspiring of Scripture as one of the constitutive elements of the process by which the Church was divinely instituted. The Scriptures were not merely occasioned by the foundation of the *Urkirche*, nor were they a result of it. God's authorship of Scripture through inspiration was an essential moment in the production of the *Urkirche* and derives its peculiar character from the divine founding of the Church. Thus, scriptural inspiration is "simply God's authorship of the Church insofar as this has a relation to Scripture as a constitutive element of the *Urkirche* itself." [20]

How does Rahner conceive God's founding of the Church? By a will-act which is absolute and which is eschatological. It is absolute because [it is] included in the decree of the Incarnation, prior to any decision of human liberty. It is eschatological because, in contrast with the election of Israel, it constituted the definitive *Heilsveranstaltung* in Christ and the Church, namely, the definitive presence of divine grace in the world as the eschatological event of God's mercy, the consummation of history.[21]

What does Rahner mean by the *Urkirche* and how does he understand its function in the salvation history? It might be called the *Church-in-fieri* during the apostolic age, which was directed by God in such a manner as to determine the character of the Church as an institution which was historically perceptible and destined to be indefectible. Involved in this work of foundation was not merely Christ alone but also the group of disciples He had gathered during His public life, who later enjoyed the absolutely unique experience of Pentecost. God's relationship to this *Urkirche* was a very special one: Only through this first generation does He have a relation to succeeding generations of Christians. For revelation closed with the death of the last apostle, and Peter and the apostolic college possessed, in addition to the office handed on to their successors, an untransferable function in the Church.[22]

But the founding of the Church took the form of an evolutionary process extended in time.[23] There were events in her coming-to-be which were not destined to specify the Church's complete status, namely, Temple worship and certain judaizing practices. Hence the eschatological character of the Church endowed her with a clear self-consciousness of her own divinely intended nature and gave her the power to prune away any pseudo-Christian phenomena attending her emergence from the matrix of Judaism.

How does Rahner justify his view that the writing of Scripture under divine inspiration formed a constitutive element of the Church's founding? Granted that by His divine direction of the historical process through which the *Urkirche* evolved into the Church God decreed to found the Church, then the *Urkiche* had necessarily to contain certain essential elements (the *depositum fidei*, the primacy, apostolic succession, the sacraments). Now the formation of (at least) the New Testament belongs to these constitutive elements because the Scriptures are the Church's book. Only she can recognize their inspired character or interpret them definitively. If the Scriptures are the word of God, they are just as fundamentally the Church's self-expression of her faith.[24] Like the apostolic preaching, the writing of the New Testament formed part of the initial phase of the Church's existence which was to remain normative throughout her subsequent history. It was because the *Urkirche* was aware of the necessity of preserving a record of her faith, her traditions, her very development, that she confided these things to writing.

This remarkable theological synthesis provides Rahner with a satisfactory explanation of the divine-human authorship of Scripture. God is Author of Scripture because He willed its composition as an essential part of the *Heilsgeschichte* through which He revealed Himself by means of a supernatural historical *Heilsgemeinde*, which thus objectifies itself in the Book. God is principal Author since this historical process exhibits within our world effects wrought by God alone. However, since God willed that the Church record in writing her awareness of her true nature and mission, the apostolic writers who evince this Christian faith are also real, yet subordinate authors. Moreover, just as the divine activity, which presided over the developments by which He formed the *Urkirche* into the Church, necessarily came to a conclusion once the Church was fully constituted, so too the history of God's authorship of Scripture *eo ipso* reached a conclusion as one of the events of this *Heilsgeschichte*.

Rahner is also able to explain how the Church recognized the inspired character of Scripture.[25] The Church's long hesitation about the canonicity of certain New Testament books makes it historically improbable that any revelation of the New Testament (or Old Testament) canon was expressly given through any of the apostles. So does the fact that the *Epistle of Barnabas* and *Pastor Hermas* were once regarded as canonical. We must, says Rahner, distinguish an implicit revelation of a book's inspiration and canonicity (which necessarily occurred before the death of the last apostle) and the expressly conscious, reflexive advertence to these qualities. He shows how the implicit awareness of the inspired character of his writings was present to the sacred author himself. Insofar as the New Testament authors were aware that they formed part of the concrete life of the *Church-in-fieri* expressing herself through Scripture (a knowledge which is supernatural), these writers can be said to have been conscious of their inspiration without perhaps reflecting upon it.

This magnificent contribution by one of the most original thinkers in the Church today constitutes a landmark in the study of biblical inspiration. I have found only one difficulty with it: No room appears to have been left for the possibility of the composition of an inspired book after the death of the last apostle. Since Rahner demands a revelation to the Church of the New Testament canon, a revelation that would of necessity have been given before the death of the apostles, it is hard to see, in his theory, how the Catholic critic could avoid an aprioristic rejection of certain fairly cogent arguments for dating 2 Peter in the second century. We shall find a rather convincing solution to this problem in the very recent article of Bernhard Brinkmann.[26]

Further contributions by Bernhard Brinkmann

This German theologian of the Jesuit faculty of St. Georgen in Frankfurt asks two pertinent questions: (1) How did the Church recognize the inspired character of the books of Scripture? (2) Why does the canon of Scripture contain only a certain number of books when, as Rahner, for instance, admits, there were other inspired writings?

He answers the first question by giving the common theological opinion that since inspiration is a supernatural event, it can only be known through revelation. He holds, however, that this fact is revealed by way of conclusion, not explicitly.[27] He rejects moreover a view (held also by Rahner) that some kind of revelation is necessary for the inclusion of inspired books in the scriptural canon.

Brinkmann's reasons for his views are based on the silence of the Vatican Council regarding the criterion of inspiration and on the belief found in both Jewish and Christian tradition that the deciding factor is the prophetic origin of the sacred books. The New Testament books were believed to contain the Christian rule of faith by the early Church because they had originated with the apostles, who, like the Old Testament writers, were prophets, instruments of

God.[28] Accordingly, everything the apostles wrote, like everything they preached, was considered part of the *regula fidei.* The selection of certain of these inspired writings to form the canon of Scripture was left to the Church's choice, a choice which is positive but not exclusive.

One important consequence of this view is Brinkmann's assertion that a book could be written by some associate or successor of an apostle in the second century and be accepted as canonical, provided it faithfully recorded apostolic revelation.[29]

Brinkmann's most important contribution, in my opinion, is his thesis that the canon of Scripture is the result of the Church's infallible choice. He rightly refuses to postulate a special revelation, of which there is no trace anywhere and which is excluded by the history of the canon.[30]

Areas of Further Theological Investigation

Since theology has made such advances in the understanding of biblical inspiration, we may well ask whether there is room for further development. I should like to indicate some questions which still invite exploitation.

In the first place, as I remarked in the beginning, the theologian might profitably reinvestigate the final cause of scriptural inspiration. Why did God inspire the sacred writers? Why is inspiration necessary to produce a book God willed to author through the medium of men? This question can be answered satisfactorily only by adopting a more religious view of the Bible than that taken by the old liberal critics. Let me illustrate from the history of Gospel criticism.

To defend the historical credibility of the Gospels, Catholic apologetics devised a system which rightly denounced the suggestion that the accounts written by the evangelists were the mere product of the faith (or imagination) of the first disciples. There was, however, a tendency to deny that any theological interpretation had been put upon the facts narrated and to maintain that the logia attributed to Jesus were the *ipsissima verba Christi.* In short, a valiant effort was made to make the Gospel stories conform to the canons of the nineteenth-century's conception of history.

Today, considerable work has been done upon the notion of religious history. It is now realized that there is such a thing as metahistory, which does not suffer the yardstick of secular history to be applied to it. We admit more readily that there is religious interpretation (and necessarily so) in the sacred history of Jesus' life and death, and that it is insufficient to treat the Resurrection like any other historical fact.

This more profound view of scriptural historical narration can provide a valuable clue to the purpose of the Bible's inspiration. If it were merely a question of profane history, the accuracy of the authors' statements could be checked by any valid historical method. If, however, the sacred writers are endeavoring to describe the irruption of the divine into human history through the Incarnation of God's Son, we find a new necessity for inspiration: to ensure the validity of that theological interpretation essential to the type of religious history contained in the Bible. This question of the relation of inspiration to symbolic history would reward the attention of the theologian.

We also need a theological investigation of God's total purpose in inspiring the sacred books. We have seen that this divine aim is not only doctrinal. Scripture is addressed to the whole man in his concrete existence, not merely to man's intellect. It was written "that you may persevere in your belief that Jesus is the Messiah, God's Son, and that, through your belief, you may have life in His name" (Jn 20:31). It provides food for the Christian life in a way in which the infallible pronouncements of the *magisterium* do not. The Bible is the "testimony of living experience, which tends to stir emotions and will, as well as enlightening the mind," whereas the Church's authoritative declarations are "intended to appeal only to the intellect. . . . Naturally the same Authority guarantees the affirmations of theology (those which are *De Fide*), but it does not *make* them; and the text that is adduced in support of the affirmation is functioning only on the rational, logical level, while its affective, imperative values are in this context necessarily disregarded." [31]

The task of defining the total purpose of Scripture and of scriptural inspiration is not easy. It involves a careful and complete elaboration of biblical theology which has yet to be done. Still it represents an ideal toward which the theologian and the biblical scholar can work.

Meantime, there are other, smaller issues to be settled. Rahner's splendid theory of the inspiration of the New Testament needs careful working out so that it can be applied to the Old Testament.[32] I believe also it would be profitable to follow up Rahner's lead by investigating the mediatorial role of the Church in the inspiration of Scripture. Could we not learn more about the function of the inspired writers as men of the Church?

The theologian might re-examine the discriminating attitude of the Church in the period when she was forming the scriptural canon, as Brinkmann has suggested. She was not concerned with selecting writings that were simply error-free, but with apostolically authentic doctrine.[33]

Finally, I suggest that two analogies with the practice of the Church with regard to the conferring of the sacraments and to preaching might help deepen our understanding of biblical inspiration. To confer any sacrament validly, the minister must intend to do what the Church wishes him to do. Might not this principle illustrate the way in which God influenced the New Testament writers? They intended to do what the Church wished, namely, to compose a written record of the apostolic preaching and teaching. Is not such an intention implicit in Paul's letter to the churches of Corinth and Galatia and in Luke's prologue?[34]

The second analogy derives from the Church's traditional attitude toward the necessity of a kind of "apostolic succession" in the valid, efficacious preaching of the word of God. To the bishop, as successor of the apostles, belongs the office of preaching. He shares this function with others by communicating faculties to them for that purpose. To preach without faculties is analogous to the hearing of confessions without faculties. This lofty conception of the preacher's role, postulating an unbroken chain that preserves communion with the apostles for the promulgation of the spoken word, provides a counterpart to the way in which biblical inspiration assures the Church of the apostolic authority of the written word of the New Testament.

References

[1] Dom Célestin Charlier, "Méthode historique et lecture spirituelle des Écritures," *Bible et Vie chrétienne* §18 (1957), 7-26. We shall subsequently refer to this article as "Charlier."

[2] On this point, the essay of Dom Gregory Dix, "The Conflict of the Syriac and Greek Cultures," *Jew and Greek* (London, 1953), pp. 1-18 is excellent. The perniciousness of such a radical error in the rationalist viewpoint can be most

palpably felt by examining the monographs on comparative religion produced by liberal critics like Holtzmann, Beyschlag, Weiss, and others, under the impression they were writing biblical theology.

[3] For it was primarily interested in the presentation of reality and in testimony, rather than in reality's analysis and demonstrative proof. "It has been said that the purpose of scientific statement is the elimination of ambiguity, and the purpose of symbol is the inclusion of it. We write in symbol when we wish our words to present, rather than analyze or prove, their subject matter. . . . Symbol endeavors, as it were, to *be* that of which it speaks, and imitates reality by the multiplicity of its significance." Austin Farrer, *A Rebirth of Images* (London, 1949), p. 19.

[4] Charlier, p. 16.

[5] *Ibid.* If we are to evaluate properly God's authorship of the books of the Bible, we must set this divine activity into its context, God's particular providential governance of the history of the ancient Near East. Only then can we do justice to what R. A. F. MacKenzie has called "the multiplicity of inspiration," by realizing that the Bible is the product of an inspired tradition extending at times over several centuries. See R. A. F. MacKenzie, "Some Problems in the Field of Inspiration," *Catholic Biblical Quarterly*, 20 (1958), 8.

[6] *Enchiridion Biblicum*, Rome-Naples (1954), #559.

[7] The same holds true to a certain extent of the prophetic writings, of the Petrine and Pauline epistles, and of the Matthean Gospel, all of which have been aggregated to the inspired books by having their *auctoritas* recognized by the synagogue or the Church.

[8] *Enchiridion Biblicum*, #30.

[9] *Ibid.*, #40.

[10] This being our Western view of truth, it is not to be wondered at that our treatises on scriptural inspiration treat of the Bible's inerrancy as its principal (often it would seem its only) effect. Scriptural inerrancy for us means a quality which is simply and solely intellectual.

[11] Not without reason has Pius XII bidden the would-be interpreter to "go back in spirit to those far-off centuries of the East," *EB*, #558.

[12] Paul Synave-Pierre Benoit, *La Prophétie*, Éditions de la Revue des Jeunes, Paris-Tournai-Rome, 1947. Benoit has a shorter essay on inspiration in Robert-Tricot, *Initiation Biblique* (Paris, 1954), pp. 6-45; for further modifications of his theory, cf. "Note complémentaire sur l'inspiration," *Revue Biblique* 63 (1956), 416-22. Thus Benoit's first contribution to the subject took the form of a monograph on the thomistic doctrine concerning prophecy and scriptural inspiration which was appended to his re-editing of the late Paul Synave's commentary on the questions in the Summa which treat of prophecy. We might add that Benoit's work deserves to rank high among the classical treatises on inspiration.

[13] He remains, says Benoit, dependent like the pupil whose statements rest, consciously or unconsciously, upon the superior knowledge of the teacher.

[14] Karl Rahner criticized this description of the writer's instrumental activity, remarking that Benoit has not made it clear just why inspiration does not reduce the author to the role of secretary.

[15] We might add that for Benoit inspiration extends analogously to certain versions of the Bible, specifically to the Septuagint.

[16] Benoit subsequently adopted the term "énoncé": cf. *RB*, 63 (1956), 419, n. 1.

[17] Joseph Coppens criticized Benoit's presentation in a review of *Initiation Biblique:* cf. *Ephemerides Theologicae Lovanienses*, 31 (1955), 671-73; also "Chronica," *ETL*, 32 (1956), 715-16. He gives a fuller account of his own

views in "L'inspiration et l'inerrance bibliques," *ETL*, 33 (1957), 36-57. Coppens (*ETL*, 31 [1955], 673) believes Benoit to have come close to Newman's system, although he admits that *Divino afflante* had anticipated Benoit's restriction of the "domain guaranteed by inerrancy," and he admits the real differences between Benoit's and Newman's positions. Coppens objects to the expression "objectively religious and supernatural truths" as equivocal.

[18] Coppens, *art. cit.*, *ETL*, 33 (1957), 44. I might add that Coppens' summary of points on inspiration which he feels are more or less settled today is well worth a little study: *Ibid.*, 52-55.

[19] Karl Rahner, "Uber die Schriftinspiration," *Zeitschrift für katholische Theologie*, 78 (1956), 127-68. See the English translation by C. Henkey, *Inspiration in the Bible* (New York: Herder and Herder, Inc., 1961) and the review by J. L. McKenzie, S.J., in *Theological Studies*, 23 (1962), 104-106; see also Rahner's essay, "Zur Frage der Dogmenentwicklung," in *Schriften zur Theologie*, 1, Einsiedeln-Zürich-Cologne (1954), 49-90.

[20] Rahner, *art. cit.*, *ZKT*, 78 (1956), 158.

[21] God wills the entire *Heilsgeschichte* in a more absolute way than He wills profane human history, because it is, as Rahner (*art. cit.*, 151) says, "God's own history." God is thus Author of the Church in a more intimate way than of other things of which He is transcendental cause. This historical divine activity, which we call *Heilsgeschichte*, reaches its climax in Christ and the Church. Before Christ, God's dialogue with men had not received its definitive pattern. Whether it would issue in a judgment or in grace was not yet finally determined: the objective realization of the divine activity bore the possibility of being voided. The divine imperative of the positive Mosaic code contained from the beginning the potency to be abolished. It is only the Old Testament's character as prehistory of Christ and the Church which remains permanent.

[22] I have discussed this point more fully elsewhere. This creation of what had been merely a group of Jesus' loyal adherents into the Church of the New Testament was the immediate result of their "baptism with a Holy Spirit." Since this unique experience, which could never be repeated in the lives of any other men, had constituted these disciples as the Church, they had no need of receiving the Christian sacrament of baptism. Yet this same consciousness of the unique character of their own experience led them, according to the evidence of the New Testament (Ac 2:41), to impart Christian baptism to those who wished to be added "to the number of the saved" (Ac 2:47). "The New Testament Doctrine of Baptism," *Theological Studies* 18 (1957), 207-208.

[23] Cf. "Kingdom to Church: the Structural Development of Apostolic Christianity in the New Testament," *Theological Studies*, 16 (1955), 1-29.

[24] To deny this would be to deny any real authorship to the New Testament hagiographers and reduce them to mere mouthpieces of a heavenly message. It would also be to deny an essential characteristic of the books of the New Testament: they are a manifestation of the faith of the writers and not only a manifestation of the divine revelation in Jesus Christ.

[25] Most theologians are ready to admit, with Bea, that "how and to whom this first revelation was made, we simply do not know."

[26] Bernhard Brinkmann, "Inspiration und Kanonizität der Heiligen Schrift in ihrem Verhältnis zur Kirche," *Scholastik*, 33 (1958), 208-33.

[27] Franzelin, Pesch, Bea, Tromp, and Benoit insist on an explicit revelation for inspiration and canonicity to be known, while Lagrange, Dewailly, and others hold this twofold fact can be (and was) revealed by way of a theological conclusion.

[28] Christ's teaching on the apostolic office, and more especially the Pentecostal experience, made it clear that, whether they spoke or wrote, the apostles in the exercise of their divinely conferred mission were governed by the Holy Spirit.

[29] Again, it is, says Brinkmann, theoretically possible that the Church could still accept as canonical some apostolic book lost for centuries and recovered, if it could be shown to be certainly authentic.

[30] How otherwise explain the Church's long hesitating in accepting Hebrews into the Canon, or the fact of her nonacceptance of Paul's earlier letter to Corinth (1 Cor 5:9), or her final rejection (after a certain acceptance) of First Clement, Barnabas, Pastor Hermas?

[31] R. A. F. MacKenzie, "The Concept of Biblical Theology," *CTSA Proceedings of the Tenth Annual Convention* (1955), p. 61, n. 14.

[32] Rahner, *art. cit., ZKT*, 78 (1956), 146, n. 13 and 151, n. 17: both passages contain some hints of how Rahner would conceive the Old Testament as part of the Church's prehistory. But he has not, so far as I am aware, worked out his theory completely, so as to include Old Testament inspiration.

[33] The early Church recognized that word and pen were complementary functions of the apostolic office: cf. Eusebius, *Ecclesiastical History*, III, 37,2. Since the preaching of the Gospel had been entrusted to the apostolic college, she sought the one "Gospel of God" in those writings which were to be considered normative for God's people: cf. Ireneus, *PG*, 7, 803b. Thus Ireneus points out that Luke's book was simply the written record of Paul's preaching (*PG*, 7, 845a), while Papias notes that Mark carefully reported the kerygma of Peter (Eusebius, *Eccl. Hist.*, III, 39,15).

[34] Cf. 1 Corinthians 15:3; 11:23; Galatians 1:6-9; Luke 1:1-2. There are many other questions we might propose for solution: namely, What relation does inspiration bear to the various senses of Scripture, in particular, to the spiritual or fuller sense? While theologians assert that *revelatio fuit cum apostolis completa*, why do we never find the statement *inspiratio fuit cum apostolis completa*? In fact, as G. Bardy points out, "L'inspiration des Pères de l'Église," *RSR*, 40 (1951-52), 7-26, it appears there was a constant patristic belief to the effect that they (the Fathers) were inspired.

RODERICK A. F. MacKENZIE, S.J.

The Concept of Biblical Theology

The careful reader will find in this classic article a discussion of questions such as these: What are the goals of the Catholic biblical movement that go beyond culture and scholarship? How is biblical theology to be distinguished from other branches and systems of theology? Why must the Church always theologize? What interest does biblical theology hold for modern man that the theology of St. Thomas does not? What is the advantage of biblical theology over the dogmatic theology of the textbooks? What would St. Thomas and his contemporaries have thought of the term "biblical theology"? What contributions have non-Catholic scholars made to biblical theology? What does the modern sense of historical process contribute to biblical theology? Why is context an important factor in biblical theology? What problems still remain and what procedures must be followed in the elaboration of the biblical theology of the future?

Father MacKenzie is the recently appointed rector of the Pontifical Biblical Institute in Rome. He formerly taught at the Jesuit Seminary in Toronto and is the author of *Faith and History in the Old Testament.*

The never-failing supernatural vitality of the Church manifests itself strikingly, from time to time, in movements that seem to spring up unheralded yet generally, and mark the Catholicism of a particular period as having special interests and tendencies. Such a

This article first appeared in the *Proceedings of the Tenth Annual Convention* of the Catholic Theological Society of America and is reproduced here, somewhat abridged, with permission.

movement, at the present day, is the so-called biblical revival. Among Catholics of various languages and cultures, both clerical and lay, there has developed, especially since World War II, a keen interest in Holy Scripture, and an evident desire for closer contact and greater familiarity with the written Word of God. This revival was well launched before the War in European countries, and it is now spreading to the Catholics of the English-speaking world.

Such a movement, encouraged and guided but not imposed by the Holy See, spontaneous and wide-spread, is certain evidence of the working of the Holy Spirit; and it is equally a blessing that the means are at hand to satisfy this appetite. The Church's scholars and exegetes have today a vastly increased understanding and mastery of the proper meaning, in details, of the sacred text and are capable of providing the understanding sought by our contemporaries, answering the questions they ask, and so breaking for them this holy bread.

But what is sought is not merely erudition. In the spirit of faith, Catholics look for substantial spiritual nourishment in the Bible. The liturgical revival has already given them an understanding of the contemporary, actual validity of the mysteries of the Faith. The doctrine of the mystical Body has helped them to integrate those mysteries into the substance of their daily lives, not leaving them on the level of merely intellectual assent. Now in seeking deeper understanding and a still more fruitful contact with the Christian mystery, they are driven to look for them in the Book that contains the deposit of God's revelation, where faith tells them that God is, so to speak, waiting to speak to them.

Thus it is not cultural formation that is sought, nor merely apologetic defence of the Bible's truth; it is theology—for theology is nothing but [faith seeking understanding], and that is precisely what the biblical revival of our day consists of. It is doctrine that is sought, the message contained in this mysterious and fascinating book, the revelation, in short, as it is expressed in the inspired words, preserved and presented and interpreted to us by the Church. Hence there is a duty incumbent upon the Church's corps of interpreters, theologians, and exegetes, to provide the theological interpretation and guidance with which Christians, both clerical and lay, can read and appreciate for themselves the sacred text, with all that it comports of unction and enlightenment and consolation. That is, the Catholic scholar's work on the Bible is not complete until it issues in a biblical theology.

First we must clear the ground by defining biblical theology, and establishing its right to be considered an integral part of the queen of the sciences. It may be provisionally defined as "the doctrine of God contained in Scripture, analyzed and systematized in biblical categories." The phrase "in Scripture" distinguishes its material from those of other branches of positive theology, patristic, symbolic, liturgical; the phrase about biblical categories distinguishes it from speculative theology, which must make use of some natural system of philosophy as scaffolding for its constructions.

Our faith tells us that God has spoken to men, has revealed Himself and His works, and that this revelation is contained in the deposit entrusted, for authoritative communication and interpretation, to His Church. A large part, if not actually all, of that revelation has been not merely entrusted to oral preservation and tradition; it has been set down in writing in such a way that God Himself has done the writing through the instrumentality of men. The object of our faith, then, that to which we give assent, is manifested both in the preaching of the Church and, in detail, in these written records which testify to the historical progress and stages in which the revelation took place.

I say "manifested" because ultimately the believer gives his assent not to formulas but to facts. *Actus credentis non terminatur ad enuntiabile sed ad rem.*[1] That is why there may be different equally orthodox ways of enunciating the Church's belief, and why the Church has had, and still has, different systems of theology; different, that is, in terminology and in use of philosophical concepts, but all of them truthful though inadequate presentations of the inexhaustible deposit committed to her care. In the New Testament, for example, St. Paul and St. John have erected two magnificent structures of theology, which are complementary but certainly different. The theology of St. Augustine is not that of Pseudo-Dionysius, and St. Gregory of Nazianzen has his system, quite distinct from that of St. Thomas Aquinas. Some have even claimed to perceive a difference between the theology of St. Thomas and that of some later thomists. Not all of these are of equal value; they are more or less complete, more or less adequate to the divine mystery which they reproduce analogously in human concepts and terms. It is for the Church to pass judgment on them. But of those which she approves, each has its own contribution to make to the understanding of the deposit.

When God speaks, man must listen, and he must respond. The written word is not a dead letter, it is a challenge, a summons to answer, and the response made possible by grace is an affirmation, an assent which is not purely intellectual but vital, a self-commitment involving man's whole being. In what concerns man's higher faculties, the revelation appeals especially to knowledge and love. An object is proposed to both these faculties, and our assent if genuine will involve the effort to know it and to love it ever better.

That is why theology in the broadest sense—theologizing, let us call it—is essential to the vitality of the individual Christian's life, and to that of the whole Church. Faith seeks to understand, to grasp and penetrate and let itself be seized by the reality revealed. If the Church ever ceased to theologize it would be a sign that she had lost interest in her very *raison d'être*. This is her business, to know and love God; and her theology is an ever-advancing movement toward the divine self-knowledge, of which revelation is a partial and necessarily imperfect communication.

Like the individual Christian, the Church *thinks* her faith with the powers of the human intellect illumined by grace—*ratio fide illustrata*. Human language, logic, science, philosophy are the tools with which she examines, analyzes, compares and combines the data of the revelation. And since this natural equipment varies in character and perfection from age to age, so her theology varies and develops, quarrying now in this section, now in that, returning at times perhaps to veins that had seemed to be worked out, but in the long run neglecting no corner of the field, and producing age after age new treasures from the truly inexhaustible wealth of her patrimony.

Through the working of the divine plan for man's salvation, the written deposit of revelation was produced by Semitic instruments; but the Church's exploitation of it has been mainly with Greek tools. Broadly speaking, neo-platonism was the philosophy which served to develop theology for the first twelve centuries; but in the thirteenth, as we all know, aristotelianism made its irruption, and in the hands of the Church's greatest genius achieved a fructification of theology unexampled till then and never matched since.

The thomistic theology, then, represents a high point, and the Church has officially made it her own—until a better one comes along. Even if that should happen, St. Thomas' theology would never be discarded nor any of it lost; theology is a progress in understanding the faith, and the gains made by it are permanent acquisitions. But there is always the urge to further advance; and in the twentieth century we cannot hope to advance further along the precise path followed by St. Thomas. The official thomistic revival is now seventy-five years old;[2] it has produced wonderful results in getting us away from cartesianism and nominalism, in getting us back to the heights reached by St. Thomas. But looking at it broadly, one can hardly say that in theology it has gone forward; that is, it has not produced a system or a development of St. Thomas' system, worthy to be mentioned in the same breath with his achievement.

And the reason—apart from the accidental one that no comparable genius has appeared in the Church—is that we do not spontaneously think like St. Thomas. We can learn his thought-patterns, just as we learn his Latin; but neither can ever be our mother-tongue, as natural to us as it was to him. The greatest theologian of the nineteenth century, probably, was Matthias Scheeben; and it is significant that the fertilizing element for his thought was especially the theology of the Greek Fathers, mostly unknown to St. Thomas.

On a humbler level, this is something very evident in the modern Biblical movement. The laity are often ill at ease, puzzled, even repelled by dogmatic theology as it is offered to them in manuals and textbooks—even when these are available to them in the vernacular. Such works are full of terms and argumentations, meaningful and indispensable in scholastic philosophy, but extremely elusive and hard to penetrate for minds formed according to the positivist, scientific, quantitative techniques of modern Western culture. Anyone who has tried to explain transubstantiation to an adult convert will know what I mean—especially if that convert be an engineer, a scientist, a mathematician, or the like. The Real Presence, the Bread of Life, the Eucharistic Sacrifice are doctrines as consoling, as nourishing to his soul, as they were to the converts instructed by St. Paul. But substance and accidents are notions beyond his comprehension, or at least they sharply conflict with the mental image he has formed of physical reality. He will end probably by accepting them on faith, too; but then they remain sterile elements in his belief, not fruitful and enlivening as are the dogmas of the Church.

Whereas with the Bible he feels himself at home. The greatest immediate appeal is in the Gospels, but he quickly comes to appreciate the rest of the New Testament, and the Old as well. The bugbear of Bible-science conflict being easily disposed of, and some notion of literary forms acquired, he revels in the realism the concreteness, the immediacy of the Bible message. It appeals to his sense of history and development (which he calls evolution). He *expects* to find that God worked gradually and that many things in the early stages of revelation were rudimentary and imperfect. It appeals to his interest in the individual person or fact, the verifiable prophecy, even the patent miracle. Above all, it gives him the contact with a personal and loving God, a responsible, freely willing, individual Being—who in dogmatic theology tends only too easily to dissolve in a cloud of "attributes."

I stress that example as something from my own experience, but the experience could be generalized. It was this desire for adaptation, revitalization, or whatever you prefer to call it, that lay behind the ill-fated effort at a "new theology" of [a few] years ago, which sought impatiently to restate the Church's dogmatic teachings in terms of various contemporary philosophies. That was doomed to failure, because such work cannot be done artificially and to order. Theology is an organic growth, and the faith which seeks understanding must always remain master of its tools and take time out when necessary to remodel the tools themselves. No existentialist philosophy of modern times could serve as handmaid of theology without a long process of purification and adjustment. But *Humani Generis*, in condemning a movement that would have involved Catholic dogma in a hopeless relativism, also recognized the constant need there is for theology to keep in touch with or return to its sources, and significantly indicated the "inexhaustible treasures" that still await exploitation in patrology and in Scripture. In view of the tremendous possibilities opened up by the modern renovation, almost transformation, of biblical studies, it does seem that one hope of a revitalized theology lies here.

It is very much to be hoped, too, that with all the growth of our specializations, the unfortunate separation between dogmatic theology and exegesis will not widen but tend to close. Down to quite recent times it was taken for granted that every exegete was a theologian, and every theologian was an exegete. It is only the enormously increased sum of positive knowledge that has split these into two separate vocations in the Church—I would say, with harm to both of them. It is still required that a specialist in Scripture studies first obtain the licentiate in theology; the exegete cannot but regard it as unfortunate that a specialist in dogmatic theology is not obliged to get his licentiate in Scripture. Anyway, if the breach is to be healed, the responsibility falls first upon the exegete, who can and should proceed beyond mere exegesis, to build up a connected theology of his materials.

We speak then of the biblical theologian, and of biblical theology as that division of positive theology for which the materials are supplied by exegesis which is both scientific and guided by faith. But the very name of "biblical" theology is somehow strange; it seems to be tautological. Any Christian of the Patristic period, of the Middle Ages, of the first millennium and a half of the Church's history, would probably have inquired, "What other kind of theology is there?" Certainly, St. Thomas would have been amazed at the suggestion that his *Summa* was somehow not biblical. As is plain in the very first *Quaestio*, to him, *sacra doctrina*, *sacra scriptura*, and *theologia* were all—at least from his particular pedagogical point of view—one and the same thing. He aimed at systematizing and synthesizing, in easily intelligible form, the sum of revelation contained in the Word of God. And his magnificent accomplishment rests on a minute familiarity with the sacred text—in the Vulgate translation, naturally, and according to the exegetical science of his time.

Just as St. Thomas was able to surpass his predecessors by the superiority of the philosophy at his disposal, so we can . . . I hesitate to say, surpass St. Thomas, because genius counts for something too; but at least, we can provide much that he had no possibility of discovering, that in fact would not have been intelligible to his contemporaries. What we have is a vastly increased understanding and command of all the sciences auxiliary to exegesis: cultural and political history of the ancient Near East, linguistics, literary forms, comparative religion, Semitic psychology, and so forth. Thus we can penetrate much deeper into the human elements of the inspired books and the mentality and intentions of the human authors. But by the same token—the hagiographers being God's instruments—we penetrate further the divine meaning, with all its wealth of implications and virtualities. And we cannot fail to notice at the same time how the later scholasticism, lacking St. Thomas' meticulous attention to the text, tended to desiccate the infinite vitality of the deposit, over-intellectualizing and so verging constantly toward that nominalism which is (not only in the fourteenth century!) the besetting temptation of scholastic theology.

Our advance, in other words, is possible mainly in the field of positive theology, though no doubt this will have its repercussions too, at some future date, in speculative theology. The question whether positive—and consequently biblical—theology properly belongs, in the strictest sense, to the sacred science need not be dwelt on here. If it was denied for a time, by many of the theologians of half a century ago, that was because of the crippling influence of historicism, which applied a too narrow notion of scientific detachment to an activity which is entirely proper and essential to the *fides quaerens intellectum.* After the studies of Muñiz and Spicq,[3] to name but two, there will be few to question now that one function of theology is the examining, stating, and defending of the datum of the faith, that is, a positive analysis of scripture and tradition. The same science of theology is to be considered speculative when it exercises another function, namely, uses a system of philosophy to develop that faith and draw theological conclusions. We may take it then that biblical theology is real theology, not a subordinate science that theology uses (as is, for example, exegesis); it is the science which studies divine revelation as it is recorded in the inspired Word of God and combines it into an intelligible body of doctrine according to the concepts and patterns of the inspired writers.

Since the divine wisdom communicated the revelation progressively and by degrees—"at sundry times and in divers manners"—the Bible contains it in scattered and partial form, in many bits and pieces, yet so arranged that there is a steady development and clarification. (And this of course has continued, *intensively* though not *extensively*, since the closing of the Canon, in the Church's ever deeper penetration of the meaning of the deposit.) But now that the whole deposit has been given, it is possible, and it is even necessary for us, to put together these bits and pieces, fitting them into their proper places according to the pattern in the divine Mind, and so doing our best to acquire a total grasp of God's revelation to us, analogous to that knowledge which God has of His own plan.

At this point it is necessary to say something of the work done in this field by non-Catholic scholars, which on the technical level has blazed the trail for Catholic theologians. This vigorous, renewed interest in biblical theology—among Angelicans and Lutherans especially—has various causes. One may be that they feel the lack of an authoritative and well-defined dogmatic theology and are attempting to supply it in this way. But there is far more to it than that. There is here a sharp reaction against the triumphant rationalism of the higher critics of the last century, who insisted on treating the Bible, the Old Testament especially, as exactly on a par with any other ancient literature and regarding the beliefs, practices, and aspirations of the Israelites as so many documents of cultural and religious history—interesting in their own right, but quite without any transcendental importance or relevance for the men of the nineteenth century. The texts were thus made the object of strictly scientific, impersonal study, and instead of Old Testament theology, they produced histories of Old Testament religion, or, more consistently, histories of the religion of Israel. Correspondingly, for the New Testament, there were histories of the beliefs and development of the primitive Church, and the like. As late as 1927, Hermann Gunkel was explaining that the day of biblical theology was over, and that the only possible scientific treatment of the contents of the Old Testament was the historical and literary one.

But even at that time the reaction had already begun. Karl Barth was loudly demanding whether Scripture was the Word of God, or not? and answering that question in the affirmative, set out to renew the theological treatment which God's Word must necessarily evoke in those who believe. Rudolph Kittel, about the same time, called for a treatment of the Old Testament which would do justice to its claim to present divine revelation. In the last thirty years an immense amount of discussion has taken place in Protestant circles, first in Germany, then in Great Britain, France, and other countries, concerning the justification of biblical theology—how to reconcile the prior affirmation of faith with the necessary submissiveness to the evidence that one studies—and its techniques—what authority belongs to the text? What criterion to use for subordinating doctrines one to another? What relationship has the Old Testament to the New? A large number of articles and monographs and some complete theologies, of Old and New Testaments respectively, have been produced. One may say that biblical theology has won, or regained, an acknowledged place as the crown and ultimate object of biblical studies—in spite of the vehement objections of a few scholars . . . who wish to remain faithful to the nineteenth-century ideal of scholarly objectivity as they conceive it, and who protest bitterly against the mingling of faith with scholarship.

The chief gain among the Christian exegetes has been the general acknowledgment not merely of the legitimacy but of the necessity of faith in anyone who approaches the Bible with the hope of receiving what it has to offer. They recognize now that coldly scientific—in the sense of rationalistic—objectivity is quite incapable of even perceiving, let alone exploiting, the religious values of Scripture. There must be first the commitment, the recognition by faith of the divine origin and authority of the book; then the believer can properly and profitably apply all the most conscientious techniques of the subordinate sciences, without in the least infringing their due autonomy or being disloyal to the scientific ideal. . . .

The chief problem that still remains unsolved for them—and I would say it is insoluble as long as they do not recognize the living authority of the Church—is that of authority: What guarantees the Bible's claim on our acceptance, and, in the last analysis, what guarantees a given interpretation of it? What criterion is to be used for distinguishing the less perfect from the more perfect? What about "demythologizing"? It is perfectly true that eternal truths must be disengaged and drawn clear of their presentation in terms of a particular language, culture, psychology, and so forth. But it is no good immediately reinvolving them, as Bultmann does, in the pseudo-scientific mythology of the twentieth century. The criterion for their "pure" statement must be the living spirit of faith, under the guidance of the Holy Spirit; and that means, ultimately, the authority of the Church.

On the Catholic side, biblical theology on any large scale has been slower in making its appearance, partly because there was not the same gap to be filled nor errors to be corrected, but mainly because Catholic biblical scholars are still occupied in assimilating and "baptizing" the literary and historical achievements of the last generation of "higher critics." Still, the first large-scale works have appeared in recent years, and there is an increasing number of theological monographs on particular sections of the sacred books.

The new possibilities of this science rest ultimately on the tremendous increase in our factual knowledge of the civilizations and cultures in which the Bible was produced. We have no time now to do more than refer to this new equipment, which was magisterially outlined . . . in *Divino afflante Spiritu.* But it has made possible a great refinement of techniques of investigation. For example, in the linguistic field, half a dozen ancient languages, unknown a century ago, are of immense help in the understanding of Hebrew, while the papyri and new Aramaic sources shed new light on New Testament Greek. Some—not all, but some—of the modern venacular translations are admirable in their accuracy, and even those who have forgotten their Hebrew are no longer obliged to peruse the text as through a glass darkly, in the Vulgate. The new understanding of literary conventions and stylistic usage has proved a great many hoary [difficulties] to be pseudo-problems, raised only by false principles of interpretation. I will mention one example: the symbolic and qualitative use of numbers, a favorite and frequent device in both Testaments. The mathematical literalism of the Western mind has made many difficulties for itself over this usage.

Then, there is the modern appreciation of development and change in history—the historical process. In both Testaments, we now recognize "the evolution of dogma" and do not try to put all affirmations in the Bible on one high level of doctrinal perfection. They must be read in context.

This is a point of considerable importance, for if the growth of revelation be neglected, the Bible appears as a bundle of contradictions. The Hegelian triad of thesis, antithesis, synthesis may serve as a convenient scheme for exposing this dialectic, one of the characteristic Semitic procedures of which the divine condescension made use to communicate with men in human speech. In the concrete, it means that revelation in the Old Testament progressed by a series of statements, each of which stressed one particular aspect of the truth, regardless of other aspects. The Hebrews themselves felt none of the difficulty that we tend to feel in following this process. No Israelite sage or prophet was ever deterred from speaking his mind by the fact that some predecessor had said exactly the opposite. Examples are numerous: the necessity of ritual sacrifice versus the uselessness of ritual sacrifice; God's wrath would utterly destroy sinners, God's love would reform and justify them; God's alliance was with the community, it was with each individual; God hated the Gentiles, God loved the Gentiles; the virtuous are rewarded with earthly prosperity, the virtuous suffer more than the wicked; and so on. Even in the same book, the institution of kingship may be presented as offensive to God and as willed by God. The Semitic speaker or writer is conscious of one thing at a time, and he affirms it with all the vehemence of his remarkably fiery temperament.

This is one of the distinguishing marks of the Semitic mentality, so different from that of the Greeks, which we have now learned to comprehend much better, thanks to literary and psychological studies. The Semitic mind has very little capacity for metaphysics or for abstraction, and little taste for colorless, rigorously exact statement. It prefers combination to distinction, operates with symbols where we should prefer well-defined concepts, is intuitive rather than rational; it is, in short, the mind of a poet rather than that of a philosopher. To take a metaphor from painting, it is impressionist rather than representational. It instructs and convinces, not by syllogistic argument but by a series of emphatic statements, impelling the mind of the hearer to build up a mental image corresponding to the speaker's. It expresses one idea at a time, with all possible emphasis, without regard for inferences which a more reflective mind might be inclined to draw from the expression. The Semite can, and often does, quite happily affirm something, *without* intending to deny its opposite.

Another characteristic concept of the Old Testament, which is difficult to accommodate to Greek philosophy, is its special anthropology. The soul-body dichotomy, of such importance in Western thinking from Plato on, is quite alien to Semitic ideas. They know only Man, who thinks (with his heart), eats, drinks, loves, begets, is born, dies, is strong or weak, truthful or false, and so forth. In all his material, animal functions he is *basar*, "flesh." In his affective, volitive activity he is *nephesh*, usually translated "soul," though "person" might be nearer the mark. And the source of all his activity, that which distinguishes a living man from a corpse (best compared to the electric current that makes a wire "live") is *ruah*, the "spirit." When God infuses it the embryo comes to life: when He withdraws it the man dies. There is probably no more frequent misapplication of texts than that which rests on the translation of *nephesh* as *anima*, soul.

Though it hardly seems to belong to our subject, it may not be out of place here to say a word on the "Scripture proof," as it is applied in textbooks of dogmatic theology. It would be easy, but rather unprofitable, to draw up a list of horrible examples, in which the casual and perhaps rather inappropriate use of a particular Latin word in the fourth-century Vulgate is made to bear the weight of an elaborate philosophical argument according to the meaning the word acquired in the late Middle Ages.[4] But it is better to be constructive; so let me suggest that nowadays a dogmatic theologian has an obligation to re-examine the "traditional" Scripture proofs, checking them by some up-to-date translation and commentary (such as the *Bible de Jérusalem*), and seeing whether in their original context the words can support the interpretation which his dogmatic thesis requires. He may thus get some salutary shocks; and in any case he will receive some rather stimulating insights into what divine revelation, at a given stage, really revealed.

Above all, one must deplore the technique which seeks in Scripture for brief isolated phrases, suitable to serve as major or minor of a scholastic syllogism; and it is here the exegete must feel most keenly, not only that the sacred text is being given less than its due respect, but that it is being distorted. Regardless of strain on pupils' memories, one would like to see a little more strain on their understandings, to help them to realize that each of the sacred writers has his own personal message which he is intent on proclaiming: a message that deserves to be heard as a whole, and which as a whole takes its proper place in the sum total of God's gracious proclamation to mankind.

Often, at the beginning of a treatise, or before a group of theses, in a dogmatic textbook, there is included a history of the development of a particular dogma in Christian tradition and the controversies that led to its clarification and definition. But how often does one see a summary of its development in the inspired text itself, its successive forms in various Old Testament books, its transformation and flowering, perhaps by stages, in the New? Yet this is, for the most part, the deposit which the dogma sums up and crystallizes in the language of the Church. . . .

The ideal biblical theology then lies still in the future; but it is already possible to describe the form it will take and the techniques necessary in producing it. There are two stages in the work: First, there must be an exact determination of the data, namely the theological truths expressed in each particular inspired book; Second, the testimonies thus determined and collected must be arranged in their right doctrinal relationships, and coordinated into a complete system according to the patterns that are implicit in them. Even the first stage requires much skill and training (to say nothing about talent); its author must not only be a theologian, thoroughly familiar with the Church's doctrine, so as to keep the *analogia fidei* and tradition as guiding principles of interpretation; he must also be an expert scientific exegete, at home in all the complicated auxiliary sciences —languages, history, literary criticism, psychology—which make up the equipment of the biblical scholar. He must be both textual critic and commentator, and in the latter capacity he must treat his subject theologically. As *Divino afflante* admonished, he must not think his work is done when he has discussed his text from every literary, cultural, and historical point of view. He has to uncover and synthesize that for which it exists—the witness it bears to some particular stage of God's saving activity toward men. In short, he must present the theology of the particular section of the Bible he is dealing with.

When—in the not too distant future, let us hope—we have an abundance of Catholic commentaries which are both scientific and theological on all the parts of Scripture, the way will be clear for the second stage, which offers new and even harder problems. The main one is the question of arrangement: what order to follow, and what central theme to make the backbone of the synthesis. Something is required, analogous to the neo-platonist idea of outgoing and return, from God and to God, which St. Thomas applied so brilliantly in the *Summa*. All we can say is that it must be something suggested by the history of revelation itself, not by any scheme of philosophy. We spoke already of . . . the Covenant theme, the most successful so far though restricted to the Old Testament. Others that have been suggested are: the Person of Christ in all His manifold activity; the Holiness of God; the idea of Election; the Kingdom of God. Whatever it is, it must be something that allows for the development and sequence of revelation, the history of God's care for mankind: the gradual preparation of the Old Testament, the decisive saving judgment that is the Incarnation, the eschatology prophetic of the last times in which the Church lives her militant life.

But positive theology is not the whole of the sacred science; as we saw, it represents only one of its functions. The faith that seeks understanding is driven on to ask questions, to compare, to speculate. And this is where biblical theology rejoins dogmatic theology, as the latter has been developed up to the present in the Church. When the former has advanced nearer to its perfection, it will offer to the speculative theologian a rich harvest in the way of fuller understanding of the deposit, an immense accretion of the materials on which speculative theology can build. When that will come and in what precise form must be left to the Providence of God, who will surely raise up in His Church thinkers as gifted and as wise as the Doctors who have served her so well in the past. In the meantime, the humbler task of biblical theology is accessible, at least in its details, to every exegete who is willing to be a theologian and to every theologian who remembers that he is by rights an exegete. At the present day, they can find no nobler intellectual task in the service of the Church.

References

[1] St. Thomas, IIa IIae, q. 1, art. 2, ad 2um.

[2] The Encyclical of Pope Leo XIII, *Aeterni Patris*, is dated August 4, 1879. The revival, of course, was primarily a return to thomistic philosophy; but whereas in the Middle Ages this had shown itself so effective a stimulus to theology, in modern times it has yielded little inspiration toward development. Theological progress is at present stimulated rather by positive studies in liturgy, patristics—and Scripture.

[3] F. P. Muñiz, "De diversis muneribus S. Theologiae secundum doctrinam D. Thomae," *Angelicum*, 24 (1947), 93-123; C. Spicq, "L'avènement de la théologie biblique," *Revue des sciences philosophiques et théologiques*, 34 (1951), 561-74. See also F.-M. Braun, "La théologie biblique. Qu'entendre par là?," *Revue thomiste*, 53 (1953), 221-53.

[4] A discussion of selected "proofs" will be found in E. F. Siegman, "The Use of Sacred Scripture in Textbooks of Dogmatic Theology," *Catholic Biblical Quarterly*, 11 (1949), 151-64; the author draws largely on the work of Ceuppens, *Theologia Biblica* (1938-39). A more fundamental treatment of the use of Scripture in dogmatic theology is J. Levie, "Les limites de la preuve d'Ecriture Sainte," *Nouvelle revue théologique*, 71 (1949), 1009-29; cf., by the same author, "Exégèse critique et interprétation théologique," *Recherches de science religieuse*, 39 (*Mélanges Jules Lebreton*, I, 1951), 237-52.

II. OLD TESTAMENT STUDIES

"My salvation shall not tarry; I will put salvation within Sion and give to Israel my glory. . . ." (Is 46:13)

RODERICK A. F. MacKENZIE, S.J.

The Structure of the Old Testament

The diligent reader will find in this comprehensive article a discussion of questions such as these: How would a modern author be inclined to write the history of Israel? How did the Old Testament authors write the same history? In what sense is Genesis the foundation stone of the Old Testament structure? Why was the Israelite concept of man's relation to God somewhat pragmatic? In what sense did this relation involve an exchange? What is the significance of the story of Moses? What is the Old Testament attitude toward man's habitual rebellion against God? How do the Yahwist and Priestly interpretations of the man-to-God relationship differ? What was the central message of the Prophets? How did the Old Testament hope for salvation become spiritualized? How does the Old Testament speak of the relation of God to the Gentiles? How do the Jewish and Christian arrangement of the Old Testament books differ? What values are emphasized in each of these different arrangements?

Father MacKenzie, author of a previous article, is rector of the Pontifical Biblical Institute in Rome.

The structure of the Old Testament is not quite the same as the history of Israel, or for that matter the history of the Old Testament. By the history of Israel we mean a history conceived and expressed in modern terms: a narrative presentation of the externally perceptible events in the life of a people, their movements, their cultural development, their progress in thought, social structure, and

This paper was first delivered at the 1960 Christmas Conference of the Basilian Fathers in Toronto. It was published in *The Basilian Teacher*, February 1961, and is reproduced here with permission.

the like. It is thus that we would write a "history of . . . [America]" or of any Western nation. We can quite legitimately do the same for ancient Israel. There is enough material in the Old Testament, enriched now with vast new acquisitions of knowledge concerning the neighboring civilizations of Egypt and Mesopotamia, to enable scholars to compose a well-developed and sufficiently detailed account of the life of this little Semitic people of the first millennium B.C. Even in those terms, the story is a fascinating one. Even without reference to revelation or Israel's historical connection with Christianity, profound religious lessons could be drawn from it. But such a work would not include statements such as "God led the people out of Egypt." History in the modern style, even though written by a believing Catholic and for use in Catholic schools, just does not mention the name of God. I am not criticizing this. It is a perfectly legitimate literary and scholarly convention. We write history in terms of secondary causes, dealing only with events on the plane of ordinary human experience.

A Modern History of Israel

In modern terms, then, what would be our presentation of this history? We would start with the situation of a group of Semitic tribes in Egypt at the beginning of the thirteenth century B.C. They are descendants of seminomads who migrated thither from the land of Canaan generations before. Now they find themselves increasingly constrained and oppressed by the Egyptian government. The Pharaohs of the nineteenth dynasty have moved their capital downriver from Thebes to the Delta and find it convenient to exploit, that is, to mobilize for the service of Egypt, the manpower of these Semites who are still recognizable as foreigners upon Egyptian territory. But one man appears, who organizes resistance to the government. The Semites are united; they successfully defy their Egyptian overlord; they make an unexpected and mysteriously successful getaway into the Sinai desert. After much wandering to and fro—in which, however, they maintain their unity—they head for that land of Canaan which their ancestors had left three or four centuries before. Partly by fighting, partly by infiltration, they establish their claim to it and settle down there. They exchange their seminomadic for an agricultural way of life, and soon find it necessary to organize themselves as a monarchical state. Only so can they preserve national unity and resist being overwhelmed by the Philistines in the west, by the nomad Bedouin from the east, or by the Arameans in the north.

There is first the one kingdom, then the twin kingdoms of Israel and Judah. They flourish for two or three centuries until the great recrudescence of imperial ambitions in Mesopotamia, represented especially by the kings of Assyria. First the northern kingdom is swept away in the eighth century B.C., then the successors of the Assyrians, the Neo-Babylonians, overrun and destroy the smaller kingdom, early in the sixth century B.C.

The surviving population of Jerusalem and its environs is deported to Babylonia. Again something unexpected happens. The deportees do not lose their identity among the teeming thousands of Mesopotamia. They stick together closely and even develop a keener sense of their racial, national, and religious separateness from other peoples. So much so that when the Neo-Babylonian power is engulfed in the vaster Persian empire, fifty years later, the Judaeans in Babylonia petition to be allowed to migrate to the land of their fathers and grandfathers, there to rebuild the temple that was destroyed and to resume the worship of their God as a functioning national community.

That prayer is granted by the Persian conqueror Cyrus. Thus is constituted, in the fifth satrapy of the great empire, the minuscule province of Judea, centered in the city of Jerusalem, containing a community which is truly the heir of the pre-Exilic southern kingdom, even of the glories of the older united kingdom of Solomon and David.

This small population is geographically isolated, yet it has connections with many similar Jewish communities in other parts of the Near East, Egypt and Mesopotamia especially, They enjoy a comparatively peaceful existence under the Persians, under Alexander, under the Hellenistic monarchies until the attempted suppression of their religion by the Seleucid king Antiochus IV, in the second century B.C., brings the violent uprising that is the Maccabean revolt. This, for a time, actually re-establishes an independent Jewish power in Palestine; but in less than a century, it is overrun and subdued by the power of Rome.

Such in barest outline might be a history of Israel, in modern style. It is all true, you see; it is all accurate, and a great deal more detail could be added; but it is utterly different from Israel's own concept of her story. The name of God has not appeared in that account at all.

Israel's Own Story

On the other hand, the story Israel has to tell is not so much her own history as a partial biography of her God; it is the account of what God has done to Israel, with Israel. Therefore the center of interest, the "formal object," is not Israel herself but her divine Creator, Lord, and Covenant-partner. The external events of her experience are narrated only insofar as they externalize and convey His promises and His acts. In those events Israel has met God, has heard His voice, has experienced His work and also has given her answer. For the sake of His glory, not her own, she bears her testimony to all that He has said and done to her. All this, the experience of the people, the word spoken through the prophets, is put on record that no particle of it may be forgotten, that the testimony may be transmitted to future generations and even to the Gentiles. Thus, the history the Israelites write about themselves is, really, theology: it is a statement about God, an affirmation of faith concerning the God who spoke to them. The structure of the Old Testament, then, is not the external history of Israel; it is the history of the divine actions upon this people.

The Meaning of Genesis

This theological history begins with the book of Exodus. Before the events therein narrated, Israel does not exist. The people are constituted by the events of the Exodus and the Sinai covenant.

How then do we come to have the book of Genesis? Where does this book fit into the structure of the account of Israel's experiences with her God? From the point of view of Israel's experience, the book of Genesis is secondary. But from our point of view as Christians, it appears as the foundation stone of the Old Testament structure.

In Genesis 12-50, we find the story of the ancestors of Israel. They are pictured as individuals who, centuries before, lived in Canaan, and with whom this same God made a covanant, by anticipation as it were: a covenant which did not directly benefit them, but which consisted mainly in a promise for the future; a covenant which guaranteed that their descendants should return to Canaan to enjoy the land, in a special covenant relationship to this God. So those patriarchs have a connection with Israel, though they are not Israelites. (Remember Abraham was *not* a Jew!) They are ancestors: they illustrate the themes of choice and of promise, which are characteristic of the whole story. In our historical terms, we can locate these figures fairly well in the early centuries of the second millennium B.C.

Before that, we have Genesis 1-11, which is again a step back in time. Now there is no Israel, and there are no ancestors of Israel who can be known as individuals. There is only mankind, the mankind out of which God was to choose, in fact to create, this people. Because He existed before Israel did, because He existed from the beginning, they must explain His relationship to the whole human race. Hence we have these chapters which are so immensely rich in theological teaching—almost in proportion, one might say, to their unlikeness to our type of history.

Israel's Practical Approach to God

In all of this, the Israelite writers' interest is in man's relationship to God. The starting point—and almost the finishing point too—of Israel's interest in their God is what He does for them. They are not, I think, interested in Him for His own sake. By that I do not mean to imply any lack of devotion or of a right religious attitude on their part, but simply that they know Him because He has manifested Himself to them, and He concerns Himself with them. Outside of that they do not speculate. (There are individual exceptions to this rule, chiefly in the later Old Testament period.) They communicate as much as they have experienced and can conceive of His demands, and what response they made to them. Further, they put on record His earlier promises to their ancestors, and convey what they know of His activity among the human race from which they sprang. But further back than that they do not attempt to go. They begin simply with His creation of the universe, the setting for man's activity. At the beginning of those creative acts there stands Yahweh alone, in all His mystery. They do not attempt to trace Him further back, into His own secret pre-existence. From the beginning, and before the beginning, He is there.

The Israelites have this much in common with the general ancient attitude toward religion in the Near East [in] that their fundamental approach is a severely pragmatic one. Their concern is with God's plan for men in general and themselves in particular. They do not go in for theological speculation for its own sake. If no activity is in prospect, if nothing is to be done about certain truths, then for them those truths quite lack interest. They do not even bother to wonder about them or to record them.

Yahweh as God of Salvation

An essential part of this structure, as it is traced through the Old Testament, is that it is an exchange. There is God's side of the work, and there is man's response. The salvation history is represented as a dialogue. God speaks to men, creatures with the gift of speech, and requires an answer from them. But speech on both sides is not mere utterance of words; it is as much deeds as words. God does things for these creatures, and expects a certain action from them in response.

What does He do for them? What is the divine activity? It can be summed up in the word salvation. All peoples of the Near East, as all peoples generally, I suppose, who are religious, looked to their gods for salvation. By this we understand the good which human minds and hearts can imagine and desire, but cannot attain to by their own resources; for which appeal must be made to extra-human or supra-human powers. This craving for salvation, whatever form it takes, is common, on the human side, to all religions alike.

The Divine Initiative

The interesting part of Israel's presentation is that her God takes the initiative in offering salvation, and what He offers is far above and beyond anything which man can imagine or desire. This may be illustrated from the opening chapters of Exodus. Remember the account therein given of the situation of the Hebrews in Egypt and the type of message that Moses brings them? We are not told, and we probably should not suppose, that those Hebrews knew of Yahweh, much less worshiped Him. The announcement made by Moses, even the very name of God, is something new to them. No doubt there had been preserved, perhaps in Moses' family, perhaps in other groups, some traditions about the patriarchs, about the God of Abraham, and the peculiar promises He had made. But in the main we have no reason to think of this "mixed multitude," as the Bible calls them, as being anything but polytheists and worshipers of Canaanite gods and goddesses. Just to drive that point home, the writers of Exodus carefully avoid saying that the Hebrews cried out to Yahweh. We read several times that they groaned and cried under their oppression, and that Yahweh heard them; but not that He heard them crying to Him. The omission is quite deliberate: it expresses the novelty of Moses' intervention, and that means, ultimately, the initiative taken by Yahweh. The plan of this great salvation act, the Exodus, did not come from men; it was Yahweh's own idea.

This is again brought out in the details of Moses' message. The people were complaining at being subjected to the same kind of government servitude as the unfortunate Egyptian *fellahin*. Possibly they had to pay taxes in kind; certainly they had to furnish, for several months in the year, manpower for Pharaoh's building enterprises. This was something unprecedented and repulsive to the traditions of independence and liberty of these seminomads. What then were they crying for? Certainly they were not asking to leave the land of Goshen and start wandering through the desert. No idea of emigrating had crossed the mind, as far as we can tell, of any of these Hebrews in Egypt. All they wanted was that the government inspectors would go way and leave them in peace. If the oppression had ceased, if the situation as it was prior to the nineteenth dynasty had been restored—the "good old days" when they owned no master but simply enjoyed a good life in the Egyptian Delta—they would have been satisfied.

Therefore the salvation announced to them by Moses is, literally, more than they asked for. He comes and tells them that the God of their fathers is taking an interest in them, has remembered now His promise to Abraham, and is about to fulfill it in His own way. This fulfillment involves their packing up and leaving, and starting on a desert journey which turns out to be much longer than anybody, even Moses, expects. It involves all the other experiences and changes accompanying their constitution as God's people. All this is a divine initiative, as much a surprise to Moses himself as to the people whom he leads.

Human Resistance to God's Plan

In the same way, the account shows how all the human factors in the situation combine to resist Yahweh's will. Moses himself protests and argues; he tries so long to evade his commission that he makes Yahweh angry. The people are at first pleased, but soon become discourged and even resentful. Pharaoh, of course, is dead opposed, and so are Pharaoh's people. All the human wills involved resist Yahweh's plan; and one after another they are beaten down and forced to submit. The Hebrews are led out of Egypt, and through the desert, as Yahweh intended they should be. This is the biblical way of stressing the "allness" of God's causality in the salvation history.

In contrast to this salvation will, there is the negative response of men. There are exceptions, certainly, men who are responsive and faithful, but in general the history of Israel is the familiar and unhappy story of repeated rebellion and infidelity to their divine Covenant-partner.

The structure of the story has to keep these things in balance: first, that Yahweh's plans are not to be frustrated by men's resistance or ingratitude; on the other hand, that men's disobedience must be duly punished, since Yahweh's justice cannot ignore the sin of rebellion. The prophets insist on both these points. The guilty generation is punished, yet even through their defection and infidelity Yahweh continues to lead His people forward toward the promised salvation. The great Isaia develops this into the doctrine of the Remnant. The majority of the people are unfaithful, and therefore to be destroyed, but always a minority will persevere, and to that minority and its descendants the promises will be eventually fulfilled.

The Yahwist Theology of "Beginnings"

The same idea is carried back into that "prehistory" that we spoke of by one of the great "traditions" of Israelite theology. The Yahwist, as he is called, who has left us Chap. 2, 3, and 4 of Genesis, along with one version of the Flood story, and the story of the Tower of Babylon, has read back the mentality or psychology of Israel into prehistoric humanity. In accounting for the frustrations, tragedies, and general unsatisfactoriness of human life, he sees that it must have a moral explanation similar to the one he is familiar with. Therefore he pictures a good and loving God, creating human creatures and making a sort of covenant with them. He bestows on them an endlessly happy existence and requires as condition of the covenant the observance of a single prohibition. And the first human beings, exactly like Israel, are unfaithful and transgress that command. From that transgression follows all that is painful and disappointing in human life as we know it.

Priestly Theology of "Beginnings"

It is interesting to notice how the other parallel treatment of the beginnings takes a different view. This is the so-called Priestly tradition, represented in Chap. 1 and 5, in the other version of the Flood story in the Table of Nations, and Chap. 11. It concentrates on God's side of the dialogue, and hence has a much more optimistic tone. The great cosmogony of the first chapter reaches its climax with the creation of the human race, elevated above all other creatures and, by virtue of the divine likeness which it bears, functioning as a kind of vicegerent of the Creator Himself. That majestic account knows nothing of any fall of man, because it is picturing what God has done for His creatures and not how the latter may have responded or failed to respond. Similarly, with the successive covenants presented by the same tradition, that with Noe and that with Abraham (Gen 17); they are pictured as gracious decrees of God's providence, and the question of human acceptance or reaction is simply passed over. This is in line with the more strictly "theological" interest of the Priestly narrators.

Doctrine of the Prophets

The position of the prophets in this structure of the Old Testament is important. The work of Moses established the foundation and the constitution of the people. But thereafter they were not left to their own interpretation, so to speak, of a dead document. There is a constant renewal and continuance of God's part in the dialogue through His servants the prophets. There is also, unfortunately, continuance of the people's infidelity in their resistance to and disapproval of these messengers of God. The prophets' warnings are abundantly verified for the Judaeans in the event of the Exile. The destruction of the Temple, the habitation of Yahweh on earth; the demolition of the city, with which all kinds of wonderful promises had been associated; the cessation of the Davidic dynasty, which was supposed to enjoy an everlasting covenant with Yahweh: those things are interpreted by the prophets as the just punishment, long foretold, for the breaking of the covenant. Yet the covenant itself was not destroyed, or at least was promptly to be renewed.

More Spiritual Idea of Salvation

The work of salvation, then, is always continued in renewed intervention and rescue by Yahweh. But the very concept of salvation was drastically purified as time went on. At first, as we said, it was presented in crude terms such as seminomads in Egypt or in the desert might appreciate: a truce to all this wandering around—give us a place where a man can sit down and rest. The perpetual longing of the wanderer for a "lasting city," the nomad's dream of a *pied-à-terre* where he can settle down and find peace—that is the "formality" under which salvation is offered: a "good life" as they could conceive it.

But that salvation doctrine was elevated and spiritualized, step by step. Through a long and painful national experience, Israel learned to understand better her own fatal weakness, the hollowness of all merely earthly goods, and by contrast, the transcendent security and consolation to be found in Yahweh Himself. The highest appreciation of that in the Old Testament is found in Psalm 72, where the psalmist proclaims his great insight, that the greatest good, above all that is in heaven or on earth, is to possess Yahweh Himself. It took the rest of Israel a long time to reach that height; but at least there is in the post-Exilic age a very marked spiritualization of the idea of salvation.

God and the Gentiles

That is one aspect of the development of doctrine and understanding that marks the structure of the Old Testament. A similar growth occurred in Israel's concept of the relationship of other peoples, of the rest of mankind, to Yahweh. At first (in the Book of Exodus), He is Israel's God alone; that is all they know about Him, and that is all that concerns them. But because they have, and continually develop, such a superlative idea of His power, His independence, His lordship, because no other gods count for anything in comparison with Him, they soon came to attribute to Him all the divine activity there ever was or ever will be. Thus, as we have seen, they describe Him as making the universe and the whole human race long before Israel even existed. But there was the further question of the present and future relationship to Him of other peoples, beside Israel. How was it possible that this one supreme God should be known and worshiped only by this small and insignificant people? Could it continue to be so? Once the question was seriously raised, there could be only one answer to it, consistent with the character of Yahweh Himself. There must be, somehow, some time, a proclamation of Yahweh to the Gentiles, and a conversion of the Gentiles to Him.

The prophets are the great heralds of this doctrine, and they combine it with vehement reminders that the choice of Israel does not mean any intrinsic superiority of the latter over other nations: rather the contrary. Thus Amos in the eighth century makes an amazingly radical devaluation of the covenant-doctrine by quoting Yahweh to this effect: "I brought up Israel from the land of Egypt, as I brought the Philistines from Crete and the Arameans from Qir." Ezechiel, in the sixth century, almost comically combines prophecies of glory and consolation with gruff reminders that his people are totally undeserving of them. One of his most trenchant remarks is in Chap. 3, where he quotes Yahweh's commission: "I am not sending you to a foreign people who speak a strange language—if I did, they would listen to you—but to Israel, who will not hear you." That unflattering comparison of Ezechiel's becomes the theme of the Book of Jona, which is one of the gems of the Old Testament. It handles the question of the relationship of the Gentiles to Yahweh, showing not only His mercy toward them but also their receptiveness and grateful response to His Word. At every point they are favorably contrasted with the most unfavorable possible portrait of Israel, personified in the ungracious and stubborn figure of Jona. The book unmercifully satirizes Jona's mentality, so out of harmony with the gracious and patient kindliness of God. The book itself, of course, is a noble example of the generous universalism to which some, at least, of Israel's teachers had attained. And we should notice how they reconcile that universalism with the privileged position of Israel, which they do not for a moment question. The Ninivites are loved by Yahweh and are saved by Him, because they respond to His message; but that message has to be brought to them from Israel, and by an authentic Israelite prophet. Unworthy and almost contemptible as that prophet is, still he is an essential intermediary. When he shirks his duty and tries to run away, Yahweh must first bring back His wayward servant before He can proceed with His salvation for Niniveh.

Composition of the Old Testament

A point which may be of some significance for understanding the structure of the Old Testament is the material sequence of the books, and here we may observe an interesting variation between the Hebrew and Christian canons. Already in the pre-Christian era, long before the Jews began to have the complete Old Testament in one volume, there was a recognized sequence of the books, at least in broad outline if not in fixed details. The law came first, the five books of Moses. Next followed the prophetic books, looked on as containing the teaching of the prophets, who were the spokesmen of Yahweh. There were two groups, the "earlier prophets" comprising the books of Joshua to Kings, and the "later prophets" found in the books of Isaia, Jeremia, Ezechiel, and the Twelve Apostles. The rest were "the Writings," Psalms, Job, Proverbs, and everything else. The concept apparently was that the Law and the Prophets were the word of God spoken to Israel, while the Writings contained Israel's response to that word, or reflections upon it.

But in Christian Bibles you have that arrangement significantly changed. (The change may actually have begun among Greek-speaking Jews in Egypt, but of that we are not sure.) The second group, the prophetic books, is divided and the parts separated. The earlier Prophets, our "historical books," are left where they were, following upon the Law, but the second part, "prophetic books" in the narrower sense, is transferred after the Writings, so that in the complete Christian Bible it closes the Old Testament and immediately precedes the Gospels.

That seems to be significant of a Christian approach. The addition of the New Testament sheds new light on the Old and puts everything that precedes it in a new perspective. Now the prophets are valued, not so much for the teaching they gave, historically, to Israel, as for the teaching they give, prophetically, to us. They are seen as precursors of the Evangelists. Thus the structure of the Old Testament itself is modified when it becomes part of the Church's complete Bible and is understood as preparatory to the Incarnation and the new and definitive Covenant.

But this modification of the structure is a completion and a perfection. This is seen dramatically in the way that the last book of the New Testament, the Apocalypse, corresponds to Genesis, the first book of the Old Testament. Through them we are led from one eternity of God to another. We begin with God stepping out of His majestic solitude to create, and we end with God returning to that eternal beatitude with the creatures He has created. We come at the end of the Apocalypse to the final consummation of all things, which is the cessation of time and the entrance to eternity, but this time along with God's creatures, which have been led through all the peripeteias of history described in the intervening pages of the Bible.

Thus, we cannot completely account for the structure of the Old Testament without referring, finally, to the New Testament. There is but one salvation history, as there is but one race seeking salvation and one Saving God. In explaining or teaching separate parts of that history, we shall be much helped by keeping its over-all structure in mind.

BRUCE VAWTER, C.M.

Understanding Genesis

The earnest reader will find in this article a discussion of questions such as these: What papal document opened the way for a new approach to the understanding of Genesis? What particular key to interpretation did this papal statement explicitly approve? What sort of historical thinking influenced the composition of Genesis? What is the theological viewpoint of Genesis? What are the principal ideas that the story of Genesis tries to convey? What raw materials and literary forms were used in the composition of Genesis? In what sense is our contemporary understanding of Genesis a positive improvement over that of the past?

Father Bruce Vawter is professor of Sacred Scripture at Kenrick Seminary in St. Louis, Missouri. He is the author of *A Path Through Genesis* and *The Conscience of Israel.*

At the beginning of this discussion, it is proper to note briefly what has occasioned it. A generation ago we would hardly have considered just such a purpose as this, to discuss nothing less fundamental than the very meaning of Genesis. A real revolution has taken place in our dealing with the Bible, a reappraisal not only of our methods of teaching it, but, far more essentially, also of our own understanding of the subject. We are, very much for the better, much more unsure of ourselves than we would have been a generation ago. We have less encouragement to confuse timeless truth with an understanding of the truth which is necessarily conditioned by time. We acknowledge that our duty is to know, not in a vac-

This paper was first published in the *Proceedings of the Sixth Annual Convention of the Society of Catholic College Teachers of Sacred Doctrine.* It is reproduced here with permission.

uum, nor in the world-view of the age of faith, but as those who are at home and not merely resident in the twentieth century. We recognize the imperative of Newman's words: "In a higher world it is otherwise, but here below to live is to change, and to be perfect is to have changed often."

The direction of our studies has radically altered. A generation ago the teaching of Scripture was dominated by the *Manuel Biblique*, which was able to compress within a few volumes all that we felt needed to be said about the biblical books and "questions." The *Manuel Biblique* was mainly defensive, much concerned with holding to traditional views and refuting their adversaries. Today the *Manuel Biblique* is no more. It has been replaced by introductions and biblical theologies, by Bible dictionaries and atlases, by commentaries and thematic studies that are positive rather than apologetic in tone. We do not yet have enough of these, and we know that those we do have need systematic revision and replacement from time to time.

The symbol and crystallization of this change . . . was the appearance of the encyclical letter *Divino afflante Spiritu* of Pope Pius XII in 1943. In it the Pope called for a positive Catholic scholarship that would abandon merely defensive positions and exploit every resource of modern scientific method to make its own contribution to biblical science. He recognized that the entire critical scene had shifted since the last papal encyclical on biblical studies, and especially since the *Providentissimus Deus* of Leo XIII, in which caution had been very much the watchword. Anyone who would understand the wholly new atmosphere in which Catholic biblical studies are now pursued should compare the lengthy exhortation to the use of textual criticism in *Divino afflante Spiritu* with the references to the same subject in *Providentissimus* and in *Pascendi*.

The Meaning of History

As far as our subject . . . is concerned, what has made all the difference is the wholehearted adoption by *Divino afflante Spiritu* of the literary form as the key to interpretation. It is true, literary forms were not previously unknown; but not until our times have they been invoked so extensively, and for eminently positive purposes as well as for the solution of difficulties.

Formerly, the exegete was expected to reason something like this:

Unless the sacred writer has made it incontestably plain that his words were not intended at their literal face value, he is to be understood as having written literal history. This principle was invoked by the Biblical Commission in a decree of 23 June 1905 against a theory of "apparent history" by which certain exegetes had sought to solve some of the historical difficulties of the Bible.[1] To be sure, the principle was sound enough, provided the interpreter was in a position to recognize the signs given him by the sacred writer, but in practice he usually could not do this. As a result, the application of the principle often enough begged the whole question. Unless the sacred writer had provided unmistakable evidence that he was not writing history as the interpreter understood history, then the interpreter was to take the text as representing history in his sense of the word.

Today we rightly take the Scripture itself rather than the interpreter as our point of departure. Rather than assume that the sacred writer was right-minded enough to share our view as to what history is, we begin with the more considerate question: What was his idea of history? This is to appeal to his literary form. This is the principle adopted by the Biblical Commission in its famous letter of 16 January 1948 to Cardinal Suhard, which modified the decree of 30 June 1909 concerning the first chapters of Genesis.[2] In this letter the Commission insists, among other things, on the necessity of examining the literary processes of ancient oriental peoples, their psychology, their way of expressing themselves, *and their very notion of historical truth* ("et leur notion même de la vérité historique").[3] Only on this basis, said the Commission, may one attempt to interpret the biblical author.

History in Genesis

Applying these principles, what are we to say of the history of Genesis? In the very first place, to be properly oriented we must remember that though Genesis is the first book in our Bibles, it is far from being the Bible's oldest book. In its letter to Cardinal Suhard just mentioned, the Biblical Commission stated that the older decrees to which we have already referred, together with that of 27 June 1906 on the Mosaic authorship of the Pentateuch,[4] are not intended to exclude further re-examination of the same questions in the light of scientific knowledge acquiring in the intervening half-century. It added that there is no one today who does not admit that the Mosaic law underwent progressive enlargement ("accroissement") through the ages, and that the historical narratives of the Pentateuch had a like development.[5] The Commission did not make it its business to decide the nature of Mosaic authorship in relation to the literary study of the Pentateuch; this question it left to the study of Catholic scholars, to be pursued "sans parti-pris." Neither are we presently concerned with this question. We will simply note that modern Catholic scholarship in general accepts the common critical view that the Pentateuch was completed in its present form in the post-Exilic period, in the fifth century B.C., a compilation from various streams of tradition, on the one hand the parallel sources designated J, E, and P by the critics, which have been combined to make up the books of Genesis, Exodus, and Numbers (Leviticus is entirely P), and on the other hand the complementary source D, which accounts for most of the book of Deuteronomy and which may originally have been the beginning of a separate history, continued in the books of Joshua through Kings. . . .

Israel's history as Israel begins with Moses, with the Exodus, and the other soul-stirring events by which Yahweh created this people. This Israel began to write its history with the coming of the Davidic monarchy and the consolidation of the state under Solomon. . . . The historical writing which dates from this period is of a high order, virtually unique in the world of its time, and of this tradition the redactor of the Pentateuch is the heir. The sources on which he necessarily depends are not properly historical writings. They too, nevertheless, are from the beginning shot through and through with an historical sense that again has no parallel among other ancient peoples. Before it wrote history, early Israel exercised its narrative gift in the aetiological story: What mean these stones? What is the origin of peoples like Ammon and Moab? How are the Edomites related to Israel? The answers to these questions are overladen with legend and the accretions of popular fancy, but they are in the order of history, based on true recollections. They are not myth, which is the characteristic of the aetiological stories of other ancient peoples. Even the most primitive stories that have found their way into the Pentateuch contain accurate historical data to a surprisingly high degree, far higher than we would have any right to expect a priori. Such has been one of the chief revelations of Palestinian archaeology.[6] The sense of history that accounts for this fact is to be traced to Israel's unique origins in its encounter with Yahweh. It was Yahweh's intervention in history that had made Israel. Yahweh was no mythical god, like the Canaanite Baal, to be experienced in the recurring cycles of nature. He was a God who had done things at determined points in time. Because Israel had experienced Yahweh in history and was itself the result of history, Israel had a sense of history.

Genesis is the product of this historical sense. It takes only the most superficial comparison of it with *Enuma eliš*, the theogonic myth sometimes called "the Babylonian Genesis," to recognize immediately the wholly different world from which it comes.[7] Genesis can make use of myth, but it is not myth. Even when it uses myth to fill out its content, its intention is historical, to tell what happened. "What happened" does not necessarily mean what is told in the stories of Genesis; I think its author was as well aware as we of the intrinsic unlikelihood of some of these. "What happened," rather, was what Israel's experience of Yahweh had taught it must have happened, and which it documented with the materials it had at hand, legend, folklore, saga, whatever they might be. All historical writing must be to some extent a reconstruction. The reconstruction of Genesis derives from Israel's knowledge of Yahweh and his purposes, infallibly demonstrated in his deeds, epitomized in the doctrine of election. Such a reconstruction, we may say, is theology rather than history. This distinction, however, would have been meaningless to the author of Genesis, who had no word for "theology" or for "history." Because his reconstruction began with history, it too was historical, the only kind of history he could write; what we call history and theology were to him one and the same.

The historical reconstruction of Genesis begins with creation, in which act are to be seen all the attributes which Israel recognized in the God of its election and covenant. The Genesis story of creation opens with an extract from the Priestly tradition, a source committed to writing during the Exile much under the influence of prophetic teaching, with some striking affinities to the militant monotheism of Deutero-Isaia.[8] But if P is more explicit and doctrinaire in its teaching, the much older J tradition, with which the author continues the story, teaches nothing that is essentially different. It is very evident that the God of P and J is one and the same: a supremely moral, only God, whose work of creation is good. That the ancient J source also began its sacred history with creation shows us again how venerable was the historical conception continued by the author of Genesis. Just as history for the Israelite was nothing if not *sacred* history, neither was creation or any other divine fact merely a theologoumenon, but part of sacred *history*. We might note, incidentally, that this Old Testament viewpoint is one that is continued in the New Testament.

History, then, begins with God and creation. Creation was good, for God was good, yet the author had to explain the evident fact of evil. Sin must have had a beginning; hence, there is a story of the fall of man. Yet if men are sinners, God remains true. Not only in the verses subsequent on the fall, the "protoevangelion," but also repeatedly, God is shown with the determination not to abandon the man created in His image and likeness. Providence rules the world, for the world remains God's good creation despite what man has made of it through his disobedience. This providence and the opposition of good to evil are the themes of Genesis.

The story of mankind is unfolded. The primitive human pair becomes a family, which divides and subdivides into many families. After the flood, which divides the story of human origins into two parts, the proliferation of humankind begins afresh, and the families of man are scattered throughout the world, now separated from one another by languages and customs. God is seen to have resigned Himself to living with the man He has created, and to have pledged Himself to deal with him by providential intervention rather than by permitting the return of primal chaos. The arts and the crafts develop. Cities are founded. And from one of these cities, from one of the many human families, Abraham is summoned to migrate to the land of Canaan, destined for his descendants four ages hence.

We may pause to remark how essentially true all this is, the history as well as the theology. Unlike the origin-myths of other ancient peoples, who put their city, their state, their race at the center of the divine act, Genesis frankly makes Israel a latecomer, lost among the families that make up world history. This realism is otherwise unheard of in antiquity. Israel's prerogatives are tremendous, certainly, but the author will deal with them where they belong historically, as the result of God's special providence. Apart from this grace of God, there is nothing in the nature of things superior about Israel or its ancestors, proximate or remote.

And so the story continues. The author uses the sources that were available, admittedly with artifices and conventions not permitted in modern historiography, but throughout with the manifest intention of writing history as he knew it. He is circumscribed by the limitations of his age in respect to many details, as we well know. We who have taken our science as we have taken our scientific history, at second hand, have better information on many of these things than the author of Genesis enjoyed. Even here, however, he stays in the realm of history, not myth or magic. His is a science of appearances, the only science that was known until fairly recent times; in its own way it makes an attempt to assign rational explanations, and it should be respected for what it tries to do rather than condemned for what it does not. The mythical conception of the cosmos is sedulously avoided. This mythical conception, the common property of Near Eastern literature, occurs frequently enough in the poetic imagery of the Old Testament, but it has no place in an historical account.

With Abraham the story narrows down to the one family in which the author is proximately interested, but the historical spirit is never abandoned. Abraham's call is not a departure from the divine covenant that has been made with all mankind, but a means of implementing it. It foreshadows the covenant with Israel that is at the heart of this sacred history. The patriarchal history, we now know more and more, is no mere artifice, but represents solid historical recollections of at least some of those who were later to make up the Israelite federation.[9] Relationship with other peoples, even hated peoples like the Edomites, is frankly acknowledged. This is part of the message of Genesis, for there is no election without selection. It is always God's providence that makes Israel, nothing inherent in itself.[10] Finally, Israel is brought into Egypt, where it is to be formed into a people, and the scene is set for Moses and the Exodus.

The Materials

So much for the author's story. There is a great deal more to it than this; of course, [there are] many ramifications of his theme and countless minor preoccupations. But this is the outline of the history he wanted to relate. It is a simplification of the past, surely, and in large part a reconstruction of it, but it remains history for all that. What were the materials he had to work with in the writing of this history? Since, as we know, the redactor of Genesis and the Pentateuch combined already complete, or virtually complete, histories to make up our present text, we are really concerned here with the materials that have gone into the sources of the Pentateuch.

First and foremost, they included genuine historical recollections, as we have already insisted. Popular folklore they may be, transmitted through the creative imagination of the storyteller, incomplete and highly selective, yet they put us in authentic contact with the past. We cannot ask of them more than this, for the past which they remembered was already too remote to be recalled other than in a simplified form. The origins of the stories were as many as the origins of the people who told them. It is now strongly suspected that the Sinai and Kedesh traditions combined in the Pentateuchal sources derive from separate histories, from different components of people of Israel. It is even more generally agreed that not all those whom we know historically as the people of Israel had ancestors who had been in Egypt. Not only were there probably two separate groups which invaded Canaan at different times, one, under Joshua from the east, and the other from the south, but there were other Hebrews who had been indigenous there from the time of the Patriarchs, and still others, originally unrelated to these by blood ties, were brought into the Israelitic alliance by treaty and covenant.[11] Most of this had been forgotten in favor of larger issues, though there are fleeting and half-remembered allusions to it in the Old Testament. Not unlike the American citizen of perhaps the second or third generation who regards (and rightly) the war of independence as part of the history of his own people, the later Israelite considered himself the heir of a unified Israelitic history.

Contrary to the views of some,[12] the earliest as well as the more recent of these traditions, that is, those of the patriarchal age as well as those of the settlement in Palestine, contain to an astonishing degree authentic historical recollections. As we have already indicated, archaeology has furnished the evidence to substantiate this statement.

Beyond the patriarchal times, to describe the vast age of mankind that preceded Abraham, it is not really correct to say that the Israelites retained historical recollections. As we have seen, the description of this age is done by conviction rather than remembrance. They knew very well, for example, that existing human institutions had had a beginning. In Genesis 4 and 10, however, when the Yahwist records these beginnings, he is writing poetry rather than history. There was no historical chronology available, and the elaborate chronology given Genesis by the Priestly writer is quite artificial and theological. Lacking scientific and critical means of getting at prehistory, Israel did what it could. Into an artistically contrived whole it used its narrative genius to combine hero-stories, legends, myths, poems, genealogies, and other miscellaneous materials; with this it bridged what it knew was the considerable gap between creation and the beginning of historical recollection. Many of these elements doubtlessly owed their existence to some real event —the flood-epic, for example, the story of the tower, the story of Cain and Abel—but their present homogeneity and continuity are artificial. Still, we can call this section generally historical, as we have done, because it is a sober reconstruction, with whatever unlikely materials, dominated by an historical sense. There is nothing, or virtually nothing, in it that borders on the fantastic, frivolous tales which other peoples supplied for their ignorance of the past.

The profound truths inculcated in the stories of creation and the fall obviously appear in narratives that are completely imaginary as to detail. These can be called "historical" only in the sense that they teach truths about real events; in this sense the term "historical" has been applied to the first three chapters of Genesis by the Biblical Commission.[13] Some of the elements in these stories can be duplicated in the creation-myths of other Near Eastern peoples, but they have been thoroughly assimilated into narratives which appear to be originally Israelitic in conception. There is no firm agreement as to what we are to call their literary form. Some authors do not hesitate to apply the term "myth," not in its ordinary dictionary definition, but as it is defined by modern philosophers and anthropologists, essentially a perception and expression of truth, specifically divine truth, though not by the processes of discursive reasoning.[14] Whatever we are to call the genre, it has been used to inform a content that would be inconceivable apart from Israel's historical encounter with Yahweh.

Conclusion

. . . Admittedly, we have been explaining Genesis along lines that have not always prevailed among Catholic interpreters, though as a matter of fact our understanding of it is a return to an earlier exegetical tradition that was abandoned because of circumstances which we have no purpose in analysing [here]. In any case, we have no choice but to accept the results of sound criticism in our dealing with this book; this our dedication to truth and the explicit injunction of ecclesiastical authority demand of us.

[It should be said], in conclusion, that, above all, our [understanding] should be positive, that our first aim should always be to deal with what the inspired author was really interested in, not with what did not enter his mind.

References

[1] *Enchiridion Biblicum* (Naples: D'Auria, 1954), §161 (hereafter *EB*); *Rome and the Study of Scripture* (St. Meinrad's Abbey, 1953), 115f. (hereafter *RSS*).

[2] *EB*, §§336-43; *RSS*, 120-22.

[3] *EB*, §581; *RSS*, 150.

[4] *EB*, §§181-84; *RSS*, 116f.

[5] *EB*, §§579-80; *RSS*, 149.

[6] Cf. William F. Albright, *The Archaeology of Palestine* (Baltimore: Penguin Books, Inc., 1954), pp. 204-208, 235-37; Nelson Glueck, *Rivers in the Desert* (New York: Farrar, Straus & Cudahy, 1959), esp. pp. 60-84.

[7] Cf. H. and H. A. Frankfort, "The Emancipation of Thought from Myth," in *Before Philosophy* (Baltimore: Penguin Books, Inc., 1949), pp. 237-48; Bruce Vawter, C.M., "Our God is the God of History," *Worship*, 32 (1958), 225-33, 287-300.

[8] Cf. Carroll Stuhlmueller, C.P., "The Theology of Creation in Second Isaias," *Catholic Biblical Quarterly*, 21 (1959), 429-67.

[9] Cf. H. H. Rowley, *From Joseph to Joshua* (London: The British Academy, 1950), pp. 43ff., 57-108; Bruce Vawter, *A Path Through Genesis* (New York: Sheed & Ward, Inc., 1956), pp. 230f., 292f.

[10] Karl Cramer, *Genesis 1-11: Urgeschichte?* (Tübingen: Mohr, 1959), pp. 17-19, interestingly points out that this is the message of the patriarchal stories rather than their being a foreshadowing of Israel's possession of Canaan.

[11] Rowley, *From Joseph to Joshua*, pp. 100-108, 125-29; H. Cazelles, S.S., *Les Nombres* (La Sainte Bible de Jérusalem; Paris: Éditions du Cerf, 1952), p. 98, note *d;* Donato Baldi, O.F.M., *Giosuè* (La Sacra Bibbia; Turin: Marietti, 1952), p. 70; G. A. Mendenhall, "Covenant Forms in Israelite Tradition," *Biblical Archeologist*, 17 (1954), 50-76; Albright, *From the Stone Age to Christianity* (Garden City: Doubleday & Company, Inc., 1957), pp. 276-82; F. M. Abel, O.P. and M. du Buit, O.P., *Le livre de Josué* (La Sainte Bible de Jérusalem; Paris: Éditions du Cerf, 1958), pp. 10-12, 103f.

[12] The school of Albrecht Alt, in general, characteristically represented by Martin Noth, *The History of Israel* (New York: Harper & Row, Publishers, 1958). See the remarks of G. E. Wright, "Archaeology and Old Testament Studies," *Journal of Biblical Literature*, 77 (1958), 46-48.

[13] *EB*, §336; *RSS*, 120.

[14] John L. McKenzie, S.J., "Myth and the Old Testament," *Catholic Biblical Quarterly*, 21 (1959), 265-82. "Some term must be improperly applied; if it is not to be theology or history, why should it not be myth? And is not myth a less improper term than these others? No doubt something should be added to distinguish these passages from the myths to which the name has so long been exclusively applied" (281). Cf. *ibid.*, "The Literary Characteristics of Genesis

2-3," *Theological Studies*, 15 (1954), 541-72; "Mythological Allusions in Ezekiel 28," *Journal of Biblical Literature*, 75 (1956), 322-27. Other authors find the difference between the Old Testatment forms and myth too pronounced to permit the use of the term; cf. J. Barr, "The Meaning of 'Mythology' in Relation to the Old Testament," *Vetus Testamentum*, 9 (1959), 1-10. On the respect shown myth as a legitimate conveyer of truth, see Ernst Cassirer, *The Philosophy of Symbolic Forms*, II: *Mythical Thought* (New Haven: Yale University Press, 1955).

BRUCE VAWTER, C.M.

Messianic Prophecies in Apologetics

The fair-minded reader will find in this searching article a discussion of questions like these: What are the shortcomings in apologetics of matching New Testament details with isolated texts taken from the Old Testament? What is the true nature of Old Testament prophecy? In what sense is Old Testament messianism developmental? Does the Old Testament expectation always center on a personal Messiah? What are the limitations of the use in apologetics of the Old Testament figure of the Messiah-King? What is the best way to explain how the Old Testament fulfills the New? In what sense does the New Testament fulfillment go beyond the Old Testament expectation? What was the attitude of Jesus toward His own Messiahship? How does the New Testament preaching of the resurrection of Christ make use of Old Testament prophecy?

Father Vawter, author of a previous article, teaches Scripture at Kenrick Seminary in St. Louis.

The Misuse of Messianology

Used as we are to the centrality of Christ in our religious thinking, we have the tendency to attribute a like centrality to the figure of the Messiah in the religious thinking of Judaism and the Old Testament. This, however, is a grave mistake. . . . The failure to recognize [this] unique emphasis of Christianity has sometimes led us in the past to expect from messianic prophecy something more—

This paper was first delivered at the Buffalo meeting of the Catholic Theological Society of America and was published in the *Proceedings of the Fourteenth Annual Convention*. It is included here, the first part considerably abridged, with permission.

or, rather, something different—than it is prepared to give. It has led to the imposition of a messianic meaning (better, a christological meaning) on texts that will not sustain it when examined in the light of sound historical criticism. It has led to the attempt to find a complete Christology in the Old Testament, according to which the most minute and even trivial details of our Lord's life and personality were systematically foretold in prophecy; parallel columns represented point by point Old Testament prediction on the left and New Testament fulfillment on the right.

I am aware that the limitations of this type of proof from prophecy are well known . . . and that its extravagances are avoided nowadays by professors of apologetics. My purpose in again pointing out its shortcomings . . . is therefore not just another, unneeded indictment of a notorious misuse of Scripture. Rather . . . I hope to show that what is wrong with the parallel-text argument is not its extravagances, but the argument itself.

What is wrong is not the selection of texts, but the entire methodology. The "A in the Old Testament = B in the New Testament" procedure inevitably assumes precisely what apologetics seeks to prove, that the New Testament is correct in regarding itself as the fulfillment of the Old Testament. This it does on the wholly fallacious premise that the Christology of the New Testament can be found point by point in the Old Testament, that the Old Testament writers, in other words, meant just what the New Testament writers mean when the latter refers to the former. By ignoring historical exegesis, the argument can make an appeal to no one who does not already accept the New Testament's account of itself. The meaning of A is defined by B; then A is pointed to triumphantly as the anticipation of B. Whatever this may be said to be, it is obviously not apologetics.

The New Testament writers, it is true, find Christ on every page of the Old Testament. The New Testament, however, is not a book of apologetics. It is a collection of writings by Christians for Christians, which in its use of the Old Testament leans on a typology already accepted in Christian faith. When Matthew, for example, cites a text like Osea 11:1 in connection with the Holy Family's sojourn in Egypt, he can do so only in view of a typology that permitted him to refer to Christ virtually anything that in the Old Testament was stated of Israel. As a matter of fact, it is only *by exception* that the New Testament adheres to the strictly historical sense in citing the Old Testament; in general, it interprets according to a deeper, spiritual sense.

Determination of the spirtual sense of the Scripture is a legitimate, in fact, a necessary task of the exegete, insisted on by Pope Pius XII in *Divino afflante Spiritu.* Without it, we can hardly have theology. Anyone who admits the unity of the Bible and believes in its inspiration by the one divine Spirit cannot ignore the validity of typology. But typology and spiritual senses have no function in apologetics. They presuppose faith—they do not lead to it.

The Nature of Messianic Prophecy

The Nature of Prophecy. What has often been presupposed in arguments, like the one we have been discussing, is a concept of prophecy verified neither in the Old Testament nor the New Testament. Whatever is to be said of the charism of prophecy in the abstract, it is a verified fact that one property of biblical prophecy is its obscurity. We simply do not look for, and have no right to expect, in Old Testament prophecy anything like a blueprint of the future.

In 22:19 Jeremia prophesies of the hated king Jehoiakim that he will have "the burial of an ass," that is, no burial at all, that his body will be cast outside the city as so much refuse. However, according to 2 Samuel 24:6 and 2 Chronicles 36:8, Jehoiakim received a normal burial with his fathers in Jerusalem. Since the king died detested by his subjects, who had already experienced the bitter and disastrous results of his policies, we can say that what Jeremia predicted might well have been carried out quite literally. But it does not appear to have been. Similarly, the prophet said of Jehoiakim that none of his descendants would sit on the throne of David (36:30). Actually, his son Jehoiachin did so, for all of three months, before he was deported to Babylon and replaced by his uncle Zedekiah, the last king of Judah. Again we can say, and truly, that the substance and spirit of Jeremia's prophecy were fulfilled. But we must also recognize that the prophet clearly had no photographic idea of the future.

A classic indication of the generic as opposed to the specific nature of the prophetic vision can be seen in Isaia's prophecy of invasion in 10:27-34 (the introduction to the messianic passage which follows in 11:1ff.). Here the prophet graphically describes the Assyrian army proceeding from the north, city by city, through Geba,

Gibeah, Anathoth, Nob, to the summit of Mount Zion. Actually, when the invasion came, Sennacherib followed the seacoast and entered Jerusalem from the west. Another classic indication is in the detailed prophecies against Babylon found in Isaia 13:17ff.; 14, 4ff.; Jeremia 50:15; 51:58, and so forth. Babylon was to be destroyed by the Medes, leveled like Sodom and Gomorrah, to remain a dwelling place only for wild beasts; her walls were to be thrown down, her gates burnt with fire, her king brought down to Sheol. Babylon did fall, not to the Medes, but to the Persians; and the conquest of the city was peaceful, with no bloodshed and no destruction.

These examples could be multiplied by the hundreds. What they prove is that while the prophet does foresee the future, he foresees it within the limitations imposed by his personal, historical, and cultural background. Messianic prophecy is no exception to this rule.

In Jeremia 33:14-26 occurs the prophecy of a messianic king: "a just shoot for David; he shall do what is right and just in the land. . . . Never shall David lack a successor on the throne of the house of Israel." Coupled with this is the equally categorical statement: "Nor shall priests of Levi ever be lacking, to offer holocausts before me, to burn cereal offerings, and to sacrifice victims." It is quite evident that to the prophet (not Jeremia himself, but one of his disciples) the perpetuity of the Levitical priesthood is taken as much for granted as the perpetuity of the Davidic kingship. It is all very well to say, as we rightly do, that the perpetual priesthood was fulfilled in a way not contemplated by the prophet; so was the messianic kingship fulfilled in a way he did not contemplate. This being so, how probable is it that we should find in prophecy details of the Messiah's birthplace, and the casual information that he would be buried in a rich man's tomb?

THE NATURE OF MESSIANOLOGY. The limitations inherent in the prophetic vision result in a multiformity of Old Testament messianism that is blandly ignored by the parallel-text argument, but which cannot be ignored by any apologetics that proposes to argue realistically from promise to fulfillment. In its broadest possible sense, what we call messianism is hardly distinguishable from Israel's conviction of its divine election and of God's continuing providence. Within this framework, the most varied conclusions emerged, all of which contribute to the messianic expectation, all of which find their fulfillment in Christ. Christianity is the fulfillment of the Israel of the old covenant, not of a few of its ideas.

By ignoring the varied forms of messianism and concentrating attention on a supposed messianology that developed only from generation to generation, here with an additional hint by a court poet, here with a further detail from an unknown prophet, we arrive at an obvious caricature of the Old Testament and of the Old Testament religion and revelation. In this acceptation, the millions who lived and died within the Old Covenant would have served no function other than to point up the lack of a redeemer. It would result that no demand of faith could reasonably have been made of anyone during Israel's long history, if there is no messianism, properly speaking, until the Old Testament exists complete, to serve as the source of the selected texts which . . . "[all were fulfilled in Jesus of Nazareth and in Him alone]."

Yet there are wide areas of the Old Testament in which there is no personal messianism whatever. If the monolithic messianism of the parallel columns were based on the historical development of revelation, we should expect to find the most clearly defined ideas about the Messiah and His fulfillment in the last of the Old Testament books. How little this expectation is justified will be apparent to anyone who pages the Books of Wisdom, Sirach, and Ecclesiastes. The author of Wisdom, who has accepted the Hellenistic conception of the soul, believes in an extraterrestrial blessed immortality; there is no room in his thinking for either a resurrection or for personal messianism. Ben Sira, on the other hand, sticks to an older view of human destiny that explicitly rejects a blessed immortality (cf. 41:4); neither does he contemplate a resurrection, and he retains only faint echoes of the messianic hope. Ecclesiastes is skeptical alike of Wisdom's optimism and of Sirach's complacency with the tried-and-true; he does "not doubt about God's existence and power, but rather concerning His readiness to intervene radically in history or in the individual human life. . . . He knows that the world was made and is watched over by God, but the tragedy of man is that he cannot achieve contact with this divine Being, which is too deeply hidden from him." [1] In such a perspective, there is no place for messianism.

The artificial conception of Old Testament messianology as a single process of development supposedly reaches a major plateau when the messianic hope has been "narrowed down" to the house of David by means of the dynastic oracle delivered by the prophet Nathan. Yet in none of the authentic words of the prophets Amos and Osea is there any reference to a Davidic Messiah. This does not mean that they have nothing to contribute to messianism, but they preached in . . . northern Israel where the dynastic oracle had no relevance. Davidic messianism is found in Isaia, Michea, and Jeremia, Judahite prophets all. But the Judahite Ezechiel, though he too speaks of a restoration of the Davidic line, appears to be a man whose heart is hardly in what he says. It is difficult to see in "my servant David" (34:23) the messianic king foretold by Isaia, since Ezechiel carefully withholds from him the royal title and circumscribes his prerogatives, lest the kingship once more should fall into the evil ways that had contributed to Israel's downfall. "His references to David are somewhat automatic, and they lack the warmth that Isaia gave them. His messianism is collective. Essentially, his true Messiah is the renewed temple." [2] Similarly, Abdia 21 explicitly restricts future kingship to Yahweh alone. Yet Ezechiel has written a vital page in messianism of which Christ is also the fulfillment: his very minimization of the kingship is part of the prophetic spiritualization of messianology.

Above in connection with Jeremia 33:14-26 we saw that the perpetuity of the Levitical priesthood was coupled with that of the Davidic kingship in the later prophetic mind. Such is certainly the messianism of Ezechiel; as just noted, the Levitical succession is far more important to him than the Davidic. Levitical messianism is the only messianism of Ben Sira (45:24f.). It is part of the messianic viewpoint of the Chronicler. In Judaism it gave rise eventually to the notion of two Messiahs, the priestly and the royal, the Messiah of Aaron and the Messiah of David. This is the messianic doctrine of the Qumrân community, with which it has become evident that primitive Christianity had much in common. There is little room for this messianism in the proof-text argument of apologetics; but room must be made for it in any argument that sets out to deal with the messianic expectation realistically.

Still within the area of the prophet's limited vision, we must face the fact that the royal Messiah of prophet and psalmist was something rather different from Christ the King. While it is true that the language they use of the king is the result of a messianic concept of the kingship, it nevertheless remains that the language is applicable to the reigning or about-to-reign monarch. We have no right to presume without necessity that the prophet was looking for the fulfillment of his prophecy anywhere but in the immediate future. As G. E. Wright has said, "the dividing line between the historical and the eschatological conceptions of kingship is very difficult, if not impossible, to draw; the second was simply the extension of the first to the age of God's fulfillment of His covenanted promises." [3] Modern critics have tried, without achieving any generally accepted formula, to define the point of this division, to determine when Israelite messianic thinking became metahistorical—when, in other words, it became apparent that the existing dynasty was not, in the normal working of divine providence, to fulfill the promises. But regardless of the point of division, we must never forget that the messianism of the Old Testament was that of a people, not of a church, and that the Messiah was conceived of as an Israelite king. The justice and judgment which he was to administer were those that had been habitually denied an oppressed people under faithless rulers. Furthermore, the eschatology of the Old Testament is earthbound. When Klausner writes[4] that our Lord's words, "My kingdom is not of this world" (Jn 18:36), "cannot be imagined in the mouth of a *Jewish* Messiah," he surely minimizes the potentialities of his own people; still, the fact remains, such a Messiah was not being expected by Israel, the prophets included. National messianism did not exclude spiritual messianism—that is not the point. The point is, however spiritual the messianic concept was, it was also national in its aspirations, and these aspirations were not fulfilled in the messianism of Jesus. St. Luke shows the Apostles themselves, after the experience of the Resurrection but before Pentecost, sharing this national hope: "Lord, will you at this time restore the kingdom to Israel?" (Ac 1:6).

Associated with this is the prevalence in the messianic prophecies of the abundant material blessings that are to be the characteristic of the messianic age. These are part of the prophets' mental framework in thinking of the return of the ideal conditions of the earthly paradise. How literally these details were taken is evidenced by the gusto with which Judaism enlarged on them in its later writings. We can hardly deny that the notion of a renewal of nature was no less real to the prophets than their notion of what the original paradisiacal condition had been; we have no right to dismiss as so much foolishness the Jewish acceptance of their words at their face value. If we have a better understanding of the meaning of these prophecies than the Jews did, we must also recognize that it is a better understanding than the prophets themselves had.

Much more could be said about the varieties of the messianic expectation. Old Testament messianism is not a single, wholly consistent, progressively developing, exclusively spiritual doctrine that has anticipated the Christology of the New Testament. It can be made this only at the expense of ignoring many of its important emphases and imposing on much of the remainder an understanding that has come only through the enlightenment of Christian faith. We cannot survey its aberrant elements and aberrant developments without acknowledging the disparate and limited concepts of the very authors from whom we draw our knowledge of the messianic hope.

The confession of Peter at Caesarea Philippi was not the casual affirmation one might think possible from the practice of lining up a half dozen psalm and prophetic texts which are called the proof from prophecy. Peter's confession, bolstered though it was by signs and the living Presence, was a step into the unknown, an act of faith. It is presented as such in the Gospel. I fear that in our apologetics we have sometimes given the impression that "Thou art the Christ!" was something less than a wonderful discovery, the acceptance of revelation.

Promise and Fulfillment

In the preceding two sections I have often adopted a more negatively critical tone than I might otherwise be disposed to use were I not dealing with the apologetical use of the Old Testament. Apologetics must be prepared to cope with such negative criticism, since it addresses itself not to the man of faith but the man seeking faith.

According to the Vatican Council (1), for such a man seeking faith, . . . ["God has willed that together with the internal help of the Holy Spirit there be joined external proofs of His revelation, that is, divine actions and above all miracles and prophecies. These show forth most clearly the omnipotence of God and His infinite knowledge and are therefore the most certain signs of divine revelation as they are suited to the understanding of everyone."][5]

The argument from messianic prophecy that would serve as such an adjunct to divine grace, I would humbly suggest, ought to be formulated in the following terms:

1. The point of departure should be not the Old Testament expectation, but the New Testament realization. The reasons for this

procedure are of both the practical and the theoretical order. (a) As far as the practical side of the question is concerned, we would do well to be guided by the advice of a master of apologetics, Dr. Frank Sheed, in his suggestions for the handling of analogous arguments.[6] Beginning with the prophecies, as I have indicated above, will involve endless discussion over the exact meaning of texts, discussion which, if honestly pursued, will as often as not end in a *non liquet*. Furthermore, the apologist does not always possess the exegetical training required for such a study. (b) This procedure is the only sound one theoretically. As I hope I have brought out, no Old Testament writer adequately foresaw the New Testament fulfillment. Thus an argument that proceeds from the Old Testament to the New Testament will inevitably commit the fallacy of having more in its conclusion than is contained in its premises. Such an argument will depend on an arbitrary selection of texts that have been chosen because they "fit." In view of the variety of the messianic expectation, and given another arbitrary selection of texts, it will be just as possible to "prove" that Jesus was not the Messiah as to prove that He was.

2. Not only must we begin with the New Testament fulfillment, we must also begin with the recognition that it is in every way greater than the Old Testament promise. Jesus is not the Old Testament Messiah, He is much more. He conceived of Himself as the culmination of the messianic hope, but in a way that far transcended anything that could have been in the imagination of an Old Testament prophet. With characteristic modernity, John Henry Newman observed the implication of this fact nearly ninety years ago:

> I think it observable that, though our Lord claims to be the Messiah, He shows so little of conscious dependence on the old Scriptures, or of anxiety to fulfill them; as if it became Him, who was the Lord of the Prophets, to take His own course, and to leave the prophets to adjust themselves to Him as they could, and not to be careful to accommodate Himself to them. The Evangelists do indeed show some such natural zeal in His behalf, and thereby illustrate what I notice in Him by the contrast. They betray an earnestness to trace in His Person and history the accomplishment of prophecy, as when they discern it in His return from Egypt, in His life at Nazareth, in the gentleness and tenderness of His mode of teaching, and in the various minute occurrences of His passion;

—and for the evangelists, we have noted, this was confirmatory argumentation, after they had recognized Him for what He was in His resurrection and glorification;—

> but He Himself goes straight forward on His way, of course claiming to be the Messiah of the Prophets, still not so much recurring to past prophecies, as uttering new ones, with an antithesis not unlike that which is so impressive in the Sermon on the Mount, when He first says, "It has been said by them of old time," and then adds, "But I say unto you." Another striking instance of this is seen in the Names under which He spoke of Himself, which have little or no foundation in any thing which was said of Him beforehand in the Jewish Scriptures. They speak of Him as Ruler, Prophet, King, Hope of Israel, Offspring of Judah, and Messiah; and His Evangelists and Disciples call Him Master, Lord, Prophet, Son of David, King of Israel, King of the Jews, and Messiah or Christ; but He Himself, though, I repeat, He acknowledges these titles as His own, especially that of the Christ, chooses as His special designations these two, Son of God and Son of Man, the latter of which is only once given Him in the Old Scriptures, and by which He corrects any narrow Judaic interpretation of them; while the former was never distinctly used of Him before He came, and seems first to have been announced to the world by the Angel Gabriel and St. John the Baptist. In these two Names, Son of God and Son of Man, declaratory of the two natures of Emmanuel, He separates Himself from the Jewish Dispensation, in which He was born, and inaugurates the New Covenant.[7]

Jesus did not proclaim Himself the Messiah, He permitted the proclamation; there is much significance in this distinction. Never did He call Himself by the most characteristic messianic title, Son of David. He had not come to be merely what the prophets had looked for; it was not the prophets' ideas but their ideals that He fulfilled. Both the Synoptic Gospels and John testify that He most characteristically thought of Himself as Son of Man, and today none but the most hypercritical will question this datum of the Gospel. (Parenthetically, one may note how the common apologetical argument from prophecy to fulfillment tends to ignore the figure of the Son of Man at the expense of ignoring Jesus' own proclamation of Himself. The reason for this, of course, is that the Son of Man is not a "messianic" title.) The Son of Man enters Jewish soteriological thinking from Daniel 7, where he evidently stands for Israel. But—and this is the point of Jesus' identification of Himself with the figure—he is a glorified Israel, an Israel that has attained salvation. Judaism had not made the association of the Son of Man with the Messiah (the association in the apocryphal Book of Henoch is still *sub iudice* as a possible Christian interpolation); the synthesis made by our Lord was to enrich the messianic concept with spiritual reality and to dissociate it firmly from earthly and political connotations. Along with the figure of the Son of Man, actually as part of it, is our Lord's proclamation of Himself as the Servant of the Lord of the Second Isaia. Again, the synthesis was Jesus' own, it had not been made by the Jews. Whatever the prophet may have known of the Servant—whether to him He was a collectivity or an individual, real or ideal—, in Jesus' life, death, and glorification He achieved His ultimate, incarnate reality.

In uniting in Himself and refining the fragmentary utterances of Old Testament prophecy—and, be it noted, in discarding some of them—our Lord did a unique thing, a thing as unique as His own person. His was a work of fulfillment—never before or after has fulfillment been so complete or so satisfying—and it was a fulfillment that the prophets would not have disavowed, though they could not possibly have foreseen it without being Christians before their time.

3. How, then, do we construct the bridge between the prophetic utterances and their fulfillment? This is the crucial question. The answer, we have seen, is not to be found in pretending that there is any equation as to the letter. The equation must rather be sought in the spirit which animated the prophecies. This means that we must really understand what the prophets were concerned with in their expectation, and we must be able to see that Jesus Christ, as He proclaimed Himself, was and is the insurpassable realization of their hopes.

a. The prophets stand firmly on Israelite soil, and their Messiah is an Israelite king. But it must be remembered, first of all, that the figure of the king in ancient Near Eastern society is not the merely political one of a modern secular ruler. The king is the anointed of the Lord and His representative, the one who furthers God's plans. What those plans might be in the final analysis, the prophets could only surmise in part. "No one can ever precisely and concretely predict what God will do." They shared the aspirations of their people, and they expressed these aspirations in varied conventional ways. But they always knew that God was not bound by their conventions. They are fully cognizant that the word they speak is God's, and that "God's word is always filled with the mystery of His Being." Thus it can be said that, however earthbound and national their expression of their hopes, they themselves expected that their fulfillment would be something greater.

b. Secondly, Israel the nation was to the prophets Israel the people of God. In the very earliest of the classic prophets (the prophet Amos) we have already the doctrine of the "remnant," a doctrine that is older than the prophets, which from the first enunciates the truth that God's concern is with the Israel of faith. Only history itself could reveal to the prophets what form the remnant was finally to take. Jeremia and Ezechiel identified it with Israel in exile, and they looked for a new covenant on Palestinian soil that would be all that the former covenant had failed to be. Their hopes were only partly realized, for the restored Israel reverted to most of the vices that the prophets had condemned through the centuries. But Ezechiel's clear proclamation of the principle of individual responsibility, coupled with the diaspora and post-Exilic proselytism, marked in principle the transition from the Israel of the flesh to the Israel of the spirit. When Jesus announced that the new covenant had finally come to pass in a form that wholly transcended national distinctions, He had brought prophetic teaching to its ultimate term, in a development that is throughout organically connected. Better than they themselves knew, the prophets had foretold the kingdom of God.

c. Because of this genuine organic development, we are not dealing with typology, a mere repetition of patterns, but with fulfillment. When Jesus combined in Himself the many disparate ideals of prophetic expectation, He did so in a manner no prophet had ever foreseen, but in a manner that is a perfect realization of their best hopes. There is nothing in His fulfillment that the prophets would have refused to acknowledge as such a realization. The time of fulfillment had been as much hidden from the prophets as from anyone else. That they may have expected the coming of the messianic age in their own lifetimes no more conditions their prophecies than the fact that the first Christians, including writers of the New Testament books, looked for the return of the Lord in their lifetimes conditions the ultimate fulfillment of that expectation. Jesus appeared at a time which, as we are informed by contemporary history and the recently recovered Qumrân literature, was alive with the immediacy of fulfillment. No one else of that time, no one before it or after it, has the remotest claim to be compared with this scion of David as the fulfillment of the prophetic hope. Neither are we to look for another. One needs no bias in favor of Christianity to concede that a more exalted conception of fulfillment than Christ's is unthinkable.

4. Finally, I would observe with Father van der Ploeg that the earliest apostolic appeal to prophecy, to the extent that we are acquainted with it from the Acts of the Apostles, joined this appeal to the preaching of the Resurrection. It was the Resurrection that proved to the apostles that Jesus was the promised Redeemer, and in the light of this knowledge they saw the fulfillment of prophecy. I have said at the outset that we must begin with the realization if we would see how it was foreshadowed in the Old Testament. Here I would add that we cannot expect the argument from prophecy to stand alone without the support of the tremendous mysteries revealed in Jesus Christ. It can never be a demonstration. It must always remain one of the external aids to the divine grace without which no man can solve the problem, "What think you of Christ?" These conditions always supposed, I believe that it can be made a convincing argument along the lines I have suggested, "[suited to the intelligence of everyone]."

References

[1] Gerhard von Rad, *Theologie des AT*, I (Munich, 1957), 452ff.

[2] Jean Steinmann, *Le prophète Ezéchiel et les débuts de l'exil* (Paris, 1953), p. 263.

[3] *The Old Testament Against Its Environment* (London, 1950), p. 64f.

[4] *The Messianic Idea*, p. 392.

[5] *DB*, 1790.

[6] *Catholic Evidence Training Outlines* (New York, 1943), pp. 57-60 (on the Marks of the Church); cf. suggestions on the handling of prophecy, pp. 209-12.

[7] *A Grammar of Assent*, p. 341f. Cf. Jaak Seynaeve, W. F., *Cardinal Newman's Doctrine on Holy Scripture* (Louvain, 1953), pp. 279-87.

CARROLL STUHLMUELLER, C.P.

Old Testament Liturgy

The general reader will find in this inspiring article a discussion of questions such as these: What motives attracted the Israelites to common prayer? What was their attitude to nature worship? How did the celebration of the Pasch gradually evolve, and why was it so important? How did the Exile in Babylon affect Old Testament liturgical developments? What relevance does the study of Old Testament liturgy have for theology and worship today?

Father Stuhlmueller, of the Passionist Fathers, teaches Sacred Scripture at the Passionist Seminary in Louisville, Kentucky, and also in the School of Theology at St. Mary's College, Notre Dame.

Our task . . . is to examine Israel's liturgy in the restricted sense of public worship. What motives attracted the Israelites to community prayer? The theology of the Priestly tradition may seem to argue for some form of nature religion. It may appear that God was adored primarily as the Creator and Supreme Lord of the material universe.[1] Has it not been argued . . . previously that God's presence was detected everywhere, at home, in the field, in the elements of nature?

Some form of nature worship would have been the true explanation of Israel's religion, if God had not directly intervened in the history of the Chosen People. Other ancient Near Eastern peoples worshiped the deified powers of nature. Vegetation, for instance, was transformed into a goddess called *Tammutz*, whose death was mourned during the dry season and whose resuscitation with the

This article first appeared in more developed and extended form in the *Proceedings of the Sixth Annual Convention of the Society of Catholic College Teachers of Sacred Doctrine*. It is reprinted here with permission.

autumn rains occasioned wild rejoicing.[2] The hostility between drought and vegetation, or the fruitful union between rain and earth, was thought to enact the loves and the hatreds of the gods and goddesses. Trembling before these mighty, mysterious powers, early man felt himself in the presence of divine beings. All of nature, therefore, was no longer an *It*, but a *Thou*. . . . The entire universe was peopled with *personal* powers.

Pocketed in one, small section of the Fertile Crescent, the Israelites quickly copied the ways of their neighbors in agriculture, in building, in language, in music, and in many other ways.[3] Their temple was built by architects from Tyre (1 Kgs 5:18); Canaanite phrases are scattered throughout the Psalms and are found in such liturgical passages as the blessing of Jacob (Gn 49).[4] The one, notable exception was Israel's idea of God. Here Israel was unique. The externals of religion were borrowed from others, but the soul of religious worship—Israel's understanding of God—could have come only from God's special intervention.[5]

The origin of Israel's religion lay not in an awesome fear of the powers of nature but in the experience of God's great redemptive acts. The Old Testament confessions of faith, like the first of the Ten Commandments (Ex 20:2), or the "credo" of Deuteronomy 26, do not acclaim the sun or the rain, but dwell upon one or more of the four great saving acts of God: the call of Abraham; the Exodus out of Egypt; the Sinaitic covenant; the royal promises to David. . . . Liturgical worship centered upon the commemoration of these four acts of salvation. Certainly, God performed other momentous and even miraculous deeds, like the fall of Jericho, the swift destruction of the Assyrians in 701, the Deuteronomic reform, the return from exile. These later events, however, were always explained in the light of God's four great acts at the beginning of Israel's history.

We will concentrate attention upon the greatest of Israel's feasts, the Pasch and the Unleavened Bread, which celebrated the Exodus out of Egypt. The same procedure to be followed here can be applied to Israel's other feast days. But before studying the historical development of the Pasch, we want to alert ourselves to three important features of Israel's worship.

The first point has many ramifications and practical consequences, but these can be pared down to the statement: The full meaning of the Pasch (or of any of God's saving acts) did not flash upon the Israelites with a sudden intuition.

In this connection we are reminded of Cardinal Newman's words:

> . . . from the nature of the human mind, time is necessary for the full comprehension and perfection of great ideas; and . . . the highest and most wonderful truths, though communicated to the world once for all by inspired teachers, could not be comprehended all at once by the recipients, but, as being received and transmitted by minds not inspired, and through media which were human, have required only the longer time and deeper thought for their full elucidation. . . .[6]

The nation had to endure oppressive sorrow in order to know really what it meant for their forefathers to be freed from Egyptian slavery; God's people must thrill anew to the exultation of victory, so as to participate knowingly in the joy of the first Paschal deliverance. As the individual Israelite was absorbed into the people of God and himself felt the force of God's saving power, to that extent did the feast of the Pasch open up its full meaning.[7] The different biblical accounts of the Pasch reflect this steady development of doctrine.[8]

This notion of doctrinal development leads at once to another feature of Israel's liturgy, to be exemplified in the celebration of the Pasch and the Unleavened Bread. God's great act of deliverance from Egypt tended to absorb other *subsequent* acts of deliverance. In leading Israel out of Egypt, God became a father who had bestowed life upon a newly born child and had freely accepted all the obligations of fatherhood. Each new, saving act of God proceeded from this same fatherly interest, and so brought the mystery of the Pasch closer to its full realization (cf. Os 11:1-11). The Pasch, as described in the Bible, attracted to itself other events of Hebrew life, so that the biblical account of the Pasch is a combination of many accounts drawn from various periods of biblical history.

There is one, last point well to keep in mind while studying the Paschal liturgy. It follows from what has just been written. Because the biblical account of the Pasch is not a diary of the life of Moses but a fabric woven from many historical events, we must not classify it as modern historiography. The plague and the exodus are told in triumphant and jubilant language, in an epic "liturgical" style, intended primarily to draw a reaction of wonder from a worshiping community and thereby to involve it personally in the original miraculous event. It is no surprise, therefore, to find in the Paschal narrative a liturgical *Te Deum* (Ex 15) and cultic responses (Ex 12:26f.). We should expect even exaggerated and symbolical descriptions, because the inspired writer's first purpose was to present before the worshiper the *hidden, mysterious wonder* of God's saving act. Instead of destroying the historical reality of a marvelous event, symbolical language presumes such a wonder. Symbolism, however, does make it impossible to reconstruct the event in every detail.

The three controlling ideas, then, for the study of Israelite liturgy are: (1) the development of doctrine; (2) through historical events; (3) in the context of liturgical assemblies. Keeping these in mind, we are prepared to investigate the history of the Pasch and the Unleavened Bread.

The term Pasch, or *Pesah*, is probably derived from an Egyptian word meaning *to strike* or *to pass over*. The feast originally commemorated the fearful "night of vigil" in Egypt (Ex 12:42), when the angel of death *passed over* the Israelite dwellings, marked with blood, and entered the Egyptian homes to *strike down* the first-born. This act of God so terrorized the Egyptians that "Pharaoh summoned Moses and Aaron and said, 'Leave my people at once, you and the Israelites with you' " (Ex 12:31). It was a frantic Exodus and the fright of the people became more intense when the Egyptians "quickly changed their minds . . . and pursued them" (Ex 14:5-9). God again marvelously intervened and saved His people by the miracle of the Red, or the Reed, Sea.[9]

The oldest account of this saving act is found in the Yahwist tradition (Ex 12:21-23). Already the story is cast in a liturgical framework. No mention is yet made of unleavened bread, but the act of sprinkling blood upon the doorposts of the homes is expanded into a ritual sacrifice of lamb. This was a nomadic or Bedouin sacrifice of the springtime.[10] The *great* redemptive act of the Passover has thus attracted to itself the *small* saving intervention of God in giving an annual increase to the nomad's flock of sheep. With the passover out of Egypt, God had marvelously saved the lives of His people and had undertaken the obligations of Father and Protector; each year with the mysterious procreation of life among the sheep, God continued to fulfill these obligations.

After the conquest of Palestine and the adoption of agricultural pursuits, the Israelites introduced many elements of Canaanite worship into their ritual. With the Pasch they associated the spring festival of barley harvest and the fast from leavened bread.[11] Gradually there evolved a very elaborate ritual for the paschal meal whose regulations were subsequently inserted into the Torah (Law Book).[12] The eating of unleavened bread was now explained as a symbol of the Hebrews' worried state of mind in quickly fleeing out of Egypt; they did not have time to mix leavened bread. From our "historical" point of view, this connection of unleavened bread with the Pasch is probably false. For the Hebrews, however, it conveyed the *theological* truth that all the blessings of the soil came from Yahweh, the God who had brought them out of Egypt.[13]

We sense a growing realization on the part of the people that the personal God who had intervened in their national existence at the Red Sea was living behind the powers of nature and acting through them. Somehow or other, all of nature was becoming involved in God's determination to fulfill His promises and to make His people happy. The wind drying up the Red Sea (Ex 14:21), the arrival of quail in the Sinai Desert (Nm 11:31), the earthquake shattering the walls of Jericho (Jos 10), the increase of live stock, the barley harvest—these acts of the natural universe deepened the realization that God controlled nature and directed its powers to bestow blessing or to inflict punishment upon His Chosen People. For the Hebrews as for their neighbors, nature was never an *It* to be analyzed but a *Thou* to be known and loved. The Israelites correctly identified this *Thou* as Yahweh, the one and only God. It was not that God was submerged in the forces of the universe, but rather that He summoned all these forces to execute His plans of salvation.

With the Hebrews the point of departure was Yahweh's saving act of deliverance from Egypt. Each year when the 14th Nisan approached on the sacred calendar, the Chosen People were able to re-enact more intelligently the mystery of the Pasch; they realized better the meaning of God's words to Pharaoh: "Israel is my son, my first born" (Ex 4:22).

Not only did God's power over *nature* fuse with His saving power at the Passover, but subsequent *historical* events were attributed to the same, strong arm of God which struck down the Egyptians, divided the sea, and led the people to freedom. Not necessarily for chronological reasons but for motives of faith, other acts of salvation were placed upon the 14-15 Nisan. Faith in God's power to deliver from sorrow was being seen in an ever deeper and wider dimension. The liturgy was the controlling factor in this development of faith.

No historical event, however, so revealed to the Hebrew people the mysterious meaning of the Pasch as the Babylonian exile. This mountain of affliction can be called the continental divide of Old Testament thought. As it lifted the people into the heights of God's redemptive plans, it provided at the same time a vantage point from which they could look back and peer ahead. One of the great prophets standing upon this mountain of suffering was Second Isaia; his message is mainly a reinterpretation of the Exodus in terms of his own contemporary situation. He saw that it is for the "poor and needy" that God provides water, as Moses had once done in the desert (Is 41:17). The true participant of the Pasch, therefore, must be a member of the *Anawim*, those poor and lowly ones to whom Sophonia had promised salvation (So 2:3; 3:8-12). The theology of the Anawim resulted from sorrow and suffering, the very conditions of the first passover from Egypt. These same conditions were necessary for later generations of Israelites to penetrate the meaning of the Pasch.

In Second Isaia three religious elements converge: *the liturgy* which greatly influenced his style and thought; *the Exodus or Paschal mystery* which he reinterpreted in the light of his own circumstances; *the power of humble suffering* which he considered a necessary condition for reliving the mystery of the Pasch. Each of these elements crossed over into the other, so that the liturgy of the Pasch absorbed the teaching or the theology of the Anawim.

In the Book of Esther another historical event is connected with the Pasch. This book describes the deliverance of the Jewish people from tyrannical persecution during the post-Exilic age. It was during the octave of the Pasch that Esther obtained from King Assuerus the decree cancelling Aman's death penalty against the Jews (Est 3:7; 5:1). About a year later the Jews were allowed to slaughter their enemies. This event was annually commemorated on the feast of Purim (Est 9:20ff.). This feast occurred on the 14-15 Adar, exactly a month before the Pasch. Even today Jews consider the four weeks after Purim a time of preparation for the Paschal celebration.[14] The nature of the historical event which gave rise to Purim and which is described in the Book of Esther is disputed, but clearly evident is the spirit of viewing this subsequent act of salvation as a "lesser" Passover, as a continuation of the first Passover.

Other redemptive acts were commemorated on the day of the Pasch. The Book of Jubilees claims that Abraham's intended sacrifice of Isaac and the boy's deliverance by the substitution of a ram happened on the Pasch.[15] The *Seder Olam*, a Jewish work of the second century of the Christian era, places the march through the waters of the Red Sea[16] and the fall of the walls of Jericho[17] on the octave day of the Pasch.

This spirit of reliving the Pasch with an ever deeper understanding, of celebrating the feast with active participation in the original mystery, explains the following words of the *Mishnah*, a collection of ancient rabbinical interpretations of the law. The words are found in its treatise on the Pasch:

> It is therefore incumbent on every person, in all ages, that he should consider as though he had personally gone forth from Egypt, as it is said, "and thou shalt explain to thy son in that day, saying, 'This is done because of that which the Lord did *for me* in Egypt'" (Ex 12:27). We are therefore in duty bound to thank, praise, adore, glorify, extol, honor, bless, exalt, and reverence Him, who wrought all these miracles for our ancestors and for us; for he brought us forth from bondage to freedom, He changed our sorrow into joy, our mourning into a feast. He led us from darkness into a great light, and from servitude to redemption—let us therefore say in his presence, 'Hallelujah!'[18]

There follows a rubric for singing the Hallel.

The study of Israel's liturgical celebrations, whether of the Pasch as done here or of other feast days, can . . . [help the modern Christian] in various ways. We will summarize a few of them under the three salient features of biblical liturgy, mentioned earlier in this article: the development of doctrine; through historical events; in the context of liturgical assemblies.

First, there is a noticeable development in the people's understanding of the redemptive act of God. This development in comprehension is true of Israel as a collective group and as separated into individual members. Such a growth in the knowledge of divine mysteries comes with time, because only time provides full opportunities for integrating one's personal life into the full scope of the liturgical mystery. In the Pasch, for instance, the sacred community had come to see *its own* passage from sin to God's friendship, from worry and oppression to happiness and peace. Years and centuries of communal worship gradually opened up the deep significance of the feast, or rather, of God's great redemptive act of the exodus at the beginning of sacred history.

Similarly, we might note . . . how the development of doctrine is usually closely linked with the liturgy.[19] The liturgy, at the same time, is guided by a divinely established Church to meet the needs of the faithful. Mariology is a case in point. As Christians felt a desperate need of help and comfort, they turned to Mary, just as Jesus had done at His birth and at the hour of His death agony. Through and in the liturgy they found their heavenly Mother. As the Mystical Christ turned to Mary through the ages, Christian theology came to realize better Mary's relation to Christ in giving Him life and comfort. The original mystery of Mary's co-redemptive role opened up its fuller meaning only with the passage of time.

In this development of doctrine through liturgical commemoration, God was always taking the initiative, as He had done in the first redemptive act which the feast celebrated.[20] If it was God who set in motion and brought to fulfillment the work of salvation, then what depths of humility, what lengths of quiet waiting, are demanded of the worshiper. The worshiper came to God on God's terms, not his own! To the worshiper belonged the attitude of *receiving* from God's merciful hands.

Here we glimpse something of the mystery of supernatural prayer. Man takes the most vital and the most dynamic part possible in the mystery of salvation, when he is most passive under God's supernatural grace. Such a humble, prayerful spirit is required today for participation in the liturgy. It banishes the fear that liturgical prayer cannot be contemplative. Moses repeats to us what he said to the people of Israel: "Fear not! Stand your ground. . . . The Lord himself will fight for you; you have only to keep still" (Ex 14:13f.).

A second, controlling factor in Israel's liturgical commemorations is the tendency of viewing each *new* historical redemptive act of God in the light of the *first, great* saving act. In the Paschal liturgy God was glorified: for the gift of children, through the honored role of the first-born; for the increase of live stock, through the sacrifice of the lamb; for the blessings of the barley harvest, through the use of unleavened bread. All of these saving acts of God flowed from *the* great act of redemption, the Exodus out of Egypt, when

Israel became God's first born child and when God freely accepted the obligations of Father and Protector.

It is the same with the Mass today. The Mass attracts to itself all other great events of Christian life. The lives of the saints, the miraculous deeds at Lepanto or at Lourdes, the graces of Matrimony or of Holy Orders—these and other acts of God are seen against the background of the Mass and of Calvary. Through the Mass, modern life is absorbed into the mystery of Christ's Passion-Resurrection.

Last of all, it was as a member of a chosen people that the worshiper arrived at the full significance of the redemptive acts of God. It was principally through Israel's liturgy that the sacred traditions were transmitted to future ages. This method of transmission greatly affected the style of the sacred accounts; they were told in a way to stir wonder and adoration, to evoke love and loyalty. Today as well, the liturgy possesses a special power to unite the worshiper to God and to make him feel in his soul the vibrant force of God's redemptive acts. Liturgical hymns, prayers, and readings bring the worshiper humbly to his knees. This attitude of prayer is evoked both by the literary style of liturgical readings and by God's determination to make the liturgy a sacramental conveyor of grace.

At prayer the worshiper is a member of a large family, all of whom are adoring their Heavenly Father. Yet, he is never swallowed up in mass anonymity, because he must contribute to the group what is the deepest, most personal secret of his being—his love and gratitude. The *inspiration* of this personal love, however, is the great redemptive act which God performed for the *group* and which is renewed in the sacred assembly.

Conclusion

Need it be said, in conclusion, that frequent references to Old Testament liturgy . . . will impart a prayerful spirit to biblical studies? It will smooth out the transition from the days before Christ to our own.[21] The vocation of being God's Chosen People will retain its glorious ideals, yet at the same time it will be seen as a practical reality. Christian feast days, like those of the Israelite calendar, will be more than memorial days of the past; they will be the scene of reliving more fully the mysterious redemptive acts of God. Earthly life is thus patterned upon a heavenly liturgy, wherein angels and saints renew the same mysteries as they prostrate before the lamb standing as if slain.

References

[1] To speak of a "material" universe is a bow to modern thought processes. Biblical man was not faced with our present day dualism; he never set apart the material from the spiritual, and only in the Book of Wisdom did he distinguish Body and Soul.

[2] Cf. Ezechiel 8:14f. Tammutz was a Sumerian goddess, adopted by other, later inhabitants of Mesopotamia. The fourth month of the year (June-July) when vegetation dried up was called Tammutz.

[3] Many studies exist, demonstrating that the Bible was not "projected as though it were a monstrous fossil, with no contemporary evidence to demonstrate its authenticity and its origin, in a human world like ours," W. F. Albright, *Recent Discoveries in Bible Lands* (Pittsburgh, Pa.: The Biblical Colloquium, 1955), p. 1. For the historical background of the Bible we draw attention to the atlases of Grollenberg, Wright-Filson and Kraeling; to J. Finegan, *Light From the Ancient Past*, 2 ed. (Princeton, N.J.: Princeton University Press: 1959); to G. E. Wright, *Biblical Archaeology* (Philadelphia: The Westminster Press, 1957).

[4] Cf. B. Vawter, "Canaanite Background of Gen 49," *Catholic Biblical Quarterly*, 17 (Jan. 1955), 1ff.

[5] This distinction between the external details of ceremony and the interior spirit of religion is ably presented by R. A. F. MacKenzie, "Before Abraham Was . . . ," *Catholic Biblical Quarterly*, 15 (Apr. 1953), 131-40, esp. 139-40.

[6] John Henry Cardinal Newman, *An Essay on the Development of Christian Doctrine* (New York: Longmans, Green & Co., 1949), p. 28; quoted by E. D. Benard, "The Development of Doctrine: A Basic Framework," *Proceedings of Fifth Annual Meeting, SCCTSD* (Notre Dame, Ind.: St. Mary's College, 1959), p. 28f. In the case of the Pasch, the mystery of divine salvation is revealed not so much in *words* as in the redemptive *act* of God.

[7] Even today, must not a person first suffer in order to know the full meaning of Jesus' crucifixion?

[8] That is, Exodus 12-13; 23:14f.; 34:18-20; Leviticus 23:5-8; Numbers 28:16-25; Deuteronomy 16:1-8; Ezechiel 45:21-25. Many differences occur in these various traditions, that is, Exodus 12:9 ("P" Tradition) calls for the lamb, slaughtered at home, to be baked; Deuteronomy 16:5f. ("D" Tradition) legislates for the lamb, slaughtered at the temple to be cooked. These and other differences reflect various ages and different circumstances in the transmission of the Paschal account.

[9] The explanation that God used secondary causes in the performance of this miracle, like a strong, blistering, desert wind, does not concern us here. Both the Israelites who passed through the sea as well as the later narrators of the event were convinced that *God* had acted with wondrous determination to save His people. The exegete must share the Israelites' faith, to recognize the "hand of God" in secondary causality.

[10] J. Pedersen, *Israel* (London: Oxford University Press, 1940), III-IV, 384ff., studies the gradual evolution of the Pasch-Unleavened Bread feast. His work must be read with great caution, but his opinion is strongly probable that the sacrifice of lamb, common among nomadic people, came to the Israelites either from their patriarchal forebears or from their own nomadic experience in the

Sinai Desert. In either case, it was not an essential element of the first Pasch in Egypt. . . . A similar view is expressed by E. F. Siegman, "Blood in the Old Testament," *Proceedings of the First Precious Blood Study Week* (Rensselaer, Ind.: St. Joseph's College, 1959), pp. 51-54.

[11] The penitential feature of unleavened bread is indicated by Deuteronomy 16:3 which calls it "the bread of affliction"; Exodus 12:8 associates it with the bitter herbs.

[12] Exodus 12:1-20, 43-50 are from the Priestly tradition.

[13] The Bible does not follow *our* laws of history writing, but *its own*. The theological truth of this passage contains true history, but not modern history-writing.

[14] On the institution of four special Sabbaths between Purim and Passover, cf. J. van Goudoever, *Biblical Calendars* (Leiden: Brill, 1959), pp. 81, 93, 145. This book is very highly recommended for a study of Israelite feasts, their historical development, and their influence upon the New Testament and upon the Christian calendar. Another excellent book is Eric Werner's *The Sacred Bridge* (New York: Columbia University Press, 1959). Its subtitle is: "The Interdependence of Liturgy and Music in Synagogue and Church during the first Millennium."

[15] Jubilees 17:15; 18:18.

[16] *Seder Olam Rabba*, v.

[17] *Ibid*., xi.

[18] Treatise Pesachim, x, 5, *Eighteen Treatises from the Mishna*, tr. D. A. de Sola and M. J. Raphall (London, 1843), p. 124.

[19] T. Barrosse, "The Senses of Scripture and the Liturgical Pericopes," *Catholic Biblical Quarterly*, 21 (Jan. 1959), 1-23, explains the gradual development of the Church's understanding and the role of the liturgy in this growth.

[20] Cf. Deuteronomy 7:7f.; or Second Isaia's insistence that God is the Beginning and the End, Isaia 41:4; 44:6.

[21] We have attempted to show the rich understanding which the Old Testament liturgy imparts to Christian worship in "The Holy Eucharist: Symbol of the Passion," and "The Holy Eucharist: Symbol of Christ's Glory," *Worship*, 34 (1960), 195-205, 258-69.

III. UNITING THE TWO TESTAMENTS

"The God of Abraham and the God of Isaac and the God of Jacob, the God of our fathers, has glorified His Son Jesus. . . ." (Ac 4:13)

EVA FLEISCHNER

God's View of the World

The heedful reader will find in this short but fundamental essay a basic statement on questions such as these: To what extent can we make our view of the world coincide with God's view? What special power is needed to see the world as God sees it? What does the Bible tell us about God? about man? about the world? about history? about faith? What does it mean to say that man meets God in Christ through the liturgy? How is God's view of the world reflected in the liturgy?

Eva Fleischner teaches theology at the Grail in Loveland, Ohio.

As Christians we have the task to live in the world, to act on it, to transform it. It seems to me that this is possible only if in the first place we have the right view of it—the proper "Weltanschauung." Obviously, our view of the world will be the right one only insofar as it coincides with God's view. What is God's view of the world?

Dare we ask? Can we know? It is important that we ask, for unless we do, His view cannot become ours. And we can know, because God has revealed His view to us in Holy Scripture. We read in the opening lines of Genesis: "And God saw that it was good." Creation came forth from the hand of God pure, holy, radiantly beautiful. This is like the Leitmotif of the first chapter of Genesis.

The original goodness was tarnished by the fall—tarnished, but

This essay was originally presented at a study group session of the North American Liturgical Week held in Oklahoma City. It was first published by the Liturgical Conference in the *Proceedings* and is reproduced here with permission.

not destroyed. God still loves the world He had made, from afar. And His project is to restore it to an even greater harmony and beauty. True, He no longer "walks with man in the garden"—but neither is He totally absent from the world. The Incarnation of the Son of God, which is the fullest possible expression of God's love for the world, is prepared for by a long, gradual, and consistent process of incarnation. God does not destroy what He has made, for, as we read in scripture, "thou hatest none of the things thou hast made." Material creation has been wounded, along with the spirit, and "groans in travail waiting for the redemption of the sons of God." But even in the process of waiting, it is an image of God through which men can recognize the face of the Creator, an instrument through which the fullness of time is brought closer and closer. Time, space, matter—all these are the vehicles for carrying out God's project of salvation, which reaches its climax in the Incarnation. In the Incarnation of Christ the hallowing of matter, of the world, of flesh, finds its fullest expression.

But this is not yet apparent to our bodily eyes. To see the world as the project of God, holy and precious—a special power is required for this, a special power to perceive the reality behind daily appearances. This power, this new ability to see, is *faith*. The question I should like to pose is this: How can a biblical-liturgical orientation help to deepen our faith, help us to see the world with the eyes of God, *in conspectu Dei*?

God's View of the World Is Revealed in the Bible

In the Bible we find *reality*. Not some man-made concept of the world, but God's own revelation of Himself—of man—of the world —of history. The world from God's point of view. What does the Bible tell us about reality?

God: The initiative is always His—He is supremely free, to call, to choose, to act. He is living, dynamic, not an abstract idea. The bold term used in scripture, the "face" of God, is indeed justified, for His features are clearly discerned in its pages: God the all-other, the infinite one, eternal, utterly beyond man's reach; but also, God the intimate friend of man, loving and caring for him with the tenderness of a mother, stooping down to the very level of the creature He has made.

Man: God's creature, called and loved by Him, precious, irreplaceable, indispensable to the working out of God's plan. Free to say Yes or No. If he says Yes, the plan goes forward. If No, it is impeded—temporarily. Man, created in God's image, endowed with a heart, a mind, a will, with all that makes him a unique person. Hence capable of encountering the Divine Person. But also capable of rejecting Him.

The world: Called into being by God's love, the scene in which sacred history unfolds, the arena of God's actions. Not an incidental background, not a necessary evil, but the building place, the quarry, out of which the project of God, the new creation, is being built. The world—fascinating, beautiful, good, but wounded—hence, also dangerous, threatening, ambiguous. Loved by God, redeemed by Christ, destined one day to be transformed into the new heaven and the new earth.

History: Not an unending circle, not a shapeless chaos, but a great dynamic forward movement. Not only a looking back to the past, but a straining toward the future, when all will be accomplished and made new. And the present time given meaning, illuminated, by both past and future. Hence pregnant with *hope*, this quality so sorely needed by modern man. . . .

This is God's view of the world as revealed in scripture. And it becomes ours through *faith*. What does the Bible have to teach us about faith? Belief in God and His word to such an extent that one is willing to do whatever He asks, to set out, if need be, on an unknown road. Not an abstract, but made visible, concrete, in the great men and women of the Bible. Belief involving commitment, leading to "metanoia," such is the biblical idea of faith. And such too, surely, is the faith asked of men and women of all time who would do the work of God.

God's View of the World Is Realized in the Liturgy

To see the world with the eyes of God means to become more and more conformed to Him. This happens above all through the liturgy, which is the meeting place par excellence of God and man in Christ.

Who is this Christ, what is He like? He is risen, glorified, totally invaded by the Spirit. This is the Christ who lives and acts now, who touches us in the liturgy, transforms us more and more into Himself, communicates to us His own new life, life out of the Kingdom of God. How does He "touch" us?

By means of material, created things. Nowhere does God take the world more seriously than in the liturgy. The sacramentality of matter here attains its full flowering. Bread, wine, water, oil, light, and so on are not things of secondary importance in the liturgy, not mere necessities with which we must put up for the present, and from which we hope to be freed as soon as possible. They are precious and holy in themselves. They are the instruments through which Christ projects the life of the Kingdom of God into here and now.

The liturgy, therefore, if rightly performed and understood, can develop our ability to see the world with the eyes of God; can cultivate in us a love for the world God has made—a world which has been wounded, but which in Christ is restored to harmony. In the liturgy we are given a foretaste of the regeneration to come in the Kingdom of God.

A biblical-liturgical orientation, therefore, can be a powerful help to attaining Christian maturity, if by maturity we understand "putting on the mind and heart of Christ."

JOHN L. McKENZIE, S.J.

The Transformation of Old Testament Messianism

The interested reader will find in this brilliant article a discussion of questions such as these: What does it mean to say that messianism is a complex of ideas? What is imperfect about the Old Testament apprehension of messianism? What is the precise meaning of fulfillment? How does the New Testament transform the messianic themes of the Old Testament? How does this transformation apply to the idea of the king? of the kingdom? of the prophet? of the Servant? of the priest? of the Son of Man? of the Savior? What is meant by saying that the New Testament sees Jesus as the new Israel? What light does messianism throw on the theology of redemption and salvation?

Father John McKenzie teaches theology and Scripture at Loyola University, Chicago. He is the author of *The Two-Edged Sword.*

In modern biblical theology messianism is the name given to a complex of ideas; . . . there is an amazing variety of opinion among interpreters on what is and what is not messianism. It is impossible to settle all these discussions here; our task is to discuss the place of messianism, understood as generally as possible, in . . . [advanced] courses in sacred doctrine. Perhaps the first service we can render the . . . [student] of sacred doctrine is to remind him that when he deals with messianism, he is handling a topic which

This article was first published in the *Proceedings of the Sixth Annual Convention of the Society of Catholic College Teachers of Sacred Doctrine.* References in the original title and in the text to that audience have been edited out; it is reprinted here with permission.

escapes facile definition and which can be simplified only by distortion.[1]

If anything deserves the name of traditional, it is the apologetic use of messianic texts to vindicate the messianic character of Jesus. By an easy extension many of these texts were also employed to demonstrate His divinity in the metaphysical sense of the word—that is, in the Nicene, Ephesian, and Chalcedonian sense. This use can be traced to the third century A.D., and it is attributed to the apologists, especially to Justin. The principle of this apologetic use was and is that a number of predictions in detail of the life and personal characteristics of any individual person can be explained by no coincidence of happy conjecture, but only by the divine revelation of these details. Now the Old Testament, it was argued, presents some seventy-five allusions to the life and personal characteristics of Jesus which can be verified in no other person; hence, His life and personal characteristics were revealed to the Old Testament prophets by God, and Jesus is recognized as the Messiah of whom they spoke. The argument seems simple and effective. It is not. The primary question—Of whom do these passages speak?—was never answered by any serious exegesis. Isaia 7:14 appears in the Greek and Latin (not in the Hebrew) to speak of a child born of a virgin; it is quoted by Matthew in connection with the conception of Jesus, presumably in illustration of its virginal character; there is no other individual of whom a virginal conception is affirmed or even suggested; therefore Isaia must predict the virginal conception. All the steps in the argument except the last are doubtfully valid. Every one of the seventy-five texts can be submitted to a similar examination. We are left with a vacuum where we used to have a demonstrated thesis; and, in addition, we are left with serious doubt whether the Old Testament has any relevance whatever to Christian doctrine, and a skepticism about the meaning of the Old Testament which may never be replaced with certainty. This is what is called progress?

This is progress indeed. As it stands, it is purely negative, but even this can be progress. It is not, and we trust never will be, necessary and proper to explain and defend our faith by anything else but the truth. If biblical science has advanced at all in the seventeen-hundred years since Justin—a development which ought to surprise no one—then there are some things we know better than the apologists did. This is one of them. And we need not end with a vacuum. We have lost some messianic texts—or rather we recognize that we never had them; we have gained understanding of others. But we have gained far more. Modern biblical studies have given the messianic belief a breadth and a depth which we never perceived in earlier generations, and they have shown us that messianism influenced the composition of the New Testament far more than we realized. Jesus was the Messiah, the fulfillment of the hope of Israel, not by verifying predictions of isolated episodes in His life but by bringing the reality for which Israel hoped.

This introduces us to the idea of "fulfillment," which has been so important in the traditional messianism of apologetics; indeed it is still important, and that is why I dwell upon it briefly. In the traditional apologetics fulfillment was one term of a duality of which the other term was prediction. This is one view of fulfillment; it scarcely seems to be the understanding of the New Testament writers (most frequently Matthew) who use the term. One's hope can be fulfilled. One's personality or destiny can be fulfilled by the realization of the potentialities which lie within one's person. One's desires can be fulfilled. In all of these the common element is the emergence of some reality which in some way is foreshadowed, demanded, needed by that which precedes it: a reality without which the preceding unreality remains unfulfilled and to that extent unreal. Jesus is the reality which gives fullness to the reality of the Old Testament; He satisfies its desires, realizes its hopes and potentialities, gives it intelligibility. He is the fullness of Israel.

This . . . sums up in one word better than any other what is meant by the messianic character of Jesus: He is the fullness of Israel. And here also . . . lie the importance and value of messianism for the . . . [serious student] of sacred doctrine. What Jesus Himself said and did, the manner in which the primitive preaching of the Church presented Him, were principally determined by the recognition that He was the fullness of Israel. The words of the New Testament concerning the person and mission of Jesus are not intelligible without constant reference to the hopes, the desires, and the destiny of Israel whose fulfillment He was. . . .

There is a caution to be entered at this point. Jesus in realizing the hopes and the destiny of Israel transformed them. The messianism of the New Testament is not simply the same as the messianism of the Old Testament. One must not only recognize the difference, but one must try to see as well as one can why these differences exist. Old Testament messianism was at best an imperfect apprehension of the destiny of Israel. The full reality of Jesus was something which was not described in the Old Testament because it could not be described. The reality of Jesus is not truly intelligible without reference to the Old Testament; and the Old Testament is not truly intelligible without reference to its fullness. The Old Testament raises questions which it never answers and arouses hopes and desires which it never fulfills. When the reality is fulfilled, it grows into new dimensions, exhibits new features and qualities. The man who fulfills the promises of his boyhood is the same individual person; but without a change of identity he has educed personal powers and performed achievements which were not perceptible in the early stages of his development.

Modern interpretation raises some questions concerning this transformation of Old Testament messianism which are difficult and complex. . . . [This is particularly true] of the literary origins and formation of the Gospels. New Testament scholars of our generation accept the principle that the Gospels are the products of faith, that they are compilations of the kerygma and the didache of the primitive Church. In the Gospels, that is, Jesus is presented as the object of faith and never as the object of detached historical investigation. The historian now asks himself how much the transformation of Old Testament messianism comes from the words of Jesus Himself and how much from the faith of the primitive Church which perceived in the light of its pentecostal experience that Jesus was the fullness of Israel. To this question the historian has not and probably never will have an entirely satisfactory answer. To the believer and to the theologian, who accept the continuity of the teaching of the Church with the teaching of Jesus Himself, the question is interesting but not peremptory. They believe that Jesus lives in the Church, revealing Himself still further and in a particular way to that generation which had personal experience of Him. They know that the fact that the Gospel narratives are propositions of belief does not make them less what they were intended to be: a true presentation of that reality which was Jesus Christ. In this discussion we have neither the time nor the occasion to enter into any detailed investigation of the literary origins of particular Gospel passages.[2]

[It was] remarked above that Old Testament messianism has been broadened and deepened by modern biblical studies. We have learned that a number of elements should be included in messianism which had no place in the traditional apologetics. [We can omit here], not without regret, the hotly debated question of the eschatological character of Old Testament messianism, not because it is irrelevant, but because the time available would permit the discussion of nothing else.[3] There is no doubt about the eschatological character of New Testament messianism, whatever be its origins; this is sufficient for our present purpose. What is lacking in Old Testament messianism is a synthesis of its elements, which are so varied as to seem discordant; indeed, some modern scholars would exclude some elements which are usually included. Sigmund Mowinckel, for instance, argues very ably that messianism is eschatological by definition, and that the king-Savior motif, which is not eschatological in the Old Testament, is not to be included in the messianic complex. In synthesizing these elements the New Testament effects the transformation which we noticed above. Disparate and even apparently irreconcilable elements are fused into unity.

Since the messianism of the Old Testament is so fluid, one should be wary of conclusions hastily drawn from the use of the word *christos* in the New Testament. The Hebrew word *mašiaḥ*, which *christos* represents, means "the anointed one," and in the Old Testament designates almost always the king, rarely the priest. It is never used in the Old Testament of the figure called the Messiah; this use of the term arose in later extra-biblical Judaism. The word *christos* consequently refers to the entire complex of messianic ideas; what it means in any given passage can be defined more precisely, if it can be defined at all, only by a study of the context and its ideological background.

Under the general heading of messianism one may distinguish several streams of thought in the Old Testament. I have myself elsewhere affirmed that the king motif is basic in messianism, so we may consider this first.[4] In the ancient world the rule of a king was the only political factor which assured an ordered, peaceful, and strong society, possessed of the resources to resist external aggression and internal corruption. The two functions of the king are said by George Mendenhall to be war and law; and these are the functions which resist external and internal attack. The royal messianism consisted in a belief in the eternity of the dynasty of David, and, after the fall of this dynasty, a restoration of the dynasty under a new and greater David.

The idea of a kingdom often appears without any explicit reference to the Davidic ruler. This idea is rooted in the kingship of Yahweh rather than in the kingship of David. The kingship of Yahweh is worldwide and His effective dominion demands that all men acknowledge His sovereignty and submit themselves to His will. This kingdom is, of course, centered upon Israel, to whom Yahweh has revealed Himself; His rule, when it is exercised over all men, will go out from the place which He has chosen as the scene of His manifestation. Nevertheless, there is no clear identification of the kingdom (or *reign*) of Yahweh with the kingdom of the dynasty of David, nor does the Davidic ruler clearly appear as the human instrument through whom the reign of Yahweh is to be established. The themes of king and kingdom are related but not integrated.

The theme of the Son of Man is late and not prominent in the Old Testament. There are many obscurities in the origin and development of this concept, much of which lies in extra-biblical literature, and scholars have not yet come to an agreement on the solution of these difficulties. But the roots of the New Testament are most properly placed in Daniel 7:13, where one "like a son of man" appears before "the ancient of days" and receives from Him a kingdom. Exegetes commonly agree that the son of man here is a personification of the Jewish people; thus the Son of Man theme is related to the messianism of the king and the kingdom. The word "son of man" in Aramaic signifies no more than a man, an individual human being; but the word in popular usage certainly acquired overtones which as yet are not entirely clear to us.

The prophetic theme in Old Testament messianism is less clear. It was the belief of Judaism that prophecy ceased with Malachi and that a prophet would not again appear until the prophet came who would immediately precede and announce the coming of the Messiah. The Messiah-king is not represented as a prophet. Judaism, however, never included in its messianism the Servant of Yahweh, who appears in four passages of Isaia (42:1-4; 49:1-6; 50:4-9; 52:13-53:12). In the first three of these passages the prophetic mission of the Servant is at least strongly suggested. In the fourth the Servant becomes one who delivers by an atoning death; the idea is original and unparalleled elsewhere in the Old Testament, and it is not surprising that Judaism failed to find any room for this theme in its messianism.

These are the common messianic themes; but messianism as a whole is much wider. Israel itself is a messianic entity, a society moving toward a life under the will of God but never achieving it, a society which will find its consummation, its "fulfillment" in the dwelling of God among His people. It is a society living in a covenant with Yahweh under the law of Yahweh, worshiping Him in His temple through the priesthood which He established. All of these are institutions through which Israel approached Yahweh; they are all institutions which look to a fulfillment of some kind. Jeremia 31:31-34 sees a new covenant in which personal knowledge of Yahweh will make law and priestly instruction unnecessary. The same prophet (3:16-17) sees the symbolic presence of Yahweh in the ark of the covenant yielding to His real presence. The redemption of Israel, according to Osea 2:14-23, cannot be accomplished without another passage through the desert. It is a new creation and a new passage through the sea (Is 51:9-11).

This, we may suggest, is the reality underlying the New Testament synthesis of messianic themes: Jesus is the new Israel who fulfills the destiny of Israel. And since He lives in the Church which He founded, this Church also is the new Israel. Israel's historic encounter with God tends to the "decisive eschatological event," as Rudolf Bultmann has well called it, of the coming of Jesus, where Israel finds its true identity. In Him Israel lives eternally. And in unfolding itself it reveals Jesus Christ in His true identity.

Is this, one may ask, the key to the mystery of salvation, . . . the comprehensive principle which will answer all questions and solve all problems? . . . [There is no intention here to] suggest . . . [a] facile comprehensive answer to anything, most of all to the mystery of salvation, whose dimensions always remain too large for us. But I do suggest that this is a fruitful approach which will remove some obscurities and afford some new insights. The new Israel which outgrows the old as new wine bursts its bottles is a paradox; but whatever we do, to understand the adult we must study the child—but not exclusively.

To begin, let us take the theme of kingship. There can scarcely be any doubt, although we have no time to argue the point, that Jesus Himself did not emphasize this feature of His mission; if anything, He dismissed it. There are too many Gospel passages which indicate this, in spite of the fact that the early Church did not hesitate to give Him the titles of royalty. We have all heard the traditional explanation that it was politically dangerous to claim royalty, and I am sure we have all felt that there is something wrong with this explanation; Jesus as we know Him made no decisions on the basis of political prudence. If He had a claim to kingship, He would have asserted it. Let us ask whether His dismissal of royal messianism did not come from the inner character of His mission. Kingship, we noticed, indicated an ordered and peaceful society, and Jesus certainly intended to move toward such a society. But He had to deny that such a society is possible by political means; it comes from the inner regeneration of each man. Jesus is the initiator and agent of this process of regeneration; He is the king-Savior by offering a principle of salvation more certain and effective than the warmaking and the lawmaking of a king. Readers of the Gospels cannot but notice that the allusions to kingship are more common in the infancy Gospels of Matthew and Luke than elsewhere; interpreters with some probability credit this emphasis to the Church herself. Surely the authors of these accounts were as well aware of the paradox which they created as we are; they could recognize, we think, the entirely unroyal character of the circumstances of the birth which they narrated, and in so describing it they succeeded, whether they intended it or not, in describing what is called in John "a kingdom not of this world."

A similar paradox appears in the triumphal entry of Jesus into Jerusalem before His Passion, an event related by all four Gospels (Mt 21:1-9; Mk 11:1-10; Lk. 19:28-38; Jn 12:12-15). The paradox is attributed to Jesus Himself, who deliberately re-enacted the scene described by Zacharia (9:9). The king appears "lowly," a term which is almost technical in much of the late Old Testament literature; it designates the great mass of the poor, the helpless, and oppressed. The king-Savior identifies himself with those who are most in need of the deliverance which He brings. Here again the placing of this event at the beginning of the Passion narratives could scarcely have escaped the notice of the authors of the account.

John contains the only explicit claim of Jesus to royalty in the dialogue between Jesus and Pilate (18:33-37). The account is a final and effective disclaimer of any secular royalty; the allegiance which Jesus demands is allegiance to the truth which He proclaims. Pilate was perhaps a bit hasty in concluding that such allegiance was no threat to the secular government which he represented; other and later Roman administrators saw that the issue between Christianity and the empire was a combat to the death of one of the parties, for even the empire owed allegiance to the truth. But Pilate spoke for many men of his time, if not for most, in believing that the pursuit of truth was such an airy and elusive occupation that it did not deserve the serious concern of practical men of affairs.

Again, we do not believe that the Gospel writers were unaware of the implications of the narrative which finally synthesizes the themes of kingship and suffering Servant of Yahweh, another event related by all four Gospels (Mt 27:27-31; Mk 15:16-20; Lk 23:42-43; Jn 19:2-7): the mock salutation of Jesus as king by the Roman soldiers and the proclamation of His kingship on the placard of His execution. Here the Gospels present the recognition and proclamation of the kingship of the Son of David. The post-Resurrection narrative of the two disciples on the road to Emmaus attributed to Jesus Himself the explanation of this theme: the Christ had to enter His glory through suffering (Lk 24:26).

This development of the theme of kingship is constant in the apostolic preaching as it appears in Acts and in the epistles. By the quotation of Psalm 2:7, "You are my son, this day I have begotten you," and Psalm 110:1, "Yahweh said to my lord, Sit at my right hand," the apostles proclaimed that Jesus acceded to His kingship when He was seated at the right hand of God after His Resurrection and Ascension (Ac 2:30-35; 4:25; 13:33-37; Rom 1:2-4; 1 Cor 15:24-27; Eph 1:20; Col 3:1; Heb 1:3,5,13; 10:12-13). By so modifying the theme of the ancient Messiah-Savior-king Jesus made it complete; the idea of kingship has been "fulfilled."

The theme of the reign of God does not experience the same eschatological transformation. The common designation of the preaching of Jesus is the announcement of the reign of God, and in one passage He declares that the reign of God is "among you" (Lk 17:20-21); it is a present existing reality. The dispute about the meaning of this passage illustrates well the tension between history and eschatology which we experience constantly in the New Testament. Indeed, it suggests that our division between history and eschatology should not be too schematic. Whether we translate Matthew 4:17 and Mark 1:15 as "The reign of God has arrived" or not, the word certainly means nearness, imminence; it cannot refer to a vague and distant event. This arrival of the reign of God is indicated in the parables of the kingdom (Mt 13; Mk 4; Lk 8), where the reign of God is described as an existing reality which passes through a period of testing toward its eschatological fulfillment. But it is an existing reality; wherever men accept Jesus, the reign of God is effective. Indeed, the kingdom contains those who do not accept the reign of God; it is nonetheless the kingdom. The idea of the reign of God as an existing reality in a small beginning is as much a transformation of Old Testament conceptions as the synthesis of the royal Messiah and the suffering Servant. As Jesus merited His royalty by His Passion and death, so the reign of God merits fulfillment by a process of growth and struggle. In this it faithfully reproduces the lineaments of the life and death of Jesus Himself.

The first generation of the primitive Church perceived that the Church herself, the community which they formed, was the existing reality of the reign of God in the world.[5] In the Old Testament the reign of God was established by the manifestation of Yahweh on "the Day of Yahweh," when He appeared to deliver His elect and smite His enemies. The Day of Yahweh, as we shall try to set forth below, also experienced a transformation in the New Testament; but here again we may borrow Bultmann's lapidary phrase to point out that the early Church saw the death and Resurrection of Jesus as the "decisive eschatological event" which established the reign of God. The description which Paul gives of the successive stages of the subjection of all creation to the reign of God (1 Cor 15:20-28) is one of the most profound and mysterious passages of this great ambassador of Christ, and one of the most moving. Here, he seems to say, the Resurrection and exaltation of Jesus begin the eschatological process which is now going on and continues until "fulfillment." The salvation process has entered its final and ineluctable phase; all the principles are established which are necessary to bring it to its conclusion. It is for the Church herself to be conscious of her role as the existing reign of God and to recognize in herself the vital force of growth and development which has been instilled in her through the communication of life from Jesus dead and risen and seated as king.

The theme of the Son of Man, we observed, is in Daniel a theme of kingship, and it appears as such in the New Testament; but it also is transformed. Jesus alone uses the title; He used it when He claimed power to forgive sins (Mt 9:6; Mk 2:10; Lk 5:24) and authority over the Sabbath (Mt 12:8; Mk 2:28; Lk 6:5). But the feature of the Son of Man theme which appears most frequently is the coming in the clouds; this feature commonly appears when the second Coming of Jesus as judge is mentioned (Mt 16:27; 24:26-31; 25:31-46; Mk 8:37; 13:26-27; Lk 9:26; 17:24; 21:27). In the three Synoptic Gospels Jesus appeals to the motif of the Son of Man when He is asked directly at the critical hour of His trial before the high priest whether He was the Messiah (Mt 26:64; Mk 14:62; Lk 22:69), and by employing this motif He furnished the court with a basis for His condemnation. The theme of the Son of Man is the principal source of the apocalyptic features of the eschatology of the Synoptic Gospels; here as much as anywhere modern interpreters ask to what extent this application of the Son of Man theme is due to Jesus Himself and how much to the kerygma of the apostolic Church. The second Coming, the Parousia, relates the Son of Man theme to the theme of Jesus constituted king by His Resurrection. It is the New Testament modification of the Day of Yahweh, a sudden coming of God as deliverer and as judge; the term used in Luke 17:24, "the day of the Son of Man," applies the Old Testament phrase to Jesus Himself.

The transformation of the phrase is somewhat obscure, but it seems possible to trace it. The title is used by Jesus in two contexts where He speaks of His human condition: His homelessness (Mt 8:20; Lk 9:58) and His ordinary manner of life and His associations with the common people (Mt 11:19; Lk 5:34). These might be merely coincidental, were it not for the imposing list of passages in which the title appears in allusions to the Passion (Mt 12:40; 17:12, 22; 20:18,28; 26:2,24; Mk 9:31; 10:33,45; 8:31; 14:21,41; Lk 9:44; 11:32; 9:22; 18:31; 22:22; Jn 3:14; 8:28; 12:34, and in particular Jn 12:23 and 13:31, where the glorification of the Son of Man is identified with His Passion). Here again Jesus transformed the theme of the Son of Man by merging it with the theme of the suffering Servant. The emphasis which He placed upon the title brings out the humanity of the Son of Man and His identification with the common condition of man as much as it brings out the ideas of the kingdom and the coming in the clouds.

The theme of the prophet, we noticed, is not prominent in Old Testament messianism. But the prologue of John (1:1-14) sees Jesus as the "fulfillment" of prophecy in a most magnificent way. The word of Yahweh made Yahweh Himself known, for the dialogue of the word is a personal encounter. In hearing His word Israel knew Yahweh as the personal reality which His word expressed. The word in Israelite thought was more than a symbol of the concept; it was a distinct reality, and when it expressed the will of a person it was a dynamic reality whose dynamism was measured by the power of the speaker. The word of Yahweh was creative, for He produced the world by His command. It was destructive, for at His word kingdoms fall. It was the hinge on which history turned, for it brought to pass each crisis which it announced. To Jeremia it was a fire burning within him. The word of Yahweh never returns to Him without doing its work; the world passes but His word endures forever. Against this rich background of the word as the revelation of God and His operative force in the world John proclaimed that this word, given to the prophets, the agent of creation and the mover of history, is a personal reality who is incarnated and pitches His tent among men. Here is the self-revelation of God through the spoken word, the new creation, the crisis of history which this Word announces and brings to pass.

We have frequently had occasion to refer to the theme of the suffering Servant of Yahweh. The importance of this theme cannot be measured by the number of quotations of Isaia 53 in the New Testament, of which H. B. Swete counts eight.[6] It lies in the implicit reflection of the passage in the large number of New Testament texts which speak of the death of Jesus as an atonement, a ransom, a deliverance. This conception of the death of Jesus is a constant theme in the Synoptic Gospels, the epistles, and the Johannine writings. The idea of the suffering Servant, we noticed above, had no place in Judaism. This is not surprising, for it is the supreme paradox of the Christian fact. It is the proclamation of success through failure, of creation through destruction, of life through death. Whether for oneself or for another, in the words of Jesus Himself, one who wishes to gain life must lose it. Does not Jesus here also re-enact the history of Israel, which had to die as a nation in order to survive as a faith? It is basic in the soteriology of St. Paul that each Christian attains salvation by sharing in the experience of the redeeming death of Jesus—without death one does not pass to a new life.

It seems captious to attribute the theme to any other source than Jesus Himself, although it is not impossible, viewed in the absolute, to consider it as a result of the meditation of the Christian community upon the death of Jesus. The Synoptic Gospels emphasize several times the fact that the disciples did not grasp before the Resurrection the truth that Jesus had to accomplish His mission by His death. The understanding of the mystery of the atoning death was a part of their pentecostal enlightenment. That Jesus Himself never even attempted to explain the character of His mission nor to show how He "fulfilled" the theme of the suffering Servant is a proposition which does not admit critical and exegetical demonstration. One who believes that Jesus contributed anything to the creation of Christian faith finds it difficult to accept the suggestion that He contributed nothing to the central truth of the Christian mystery of salvation. For the atoning death is the point of synthesis of the various streams of messianic thought in the Old Testament. Without it the other motifs of messianism lose all meaning and significance; they become pieces of ancient oriental mythology, interesting as stories of the adventure of the human spirit exploring the dark mystery of life and death, but no more relevant to modern man than the victory of Marduk over Tiamat. If the apostolic preaching was the creative agent of this synthesis, then the disciples were greater than their master.

Let us now return to what we said was the dominating theme of New Testament messianism: the theme of Jesus as the new Israel. It is this conception of Jesus as "fulfilling" in Himself not only the gifts and mission of Israel but also Israel's historic experience which permits the New Testament writers to employ allusions to the Old Testament which sometimes appear far fetched. Like Israel, Jesus came out of Egypt (Mt 2:15; Os 11:1). His forty days in the desert and His temptation are re-enactments of the forty years of Israel in the desert and its temptations (Mt 4:1-11; Mk 1:12-13; Lk 4:1-13). The storm of the Sea of Galilee gives Jesus an opportunity to exhibit the power over nature which was shown in the passage of Israel through the sea (Mt 8:23ff.; Mk 4:35ff.; Lk 8:22ff.). The feeding of five thousand in the desert recalls the manna (Mt 14:13-21; Mk 6:30-44; Lk 9:10-17). John connects this episode both with the manna and with the bread of life which Jesus gives, His Flesh and Blood (Jn 6:31-35, 48-58). John also presents Jesus as the new Moses who through faith in Himself produces the water of life (7:37-38). The transfiguration of Jesus presents Him between the two pillars of the Israelite community: the Law, represented by Moses, and prophecy, represented by Elijah (Mt 17:118; Mk 9:2-8; Lk 9:28-36). These were the two channels through which Yahweh spoke to Israel; they are joined by the Son, who "fulfills" them by completing the revelation which they initiated. Paul draws an antithesis between the brilliance of the religion of death and the greater brilliance of the religion of the Spirit (2 Cor 3:7-11). Jesus is the seed of Abraham to whom the promises were made (Gal 3:16), and the community which He created is the Israel of God (Gal 6:16). The apostles shall sit on twelve thrones judging the twelve tribes of Israel (Mt 19:28; Lk 22:28-30); they rule the Church, the new Israel.

The Epistle to the Hebrews draws upon other Old Testament themes less prominent elsewhere in the New Testament. Jesus is the fulfillment of the priesthood and sacrifice of the Old Testament. The use of sacrificial terminology to describe the death of Jesus appears also in the Synoptic Gospels and may go back to the Servant passage of Isaia 53:10; but the author of Hebrews goes beyond Isaia. By comparing the death of Jesus with the regularly repeated ritual of sacrifice the author of Hebrews is able to give a peculiar emphasis to the total efficacy of the atoning death.

The Epistle to the Hebrews also combines the themes of kingship and priesthood. The ancient Sumerian and Semitic priest-king represented the people whom he incorporated before the gods; he was the head of the cult as well as the head of the state. Melchizedek (Gn 14) was such a priest-king. This conception of priest-king did not appear in the Israelite monarchy; the reasons for the Israelite modification of the common ancient Near Eastern conception are not entirely clear, but it is clear that the Israelites were unwilling that the king should become a sacral figure. Now Jesus, a priest according to the order of Melchizedek, who was priest-king, and not of Aaron, who was priest alone, restores the ancient conception. The roots of this idea may lie partly outside the Old Testament. Jewish apocryphal literature in some places exhibited the idea of two Messiahs, one royal and one priestly, and the Qumrân literature has again raised questions concerning this peculiar feature of messianism.[7]

The Epistle to the Hebrews also uses the theme of covenant to present Jesus as the new Israel. The word covenant (*diatheke*) appears in the Synoptic Gospels only in the words of institution of the Eucharist (Mt 26:28; Mk 14:24; Lk 22:20; Lk 1:72 refers to the Old Testament covenant). Paul also uses the word in his formula of institution (1 Cor 11:25). But outside of Hebrews the New Covenant is mentioned elsewhere in the New Testament only in 2 Corinthians 3:6. This is really not surprising, in spite of the fact that the covenant theme is so basic in the Old Testament. For the idea of covenant carried with it the correlative idea of the Law, and the relation between God and the new Israel established by Jesus was such that the word covenant with its implications of law could hardly be an accurate designation. Where the ideas of fatherhood and adopted sonship enter, the covenant is "fulfilled" in such a way that it can no longer be mentioned. Thus for Paul in Galatians, law and covenant are fulfilled in freedom and sonship. The occurrence of the word in the formula of the Eucharist is an allusion to the sacrificial victims of the covenant rite of Exodus 24:8; the application of the blood of the same victim to the two parties of the covenant—Yahweh, symbolized by the altar, and the people present—signified their community in covenant. Jesus is the victim who established communion between the Father and the new Israel, to whom His blood is applied sacramentally. But the nature of the relationship is as different as the quality of the victim.

We ought to mention another factor which was active in the transformation of messianism, a factor which itself arose from messianism; and this was the preaching to the Gentiles. . . . This arose from messianism itself, and in particular from the theme of the reign of God. It is evident that the apostolic Church was slow to see the full scope of its mission. Jesus Himself had limited His activity to Judaism. When the question of admitting Gentiles to the new Israel arose, the response of many if not most of the community was that they could be admitted if they first became Jews. Not, it seems, until the question was put in these terms did the Church see clearly that it was the fullness of the new Israel, and that it had to become as spacious as the reign of God itself, which knows no limits. Once this became apparent, the Church, by reflecting on the Old Testament, perceived that this fullness was a legitimate development of another biblical theme, and that to make Jesus and His Church, the new Israel, depend upon the old Israel, was to deny the newness and the fullness of the Christian fact. If the Judaizers were right, then Jesus and His Church were not a "fulfillment," but simply another stage in the development of the synagogue. Thus the Church recognized her identity with Jesus as Messiah-Savior, and her mission as a continuation of His.

But in taking the world as the unsubdued kingdom of God the Church transformed the concept of messianism still more. The peculiarly Aramaic title of "Son of Man" does not appear in the epistles, although the theme of the coming derived from it remains. The words "savior" and "salvation" occur twice in John, more frequently in Luke, Acts, and the epistles, and in Matthew and Mark not at all. The title "savior" (*soter*) is given frequently to Hellenistic kings and to the Roman emperors, and it is hardly doubtful that this Hellenistic conception of kingship influenced the presentation of the royal dignity of Jesus to the Gentiles; it was a conception more familiar to them than the Old Testament conception of kingship. The most important modification is the appearance of the title of "Lord" (*kyrios*). Vincent Taylor has shown, I believe, that this is a title conferred upon Jesus after the Resurrection and Ascension; the occurrences in the Synoptic Gospels as a form of address mean no more than "Sir." He also shows that the origin of the title cannot be explained from the terminology of Hellenistic mystery cults; it is an old title and was used by those who spoke Aramaic as well as by those who spoke Greek.[8] This does not imply that the influence of the Greek-speaking communities was not strong in the development of the term; the Aramaic world, after all, was itself subject to the pressure of Greek usage. As a royal title *kyrios* was extremely common, and its application to Jesus puts in a Greek form the transformation of the idea of kingship which we noticed above; the New Testament conceives kingship as received by Jesus in His Resurrection and Ascension.

It may seem now that we have become so enraptured with the present subject as to have forgotten messianism and wandered into ecclesiology and Christology, not to mention sacramental theology. But these excursions were not digressions; our theological areas are divided by artificial lines which do not always hew to reality. The concept of messianism is very complex, as we have observed; it is also basic and touches upon most of Christian revelation. To treat it as merely apologetic is to simplify it by distortion; in fact, this comes near to making it theologically irrelevant.

But what about the contemporary student of theology? We have done our best, as others have done before us, to show that the traditional apologetic messianism has no place in a modern course of theology. Messianism as we have outlined it here does not belong to apologetic theology at all, but to dogmatic theology. The messianic character of Jesus and of His mission shows us the context of His historical reality. We should not waste time on useless discussion of "messianic claims," which there is no record of His making, but try to see how His character as the new Israel gives sharpness of outline and contemporary urgency to His words. The incarnate Word is a timeless reality precisely because He is so deeply identified with time, with a definite history and a definite culture. We shall by the exploration of this theme perhaps reach a more profound insight into the identity of Jesus and the Church, an insight which is as necessary now as it always has been. Catholics have not always seen as well as St. Paul saw that a theology of the Church is a theology of the Incarnation. This truth may become clearer and more meaningful when both the Incarnate Word and the Church are seen as the new Israel.

Messianism, we have seen, is deeply involved in the theology of redemption and salvation. What the New Testament means by salvation is largely put in terms of the messianic hope, and we must explore the messianic themes if we are to comprehend its teaching. In our theology the social character of redemption and salvation will become clearer and more relevant to us and our times. Jesus as king is ruler of a society, not of a collection of unrelated individuals, and the reign of God is a social fulfillment, not a group of individual achievements. The tension between history and eschatology will remind us that the Church is an incarnation in history and culture as was the incarnation of the Word. Perhaps no greater falsification of the mission of Jesus and His Church was ever proposed than the theory which made Him the founder of a tight little eschatological group which was willing to let the world go to perdition while it awaited the coming of its redeemer on the clouds. And perhaps there is always a tendency to such eschatologism; it relieves us of our missionary obligations.

And here, in conclusion, may be the most fruitful effect of the treatment of messianism in sacred doctrine: a deeper awareness of the mission of the Church, and of the place of each of her members in that mission. If sacred doctrine . . . can contribute to this end, it will have justified itself beyond all demands.

References

[1] Recent surveys of messianism: the papers of Cerfaux, Coppens, de Langhe, de Leeuw, Descamps, Giblet, and Rigaux collected in *L'Attente du Messie* (Desclée de Brouwer, 1954); A. Gelin, "Messianisme," in *Dictionnaire de la Bible: Supplément* (Paris, 1955), Vol. V, cc. 1165-1212. The 1956 meeting of the Catholic Biblical Association of America presented a collection of papers on messianism which appeared in the *Catholic Biblical Quarterly:* E. F. Siegman, "The Stone Hewn from the Mountain (Daniel 2)," 18 (1956), 364-79; R. E. Murphy, "Notes on Old Testament Messianism and Apologetics," 19 (1957),

5-15; Eamonn O'Doherty, "The Organic Development of Messianic Revelation," 19 (1957), 16-24; J. L. McKenzie, "Royal Messianism," 19 (1957), 25-52; R. E. Brown, "The Messianism of Qumran," 19 (1957), 53-82; J. E. Menard, "*Pais Theou* as Messianic Title in the Book of Acts," 19 (1957), 83-92; Alphonsus Benson, ". . . From the Mouth of the Lion," 19 (1957), 199-212; E. H. Maly, "Messianism in Osee," 19 (1957), 213-25; F. L. Moriarty, "The Emmanuel Prophecies," 19 (1957), 226-33; R. A. F. Mackenzie, "The Messianism of Deuteronomy," 19 (1957), 299-305; Antonine De Guglielmo, "The Fertility of the Land in Messianic Prophecies," 19 (1957), 306-311; R. T. Siebeneck, "The Messianism of Aggeus and Proto-Zacharias," 19 (1957), 312-28. Additional bibliographical material will be found in these works.

[2] The question can be easily pursued in the articles of D. M. Stanley: "*Didache* as a Constitutive Element of the Gospel-Form," *Catholic Biblical Quarterly*, 17 (1955), 216-28; "The Conception of Salvation in Primitive Christian Preaching," *CBQ*, 18 (1956), 231-54; "The Conception of Salvation in the Synoptic Gospels," *CBQ*, 18 (1956), 345-63; "Balaam's Ass, or a Problem in New Testament Hermeneutics," *CBQ*, 20 (1958), 50-56; "Liturgical Influences on the Formation of the Four Gospels," *CBQ*, 21 (1959), 24-38; "The Conception of the Gospels as Salvation History," *Theological Studies*, 20 (1959), 561-89.

[3] Cf. my discussion in *CBQ*, 19 (1957), 49-51, and references therein given.

[4] *Ibid.*, 25-52.

[5] Cf. D. M. Stanley, "Kingdom to Church," *Theological Studies*, 16 (1955), 1-29.

[6] H. B. Swete, *An Introduction to the Old Testament in Greek* (Cambridge, 1914), p. 386. Mark 15:28, a contamination from Luke 22:37, is not found in the critical text.

[7] Millar Burrows, *More Light on the Dead Sea Scrolls* (New York, 1958), pp. 297-311; J. T. Milik, *Dix Ans de Découvertes dans le Désert de Juda* (Paris, 1957), pp. 83-85; F. M. Cross, *The Ancient Library of Qumran and Modern Biblical Studies* (New York, 1958), pp. 65-66, 165-66.

[8] Vincent Taylor, *The Names of Jesus* (New York, 1953), pp. 38-51.

BERNARD COOKE, S.J.

Christ in Scripture

The judicious reader will find in this penetrating article a discussion of questions such as these: How does the notion of covenant election unify the various elements of Old Testament revelation? How is Christ the culmination of all that God reveals about Himself and about man? How can the Old Testament understand Christ as God? How can the Old Testament mediators between God and man help us understand Christ as mediator? How can an understanding of the people of God in the Old Testament illumine our understanding of Christ as the new Israel and of the doctrine of the Mystical Body?

Father Cooke is chairman of the theology department at Marquette University in Milwaukee, Wisconsin.

As the Epistle to the Hebrews tells us (Heb 1:1-2), God spoke in diverse ways before that fulfillment came when He spoke through His own Word become flesh. Those centuries of Old Testament history when God was speaking in incomplete form are part of that same process by which God finally speaks in Christ. One intelligibility runs through this whole process of revelation, and everything in God's Old Testament actions is part of the revelation of Christ. We must be disabused on the point of view that sees certain so-called messianic passages of the Old Testament as pointing in somewhat isolated form to Christ; the *whole of the Old Testament* points to Christ and finds its fulfillment and meaning in Him.

In the actions of Israelitic history God spoke His basic revelation

This paper was first delivered at the 1960 workshop held at Barat College and sponsored by Marquette University. It was published in *Apostolic Perspectives* and is reproduced here with permission.

to men: His salvific love for them. This revelation was gradually unfolded to an uncultured and unreceptive people through the paradigmatic actions of the Exodus and the Sinai covenant, in the conquest and settlement of Palestine, in the establishment and protection of the Davidic kingship, the raising up of the prophets, the restoration of Jerusalem under the post-Exilic leaders. Each stage in the history of Israel marks a step forward, not in the sense of abandoning what preceded, but rather of transforming and absorbing it into a new reality governed by a new and deeper insight. The covenant preached by the prophets is the covenant of Sinai, but it is seen in the light of a promised land gained and then lost, in the light of a relationship to Yahweh that is likened to that of a bride. New depths of personal responsibility and dignity enter into the prophetic use of the word *berith*, yet the governing influence in the understanding of this word is the experience of the Exodus.

I would like to emphasize this notion of the transformation effected by God's Old Testament actions, for I believe this is one of the most important aspects of our understanding of the Old Testament and its revelation. As the centuries of Israel unfold, the people's understanding (or at least that of the elite) regarding man, his life, his sanctity, his relation to God, his society, his law, and so forth are radically changed. Throughout this transforming process, the principle of transformation—the core of the revelation—remains constant; but only bit by bit does this manage to alter Israel's understanding of human life. That which enters human history with the Exodus—supernatural and revealed religion—is so drastically different that it is no wonder that 1300 years were required to work to the pre-Christian understanding of Yahweh, and 2000 additional years of Christian faith have far from exhausted the understanding of this God. To study the process by which the natural religious insights of mankind, which to a large extent Israel borrowed from its ancestors and its neighbors, were radically transformed by supernatural revelation is one of the most instructive experiences we can have in learning the relation between the natural and supernatural orders.

One of the great advantages of modern biblical scholarship is the fact that it is making it possible for us to date more accurately the different elements in the Old Testament revelation and so to trace with greater exactitude the gradual clarification of religious ideas that took place during the centuries of Israel's history. This gradual unfolding of the revelation took place in terms of men, of institutions, of events, and of eschatological expectations and idealizations; and I believe that it is by studying this complex process that we can come to our best understanding of typology. There is a constant and recurrent meaning that ties together Moses and Joshua and Samuel and David and Zorobabel, and this meaning reaches its highest expression in the messianic passages of Deutero-Isaia; there is an associated meaning that links the crossing of the Red Sea with the crossing over the Jordan and the return from the Babylonian Exile and the eschatological triumph of the kingdom of the saints.

The key to this meaning seems to be a recurrent pattern developed around the central notion of covenant election, a notion which is deepened in its meaning as we progress through Old Testament history. There is always a mediator through whom God acts; there is always a call to the people: a conversion of the people is required, and then there follows a more definitive election of the people, solemnized in a covenant action and memorialized in some permanent symbol. This pattern is not one that we arbitrarily impose on the Old Testament texts; it is one consciously recognized by Old Testament writers as we can see by the way it is artificially projected back into the story of the flood. In this series of recurrences, the second realizes the constant central significance more fully than does the first, the third more fully than the second and so on; yet the understanding of the later occurrences is intrinsically dependent upon the earlier ones. Unless we knew of the Exodus and the Sinai covenant we could never grasp the Jewish understanding, that is, the revealed significance, of the return from the Babylonian Exile. It seems to me that this is where we encounter typology—each earlier occurrence is a type of each of the later occurrences. For our present discussion, on the . . . [study] of Christ from Scripture, there seems to be a special relevance in this typological pattern, for the Gospels depict Christ as the full expression of this covenant pattern which then continues in His Church and its life of the sacraments.

Nature of Yahweh

In the course of His Old Testament action of revealing, God gradually deepened and clarified the supernatural understanding of three things: God Himself, man, and the relation of man to God, that is, religion. The very earliest elements of Israelitic revelation, the law given Moses, reveals the nature of Yahweh as a personal being with a will which directs human actions, clarifies by its dictates the behavioral orientations of man's nature, and points to what man must do to fulfill his responsibilities (especially to God) and so attain his destiny. As the centuries pass, the understanding of God, man, and the relation of man to God is given increasing clarity and depth, until we come to Christ, the fullness of revelation in all three areas: He is the fullness of revelation regarding the nature of God; He is the fullness of revelation regarding the dignity and role of man; He is Himself, as mediator, the relation between man and God. It is only when we see and present Christ as the fulfillment of these three great areas of revelation that we are genuinely and adequately presenting Him as the object of faith. Nor can we hope to reach an understanding about God, about man, about Christianity, unless we study Christ in this context.

There is one last suggestion drawn from Sacred Scripture to which I would like to advert before going on to a concrete and detailed proposal. St. Paul (1 Cor 1:23) tells us that the Gospel which he preaches is that of a crucified Messiah—a stumbling block to Jews and foolishness to Greeks, but power and wisdom to those of the faith. While our task . . . [as students] is theology and not kerygma, we cannot ignore the point of St. Paul's remark. There is only one Christ; and He reveals Himself supremely in the actions beginning with the Last Supper and extending to the Ascension. Only in the light of the death and Resurrection of Christ can we really grasp the meaning of St. John's remark that God is love; only here can we understand the depths of our human dignity and weakness and destiny; only here can we understand exactly how man is to be brought to God in a supreme act of sacrificial worship.

A presentation of Christ, whether emphasizing Scripture or dogma or liturgy, that does not focus upon the key redemptive actions is an insufficient explanation. Only in these three actions—the Cenacle, Calvary, and the Resurrection—does the meaning of Christ come to full expression. And only if we can see Christ revealed in these actions can we come to any adequate understanding of the Church and its sacraments through which these redemptive acts continue.

So, with these as preliminary remarks, let us approach a suggested way of studying Christ from Scripture. My purpose here is to indicate certain elements in the scriptural depicting of Christ that I believe should find a firm place in any adequate study of the subject. I will try to align things under three headings and then proceed quite systematically, even at the risk of being dry and unliterary. The three headings are: Christ as God; Christ as Messiah or mediator; Christ as the people.

Christ as God

As Giving Life. One of the most fundamental points of Old Testament revelation is the fact that Yahweh and He alone, by His all-powerful word, is the source of life to men. Against the attraction of the vegetation cults of surrounding Canaanite peoples which so strongly tempted the sons of Israel, the prophets spoke out by word and work. Yahweh had proved His role as sustainer of life by giving manna and water in the desert years, and He it is who gives fertility to the promised land. Playing a key role in this communication of life is the word of God, a life-giving force in its own right, creative at the beginning of time, passing in Israelitic history through the Law and prophets and before that through the patriarchal blessings. To listen to this word was life and wisdom, to ignore it was to die.

Scene after scene of the New Testament links Christ to this Old Testament revelation of Yahweh. Christ's words heal and raise the dead to life, Christ feeds the multitudes miraculously in what is called a desert place, Christ invites those who hunger and thirst to come unto Him; John's prologue reminds us that Christ is the source of life and that all things were made by Him, for He is the *davar Yahweh*, God's own creative word. Obviously, this aspect of the revelation of Christ as God giving life reaches its climax in the scene of the upper room, where in unexpected and transcendent fulfillment of His promise to give the bread of life, Christ institutes the Eucharistic action.

As Putting Order into Life. If Yahweh was seen in the Old Testament as source of life, He was also revealed as source of order—for He was Law-giver, Wisdom, and the Light of Israel. God initiated His direction of Israel by giving them a law; and it was this law, derivative in large part from other ancient law and customs but controlled in its most fundamental orientations by the Yahwistic revelations, that organized Israel as a people. Human law-givers and rulers there are, from Moses through the judges to the kings; but it is always Yahweh who is the source and the sanction of the law in Israel.

So, too, when Israel, like other ancient peoples, sought for the answers to human life and its problems, sought for a wisdom that would be a sure and adequate guide for human life, the quest led to Yahweh Himself. He alone possesses wisdom; He alone by His knowledge is competent to direct the course of human events. He alone possesses the ultimate values by which to weigh the importance and goodness of men and their deeds.

And He, the God who in the theophany of a fiery column guided them in the Exodus, illumines their minds to know the right and orderly path. If Israel, and above all, Israel's leaders, will open their minds to this illumining action of Yahweh, salvation will be attained; they will be led from darkness into light.

Christ of the Gospels

When we come to the Christ of the Gospels we see that He lays claim to be Yahweh under these precise formalities, and this is part of the depth of His claim to be God. Page after page of the Gospels attests to Christ's claim to be a supreme law-giver, teaching the new law that replaces the law given on Sinai. And who but Yahweh could alter the law of Yahweh? Christ is depicted, not just as a new Moses speaking for God in conveying a new Torah; Christ legislates in His own right: "but *I* say to you." Not only that, but a close examination of the Gospels shows how the Old Testament's "be holy because I am holy" is succeeded by Christ's "come, follow me." He is the *way*, the new Torah.

One of Christ's most profound claims to strict divinity lies in His claim to be divine Wisdom, the same Wisdom identified with Yahweh Himself in the Wisdom writings of Israel. The magnificent eleventh chapter of Matthew would suffice to establish the point: it is here that the Gospel links the words of Christ with the final chapter of the book of Sirach, and the words "All things have been given me by my Father; no one knows the Father but the Son . . ." point to a knowledge possessed by the infinite God alone.

And Christ comes to illumine men's minds: He is the light of the world; He is not only the *way*, He is the *truth*. While they do so in more implicit and concrete form, the Gospels contain the same teaching that we find in the opening chapter of Colossians: Christ is the mirroring of the infinite God.

As Promised Land. Another most interesting and metaphysically profound aspect of Christ's claim to divinity is His fulfillment in

Himself of the revelation of a promised land. We know how at the beginnings of Israelitic history, Yahweh in dealing with the primitive, earth-bound people could give them little idea of their true destiny and goal except in terms of land which they could conquer and possess in peace, where they could abide and prosper. It took the sad centuries of Jewish decline and the experience of the Exile to break the hold of such a materialistic notion of Israel's destiny, but bit by bit the revelation of the Old Testament is able to stress the more profoundly human aspects of man's destiny, and by the end of those centuries it is becoming clear that Yahweh Himself is the promised land, He is the goal and abode of the just.

If one makes even a hasty examination of the New Testament uses of the word *meno*, "abide," he will see the fulfillment of this idea of promised land in Christ. Both in the Gospels and in the Pauline writings, Jesus is described as the abode of men, as their exceeding great reward.

As Kyrios. Finally, though there are a number of other titles to divinity which we must leave untouched, Christ is depicted in the New Testament as Kyrios, as the Lord who rules the world and its history, the Adonai of the Old Testament. The pages of the Acts of the Apostles and the Epistles of St. Paul, particularly those of the captivity, bear witness to the awareness that Christ, the Lord of Old and New Testaments, dwelt in His infant Church as in His Temple. And with this realization came the knowledge of that eternal preexistence of Christ as the Word to which John's prologue gives such eloquent witness.

To understand and present Christ as God in this fashion is not to dig into New Testament texts to find an apologetic for Christ as divine in order to answer those who deny this fact. It is rather to understand the fullness of God's revelation of Himself as God in Christ, God incarnated. Only in Christ as God do we come to know God as He intends us to know Him: Lord of history; source of all life and of all order, wisdom, and goodness; goal of man's existence.

Christ as Mediator

The second great area in which the New Testament depicts Christ against the emergent revelation of the Old Testament—and this is one with which we are somewhat more familiar—is that of mediator. In general, there are three great mediatorial functions that play a role in Israel: prophet, king, and priest. The great figures who exercised such mediation foreshadow and typify Christ, who is in all three functions the mediator par excellence. When Christ is depicted as fulfilling these mediatorial roles, it is more than a revelation of His excellence and His revelation to all that preceded Him; it is a most important and transforming revelation of the nature of mediation as it now exists, which is another way of saying that it is a revelation of the distinctive nature of Christianity as a religion. While the New Testament's relating of Christ to the great figures of the Old Testament is very rich and complex, let us simply take a few cases by way of illustration.

Christ, a New Moses. Comparison of Christ to Moses is one of the most basic and recurrent themes in the Gospels. This is not surprising, for the two hold parallel positions: Moses stands at the origins of the Old Testament religion and combines in his own charismatic office the three mediatorial roles which then receive differentiation in later Israelitic history. So, too, Christ stands at the beginning of Christian history, but in how different a way: Moses did not live on in the people he founded; Christ lives on in His Church which is His continuation.

The very paralleling of Christ and Moses affords the inspired writers a chance to contrast them and to point to the uniqueness of Christ—which we, too, can do in our teaching. When the people were under Moses in the desert years Israel was in many respects closest to God, most dependent and most reliant upon Him, and God's providential care was most apparent. Yet this era fades before the Christian dispensation: "Your fathers did eat manna and are dead; he that eats this bread shall live forever." What really makes the great difference between Christ and Moses is the fact that Moses did not found the Old Testament religion. He was the instrument of its founding, but Yahweh was the founder; whereas when we come to Christ, He is the founder in the fullest possible sense of the Christian religion.

Christ, a New David. Surely the most controversial, if not the most important, mediatorial office of the Old Testament era was that of the kingship. Israel never took to kingship, for Yahweh was really the ruler of the people, and the human kings who succeeded David seldom realized their place as Yahweh's vicars. So, the Davidic dynasty declined, though the expectation of a great Davidic prince persisted, even increased, over the years. Around this expectation grew the whole messianism of the later centuries, an interesting process in which the figure of David as king is gradually idealized (compare Chronicles to 2 Samuel) and projected onto that hoped-for ruler who will one day bring justice to Israel.

It is clear from the Gospels that the early Church saw Christ as the fulfillment of the Davidic promises, as the hoped-for prince of peace, even though the passages linking Christ with David are surprisingly few. What is important, however, is that Christ is not depicted as the fulfillment of the Davidic dynasty as it was; rather He is its fulfillment as it should have been. Christ, it is true, is paralleled to the historical figure of David, but He is seen much more as the final expression and revelation of the idealization of David. Christ as king tells us what kingship should be, what establishment of justice really means, how law can be made and executed most profoundly. One can learn a great deal about the mediatorial role of law in religion—a most important thing intrinsically and historically—by studying Christ as human law-giver.

Christ, the Great Prophet. There is still a tendency, I believe, in teaching Christ to Catholic students and explaining how He is the fulfillment of Old Testament prophecy, to relate Him simply to certain verbal predictions of the prophets. Rather, Christ's fulfillment of the prophets is much wider and much more profound. Even if, for the moment, we wish to prescind from the fact that the entirety of the Old Testament predicts Christ, and confine ourselves to Christ's relation to the prophets, He fulfilled not just what they said, but what they were. We know the importance of the prophetic movement for Old Testament times, how much of the preservation and evolution of the spiritual insight of Israel was dependent upon these great charismatic leaders. We are aware, too, that the word "prophets" as applied to these men in Israel denominates not so much their role as seers of the future as it does their tasks of witnessing to Yahweh and His covenant. Aware that their actions, their lives, and their very persons were as important a witness as were their words, many of the prophets performed (under divine guidance) certain rather strange but symbolic actions. The prophet was always a man of his times and his people, immersed in the thought-currents and social problems of his day, aware of and protesting against those ideas and patterns of action that were not consonant with God's action in Israelitic history.

Christ's parable of the unjust caretakers of the vineyard indicates quite clearly that He saw Himself as the heir and fulfillment of the prophetic vocation and movement in Israel. Christ performed actions which made even the masses acclaim Him as a great prophet, and He continued in His teaching all the major currents of prophetic thought; yet how transcendentally different is the word of God channelled through Him. Christ is compared, at least in His human mentality, to all the great prophets of the Old Testament. Above all, it is the death and Resurrection of Christ, the unique witness to the salvific action of Yahweh, that confers upon the prophetic movement of Israel its final glory and intelligibility.

CHRIST AS WISE MAN. For many centuries before Christ, the peoples of the Mediterranean world (as a matter of fact, of the Far East, too) were fascinated by the search for human wisdom, for the answer to human life; the sage, who pronounces upon man and his doings, is a widespread phenomenon. Israel, too, has its wisdom movement, extending at least as far back as Samson's adroitness with riddles, reaching a traditional climax in the wisdom of Solomon, but actually flourishing some centuries later. Like everything else in Israel, wisdom literature was transformed by the content of the Yahwistic revelation, by the Law, above all, and wisdom was seen in Israel to consist humanly in conformity to God's directives and divinely in the Providence that guided the affairs of men and of Israel in particular. Bound so closely to the Law, it is not surprising that the wisdom movement in Israel is closely allied with the whole scribal and rabbinic development of the post-Exilic centuries.

As early as His teaching in the Temple at the age of twelve, Christ is seen as the fulfillment of wisdom in Israel. His unbelievably shrewd answers to the verbal traps of the Pharisees and Scribes, His aphorisms that are so reminiscent of the Book of Proverbs, His use of parables in the tradition of the rabbinic *mashal*, above all His own statements of superiority to Solomon—all these point to His role as a supremely wise teacher. Actually, the questions that plagued the wisdom movements of all peoples—the problem of evil, the meaning and destiny of man, the criterion of genuine good and success—these find their sole answer in Christ, and this only in terms of those mystery-filled actions of Holy Week which summarized, completed, and transcended the earlier revelation.

CHRIST AS SERVANT. The famous Servant Songs of Deutero-Isaia are much more than a hopeful sketching of a coming redeemer. They are the high point of Old Testament messianism and for that very reason the high point of the spiritual insight of the Old Testament. Great men had always epitomized the sanctity expected of the people of God, and the figure of the Servant is the idealization of such personal realization of covenant holiness. Most appropriately is He called Servant, for service is the keynote to the specific and characteristic spirituality revealed to the people of Israel; only the greatest ever deserve and receive the acclaim "Servant of Yahweh"—Moses, Samuel, David, some prophets. Now, in the Servant Songs, that service is seen to consist in vicarious suffering effecting a new covenant dispensation that extends beyond Israel to all peoples and frees mankind from its sins.

Christ's affirmation that He is the Servant, that He realizes and absorbs and transforms thereby the spirituality of the Old Testament, extends into the very warp and woof of the Gospel narrative, above all into the description of Holy Week. If there is anything that is unquestionable in the Gospels, it is that Christ Himself, the primitive Church, and the Evangelists, see Christ as the Servant of Yahweh. And, I might add, if Christ is not to be identified as the Servant, the New Testament orientations toward the understanding of the Christian sacraments become completely unintelligible. No place else does the nature of Old Testament mediation become more intelligible than in seeing Christ as Servant in His Eucharistic action of sacrifice, on Calvary, and risen gloriously from the dead.

To teach Christ as Servant is to teach a whole spirituality, a revealed holiness of sacrificial dedication, one that is consonant, as indeed we would expect it to be, with that sacramental spirituality which should mark each Christian. To teach adequately Christ as Servant, one would have to teach a great deal about the Old Testament, indeed everything of importance. Hence, it provides a magnificent point of integration in a biblical theology.

Before leaving the topic of Christ as Mediator, there is one observation that should be made. In teaching Christ this way, one would have to beware of presenting Christ as if He were only the very best in each of these categories of mediation. Actually, as we know, the mystery of the Incarnation introduces a note of specific difference into Christ's situation which we must always emphasize. A religious mediator reveals, and unless the divine in Christ is kept in view, the depths of His mediation are not understood; we must not fall under the chiding of Christ: "Have I been with you so long and you have not known me? He who sees me, sees the Father."

Christ as the People

Not only is Christ the great revelation of God as initiating the new covenant, and the revelation in His own role and action of what mediation means in the Christian dispensation; He is also in Himself the great revelation of mankind as redeemed, as recipient of the covenant. In other words, Christ is the people and is so revealed in the New Testament; that is to say, He is seen as being the recapitulation at once of Israel and of the Church.

SYNOPTIC VIEW OF CHRIST AS ISRAEL. One of the most fascinating aspects of the Synoptic presentation of Christ is the way in which it relates Him to Israel. It is clear that He is the fulfillment of Israel because He is Israel's only perfect Son, and because His thought and teaching catch up and perfect every positive insight and religious value of Old Testament revelation; fulfillment also because all the institutions of Israelitic society are realized and transformed in Him. But there is another kind of fulfillment; that is, Christ recapitulates the events of the Old Testament by Himself, reliving in compressed form the key happenings and development of Old Testament.

Take the Synoptic description of the Baptism of Christ as an example. Like Israel of old, Christ is called out of Egypt; St. Matthew is careful to point this out. Like Israel at the Red Sea and the crossing of the Jordan, Christ must pass through the waters; as He does, there occurs His public election by His Father and the announcement of His vocation. Like Israel of old He is led into the desert, there to encounter three trials which summarize the three recurrent temptations of Israel. This runs throughout the Gospels, though in less obvious form, and emerges again in even greater fulfillment at the moment of the transformation of Old Testament liturgy in the Pasch into the Eucharist. When we begin to grasp this process, we can see much more deeply how Christ redeemed by recapitulating, by reversing, as it were, the previous life of Israel and its sinful failures, in doing now what Israel always should have done.

CHRIST'S APOSTLES, THE NEW ISRAEL. In the Synoptic Gospels, however, the notion of Christ as the new Israel is extended beyond Him to His apostles: as a kingdom has been given to Him, so He extends it to them. He is the first-born, the bearer, as it were, of the people's life force, but He is the first-born among many brethren.

And it is quite clear in the Synoptic writings that not just Christ, but His immediate followers, are the Remnant, the *anawim;* from them will come a whole new generation of the people of God. As the Old Testament people had their God with them, dwelling in their midst by covenant, so the followers of Christ have a much greater presence of God with them, a presence that centers in the new covenant action, the Eucharist.

As the Law had bound the Old Testament people into a unit, so the Church will be held together by Christ's command of fraternal love. As Israel descended from the twelve sons of Jacob, so the Church is built upon the twelve Apostles—and this in a very profound and manifold sense. Christ lives on in His followers as did Jacob in Israel, which bore his name, but now that continuance of life takes on a transcendentally different meaning.

CHRIST, THE TRUE VINE. When we come to St. John's writings, we remain in a profoundly Old Testament atmosphere, one dominated by the notion of *davar*, the word. It is this creative word of God, introduced so solemnly in the prologue to John's Gospel, that is the source of life; and we are not surprised that so much of the "life" imagery of the Old Testament expression of revelation is encountered again in St. John. It is sufficient for our present purposes to recall the interesting fulfillment of this imagery that is contained in John 15, where the key image of the vine receives an unexpected depth of realization in Christ's words: "I am the true vine . . . you are the branches." In this one statement, we find symbolic expression of the mystery of Christ's recapitulation of both Israel and the Church.

PAULINE TEACHING ON THE MYSTICAL BODY. Finally, there is the doctrine of the Church as Christ's Mystical Body, which is explained so richly and with such compression in St. Paul's letters. In Christ both Jew and Gentile come together; the Church is built upon prophets and apostles with Christ as the cornerstone; the people of God who are the infant Church are the heirs of the promises made to Abraham. Somehow, in mysterious fashion, the members of Christ's Church derive from Him, their head, the new life that they share by virtue of His death and Resurrection. More than just a moral unity, yet safeguarding the individuality of each Christian, the Church is actually Christ living on and expressing Himself in those who are His members.

Conclusion

Obviously, in these few remarks we have not exhausted the teaching of Scripture regarding Christ. Books will be written to the end of time on the Christ of the Gospels, or on Christ in the Pauline literature; and the mystery of Christ will still remain unplumbed. Perhaps we can, though, hazard a few conclusions:

1. The mystery of Christ must be seen in an historical and not merely an analytical way; His position in the historical process of man's religious development is a fact of utmost importance, and (it would seem) we must look at this fact historically, though not by purely profane historical inquiry.

2. Perhaps only in seeing Christ as related to the Old Testament can we appreciate the depths of transformation wrought by the Incarnation in man and his religion, even in the revealed religion of the Old Testament. In seeing the profound dimensions of the transformation we will better understand the meaning of "Christian" and of "supernatural."

3. In studying Christ as revealed in Scripture, more than just an isolated Christology emerges; the whole mystery of God, of the supernatural, of human destiny, of the Church and its sacraments, of the nature of religion, is involved. In a very graphic way one sees how central and all-embracing is the mystery of Christ.

4. To have studied Christ scripturally, and so to have seen the principle of typology operative on several levels, is excellent background and preparation for grasping the typology involved in the Christian sacraments and in Christian spirituality.

5. So to have seen Christ against the background and providential preparation of the Old Testament is to have entered into the mind of Christ and that of the primitive Church. Both Christ Himself and the early generations of Christians seem to have had this view, a view that contains the deposit of faith.

6. Finally, to begin to see Christ and His significance in this "emergent" historical fashion is an important conditioning, I believe, for realizing and understanding the fact of Christ's expression of Himself in the present, living mystery of the Church.

CARROLL STUHLMUELLER, C.P.

The Sacraments in Scripture

The keen reader will find in this stimulating article a discussion of questions such as these: Can we find a basis for traditional concepts of sacramental theology in Sacred Scripture? How can the Old Testament feasts be considered a celebration of God's redemptive acts? Is there evidence of development in the Old Testament understanding of its liturgy? How did the Old Testament notion of worship affect the Christian Mass and sacraments? What does the biblical attitude toward nature contribute to sacramental theology? What parallel does the Bible offer to the concept of sacramental form? How does Scripture speak of the power and efficacy of God's word? What has this to do with sacraments? What parallels do we find to sacramental matter in Old Testament ritual practices? What is the Old Testament idea of sacrifice and how does it influence the New Testament presentation of Calvary and the Mass?

Father Stuhlmueller, also the author of a previous article, teaches Scripture at the Passionist Seminary in Louisville.

The subject of the present paper, "The sacraments in Scripture," entangles us in controversy. Questions such as these arise: Can Scripture prove the nature of the sacraments? Do scriptural texts contain deeper meanings which were unknown to the original author? Are we dealing with biblical theology or with scholastic theology? In regard to these important introductory questions, we do not intend to argue, but simply to state our position, and then, to proceed with our subject matter. This method may

This article, like the previous one, was delivered at the 1960 Barat College workshop and was published in *Apostolic Perspectives*. It is reproduced here with permission.

seem high-handed, but a definite stand must be taken, lest our ideas be shot to pieces in a no-man's land between two contending sides!

The first question is this: Can we *prove* from Scripture the dogmatic Catholic teaching on the sacraments? For instance, that the Mass is a true and proper sacrifice? That Christ is really and substantially present in the Blessed Sacrament? The position which we assume in this paper is this: The sacraments belong to the realm of faith, to supernatural truths revealed by God and accepted only through the divine light of faith. Therefore, neither the Old Testament nor the New Testament provides such forthright statements that the inner, essential meaning of the sacraments becomes unmistakeably clear. A study of the Old Testament and the New Testament, consequently, does not prove sacramental theology to the unbeliever, but it does clarify and enrich the faith of the believer. In this paper, our study of the Bible belongs on the supernatural, not the natural, level of thinking. It presumes faith and the divine nature of the Church.

Another hotly disputed question, enveloped in the black clouds of controversy, is the matter of the *sensus plenior* or the *fuller sense*. Personally, I see no need of this sense of Scripture; this paper deliberately avoids calling upon its services.

Neither will we make use of typology. Even though an investigation of the typical sense is a legitimate and fruitful way of discovering God's message in the Bible, nonetheless typology is too often employed without proper restraint. In every instance it must rely upon a determination of the literal sense which Pope Pius XII called "the supreme rule of interpretation" (*Divino afflante Spiritu*, n. 34). In order to orientate our thoughts properly, it seems more in accord with our purpose to examine what the sacred writer "intended to express" (*Ibid.*).

Lastly, . . . [studying] the sacraments from Scripture involves us in the thick of another dispute: that of biblical theology, its scope and method. Let me honestly admit: I have no intention of presenting a *biblical* theology of the sacraments. Biblical theology arranges its data, not according to the thought-framework of scholastic philosophy, but rather according to the concepts and the thought-patterns of the ancient, biblical world. This paper appropriates contemporary ideas about the sacraments and seeks a clarification and enrichment of them through Scripture, and especially through the medium of the Old Testament.

Modern theological thinking divides each sacrament into matter and form. A separation such as that, as well as other divisions into sacrament and sacrifice, into remote and proximate matter, into sacred and profane signs, was not appreciated, if even known and recognized in biblical times. A practical consideration for theology as taught in our schools dictates our method of incorporating particular elements of the Old Testament into a scholastic framework.

Our first section will fix attention upon *some ideas basic for understanding the scriptural contribution to sacramental theology.* Here we will investigate the relation of the redemptive acts of God to Israelite ritual and briefly study the biblical attitude toward nature and the use of physical elements like water, bread, and animals in the worship of God. The next major section will center around *the sacramental form* and its biblical counterpart, *the Word of God.* Last of all, corresponding to *the sacramental matter, the ritual acts of the Old Testament sacrifice* will be considered.

Basic Ideas for Sacramental Theology

God comes to man, not through sentences written in a book but through acts of redemptive love. This first, basic idea has important consequences for the Old Testament sacramentary. It will mean that the Israelite liturgy was more than sacred recitations of *past* history. The liturgy imparted to the dead, written word a new, living power. For example, when the account of the Exodus from Egypt was recited in liturgical ceremony, the worshiper felt himself personally involved in a mystical but very real renewal of that saving event. Thus God's redemptive acts were constantly recurring in much the same way as the mysteries of Christ's Passion-Resurrection are continually being renewed through the liturgical words and ceremonies of the Mass.

It is quite evident, even from a cursory reading of the Bible, that the Sacred Scriptures were not the product of philosophical geniuses who sat at their desks in studious solitude and wrote down their *Pensées* on the nature of God. The Bible does not tell so much what man thinks about God as it tells what God reveals Himself to be. Once again, God reveals Himself, not in glowing, periodic sentences which describe His nature and attributes, but rather by redemptive acts performed by the strong arm of His love. The few times that the biblical writer discoursed on the nature or attributes of God, he stopped short in awe and wonderment. The psalmist cried out: "Such knowledge is too wonderful for me; too lofty for me to attain" (Ps 138:6). Ben Sirach concluded his account of the works of God in nature with the question:

> Who can see him and describe him?
> or who can praise him as he is? (43:33).

It seems that, if God had revealed Himself in statements and formulas, man would have shaken his head and said: "Would that there were a God so wonderful as that, but, no, He cannot be!"

God, therefore, *acted*, and by means of His saving activity forced man to admit: "Yes, God is that wonderful." God thus brought man into immediate, personal contact with Himself. From this contact man came to a living knowledge of God, so mysterious and so infinite as to surpass all ideas, and yet more certain and undeniable than any sentence cut in the rock forever with an iron chisel (cf. Jb 19:23f). The Bible records God's acts of salvation; it tells of His personal intervention in human life and of His gradual preparation for *the* act of salvation in His only Son. Both the Old Testament and the New Testament profess more concern with how God acts than with how God is defined.

Israelite feasts and ceremonial profess God's redemptive acts in the form of prayer and worship. Each feast was associated with God's personal intervention in behalf of His Chosen People. The weekly Sabbath renewed the act of creation by which God subdued hostile, chaotic powers and provided man with a beautiful world of peace (Gn 1:1-2:4a). The yearly festivals of the barley and the wheat harvests were associated with God's mighty intervention in the Exodus out of Egypt and in the revelation of His law on Mount Sinai. The feast of In-gathering (Ex 23:16; 34:22), the final harvest festival of late September or early October, was linked at first with the dedication of Solomon's Temple (3 Kgs 8) and after the Exile either with the reconsecration of the Temple area (Ez 3:3f) or with the messianic glory of the new Temple (Ag 2:1-9). In this late period the feast also commemorated the huts or booths in which the Israelites were thought to live while wandering in the Sinai Desert (Lev 23:33-43). Hence, the feast came to be called *Sukkoth* or *Booths*. The connection with the desert wandering reminded the worshiper of God's loving care during the Mosaic era. Also by associating the feast of *Sukkoth* with the building of the Temple, another redemptive act of God was brought to the Israelite mind: namely, Yahweh's solemn act of taking possession of the Promised Land, conquered through His assistance and now ruled through His presence at the Jerusalem Temple.

Liturgy and Redemption

The close link between the liturgy and God's redemptive acts constantly comes to our attention in Bible reading. We find it not only in the feast days but also in other ceremonies. Deuteronomy 26 quotes the words to be spoken by the worshiper on the occasion of offering first-fruits. Scholars recognize in this chapter one of the most ancient parts of the Bible. It is a Hebrew Credo, professing the acts of the Lord's "strong hand and outstretched arm" in giving the land and its fruits to His people. Temple worship was Bible history, not inscribed upon scrolls but re-enacted in public prayer and adoration.

The Israelite liturgy, like sacred history writing, was not a wistful sighing for the past. It was primarily concerned, not with what had happened in "the good old days" but with how the initial events of salvation continued taking place in the liturgical assembly. This repeated observance clears up certain difficulties which we encounter in Bible study. The various accounts of the Pasch, for instance, were at times oblivious of one another. The Yahwist account (Ex 12:21-23) says nothing about Unleavened Bread, while the Priestly tradition (Ex 12:1-20) gives it a prominent place. At other times, the accounts even openly contradict each other. This same Priestly account legislates that the lamb "shall not be eaten raw *nor boiled*, but roasted whole" (Ex 12:8), while Deuteronomy states in its law code: "you shall *boil* and eat it . . ." (Dt 16:7). Each tradition employs the same Hebrew word *basal*, to boil or to cook, in the intensive Piel form. If these accounts present the "history" of the Mosaic era as we write history today, then surely God contradicts Himself. Moses could not have legislated "to boil" and "not to boil" the lamb. If, on the contrary, the Bible presents various paschal liturgies of different places and times, which were gradually inserted into the Mosaic tradition, then what we find in the Bible is a record of the same paschal mystery as constantly relived among the changing circumstances of God's people. We can note a similar phenomenon in modern liturgical rules regulating the reception of Holy Communion.

The most valuable contribution of liturgical worship to the Bible, however, does not consist in ritualistic details like boiling or roasting the lamb, but in the ever fuller understanding of the paschal mystery on the part of the Chosen People. What God actually accomplished at the Red Sea and on Mount Sinai in delivering the fugitives from Egypt and in bringing them to covenantal union with Himself was seen in deeper and broader dimensions by *later* generations of Israelites. This deeper appreciation came only after the nation had personally relived the mystery through suffering, prayer, and deliverance. Intervening years of sorrow and joy were sustained and directed by community worship; the liturgy, in its turn, absorbed what the nation gained in spiritual insight. Through repeated sacramental observance, redemptive acts of God, like the Paschal Mystery, were personally experienced by later generations, and by that very means were gradually seen in their full spiritual significance.

Israelite Liturgy

The Old Testament notion of worship profoundly influenced the liturgy of the apostolic Church and appears today in the Mass, the sacraments and the religious calendar. The Mass commemorates the redemptive acts of God performed by His beloved Son. Immediately after the consecration, we confess how mindful we are of "the blessed Passion of the same Christ, Thy Son, our Lord, and also of His Resurrection from hell and also of His glorious Ascension into heaven." New Testament references to the sacraments proclaim the inherent power of these rites to renew the redemptive acts of our Lord. Some of these references are easily recognized, such as St. Paul's explicit words about the sacrament of Baptism in Romans 6. Baptism, according to St. Paul, buries us in the death of Christ that we might rise with Him to newness of life. Other references appear more implicit, as the baptismal liturgy in 1 Peter (1:3-2:10) which develops the Exodus theme and the mysteries of Christ's Passion-Resurrection. Still other examples include the allusion to Extreme Unction in the anointing of Jesus at Bethany in John 12:1-11 and to Matrimony in the account of the marriage feast of Cana (Jn 2:1-11). Father Bruce Vawter presents tentative ideas on these last two examples in his article, "The Johannine Sacramentary." [1]

Not only the Mass and the sacraments, but also our religious calendar brings the worshiper into personal contact with the redemptive acts of our Lord. We have no feasts honoring the nature and the attributes of God, unless it be the feast of the Most Holy Trinity. There is no day dedicated, for instance, to God's eternity, wisdom, or infinite love; the Church celebrates instead, the great moments of our Lord's life: His birth, His holy week, or His spiritual presence through the Pentecostal gift of His Spirit.

This explanation of Israelite liturgy leaves many questions unanswered: that is, Did an ordinary Jew of the post-Exilic era better understand the meaning of the Exodus than a spiritual giant like Moses? Does not a similar question, however, face us when we study the development of doctrine in the Christian era? Do we today enjoy a deeper insight into Mariology than St. Thomas or St. Gregory the Great? Has there not been a great advance, not in the accumulation of new truths, but in the fuller appreciation of old ones like the Real Presence, the Mystical Body, St. Joseph's role in the Church? In explaining this growth, no small part can be assigned to the liturgy. This Old Testament background to sacramental development continues in the life of religion after the apostolic period. It helps to explain the modifications sanctioned by the Church in the administration of Baptism, Confirmation, and Holy Eucharist. An "apologia" is offered as well for changes which might have affected the purpose of the sacrament of Extreme Unction, which, according to some ranking theologians, in the early Church was more an anoiting of the sick rather than, as it now is, a final preparation for death.[2]

Besides what we have just been considering on the relations of God's redemptive acts to Israelite ritual, sacramental theology is also dependent upon the *biblical attitude toward nature*.

In this matter of sacramental theology, we have always been aware that God comes to us by human instruments and by natural means. For the work of salvation God condescends to put to use the physical elements of this universe, even to the point of Himself "appearing in the form of a man . . . becoming obedient to death, even to death on a cross" (Phil 2:7f). God uses a lamb, bread, water, or oil to mediate grace. Sacramental anointing put an electric charge into the material world, making it hum with the presence of God.

The Israelites never felt spiritual unease, nor did they complain of any spiritual disadvantage, because of the physical world in which God had placed them. Dualism, Manicheism, Puritanism, or any other kind of false asceticism which split the "material" from the "spiritual" had no part in their religion. Too often have Abraham, Moses, and David been tagged "materialists," when they were really divine humanists, joyfully accepting every material object as a personal gift from God, to be used according to the divine will, for God's greater glory. The biblical attitude toward nature, making no distinction between body and soul or between material and spiritual, forms a necessary preamble to teaching the sacraments from Scripture.[3] It fills out our portrait of the biblical man. We see him to be extremely practical. He understood God's redemptive acts by the experience of life; this experience found expression in the liturgy which called upon the elements of this earth to renew God's saving acts.

Basic then to [the study of] the sacraments from Scripture are these two facts of Old Testament ritual: the liturgy enabled the Chosen People to relive the redemptive acts of God; the liturgy also sanctified the entire physical universe as a mediator of grace.

Sacramental Form and the Word of God

We now advance to the next section of our paper, which will revolve around the *sacramental form.* Because the "form" usually consists of a spoken word, our inquiry naturally turns to the scriptural teaching on the *Word of God.* Here is a much neglected point of contact between Scripture and sacramental theology; it possesses great potentiality for enriching and clarifying both apologetics and theology. Our concern is with theology.

To investigate the biblical doctrine of the Word of God is like being lowered into a cave, and when the lights are flashed on, suddenly to behold marvelous crystal formations, sparkling in the bright illumination. The doctrine of the Word of God brings us to a new world, at first strange and dark, but when illumined with the light of the Semitic mind, the doctrine catches us with its brilliant fascination. We have no time to look closely at these special formations of Semitic thought-processes. We must summarize them quickly. The Hebrews never split man apart into body and soul, nor the soul into intellect and will. The Hebrew felt himself to be a *one*-thing, a totality. His thought, like himself, was a *one*-thing, a total contact between his whole being and reality. He certainly felt himself to be knowing the truth, but it was truth not so much for the sake of truth, but for the sake of love, for the sake of esteem and of action.

In a similar way, the thought or the wisdom of God was considered an act of God's *total* being. It certainly included what Greek philosophers defined as wisdom and knowledge, but it didn't stop on the speculative level. The wisdom of God, in biblical language, pulsated with the beat of love and mercy. It was fibered with a steady fidelity to promises and with omnipotent power to adapt means to a foreordained end.

The biblical notion of the word, therefore, must not be limited to a speculative concept nor to the expression of an eternal truth. The Bible considered the divine word as a direct and personal intervention of God in the life of man. Rather than a discourse about God, it was the presence of God, living and acting now, with the infinite reserve of His divine being. God who is speaking the divine word is at once God who is loving with tenderness, acting with irresistible power, directing with mature judgment. The word of God vibrated with a dynamic, as well as with an intellectual, element. For the Israelite the Word of God was somehow God Himself.

This notion of the Word of God is developed in the biblical theologies of Van Imschoot, Jacob, Vriezen, Eichrodt, and others. They point out that the Hebrew *dabar*, ordinarily translated as *word*, had a peculiar meaning in pre-biblical Hebrew. It had once conveyed the idea: to thrust forward, to push, to go away with. Even in our present Hebrew Bible, *dabar* often enough designates action: that is, in Genesis 20:10, "What had you in mind in doing *this thing?*" (*hazzet haddabar*).[4] We note in passing what a different etymology *dabar* has from the Greek *logos* or *legein*, whose original meaning was "to collect," "to order," or "to arrange."

Power of the Divine Word

The power of the divine word is manifest throughout the Bible. Vriezen writes: ". . . in the history of the patriarchs . . . the word of God again and again precedes the event, introduces it, and even brings it about."[5] Later happenings are explained as though God beforehand had pronounced a blessing or a curse, as we see in the case of Noe (Gn 9:25-27), of Jacob (Gn 49), and of Moses (Dt 33). If the word really came from God, then something divine resided within its syllables. In the famous passage of Deuteronomy 18:18, which reads, "I will raise up for them a prophet," the people were advised that they could judge a true prophet from a charlatan by the fulfillment of his word. If the word was truly God's, then it possessed an irresistible power.

The classical prophets relied not upon prodigies and wonders, but upon the conviction that their word came from God. It was, therefore, invincible. God says in Osea: "I will slay them by the word of my mouth" (6:5). In the Bible, God's word was just as much the source of life, as in the familiar passage of Deuteronomy: ". . . not by bread alone does man live, but by every word that comes forth from the mouth of the Lord" (8:3).

No prophet, however, so extolled the power of God's word as Second Isaia. The re-creation of the Jewish nation, like the creation of the universe, is attributed by him to God's omnipotent word. His entire prophecy is cast in a general context of God speaking. Listen for a moment, as God comforts His people:

> When the poor and the needy seek water in vain,
> And their tongue is parched with thirst,
> I the Lord *will answer* them (41:17).

God's comfort, be it noted, comes in the form of His all-powerful word. We are familiar with another passage from Second Isaia, comparing God's word to rain and snow that water the earth and make it bring forth and sprout.

> So shall my word be that goes out of my mouth—
> It shall not return to me fruitless . . .
> Without having accomplished the purpose for which
> I sent it (55:10f).

Post-Exilic Israel carried still further this teaching on the power of the word. The acts of creation in Genesis 1 depend upon the repetition of the Hebrew *wayyomer* ("And God said"). Ben Sirach concluded: "At God's *word* his works were brought into being" (42:15). Finally, in the Targums, the Aramaic *Memra* (or *word*) is used as a substitute for God, as, for instance, in Genesis 3:8, "They heard the sound of the *Memra* walking in the garden." In this last example the *word* is almost identified with God.

In his article on *lego* or *logos* in *Theologisches Worterbuch zum Neuen Testament* (IV, 116-20), Rudolf Kittel traces this teaching on the Word of God through the New Testament. The apostles, God's instruments for actively bringing salvation to the world, are called *ministers of the word* (Lk 1:2; Ac 6:2-4). St. Paul speaks of "the word of the cross" (1 Cor 1:18), "the word of reconciliation" (2 Cor 5:18), and "the word of salvation" (Ac 13:26). Every means of salvation, even the Savior Himself, are rightly called the Word of God.

St. Peter applied the Old Testament teaching on the Word of God to the Christian sacraments. He wrote: "You have been reborn . . . through the word of God" (1 Pt 1:23). As noted earlier in this paper, 1 Peter is either a transcript of an early baptismal liturgy or else an exhortation modeled upon this ceremony.

We can profit from observing more closely this comparison between the Word of God and the word of the sacramental form. Each of these two words brings the worshiper into immediate contact with God's redemptive power. In both instances, the divine word does more than communicate an idea or express an image. This word is not so much a teaching *about* God as it is the *presence of* God. To reject the word, therefore, is to reject God; to receive the word with faith is to be saved.

Our Lord's parting words in St. Mark's Gospel declare: "He who believes [that is, humbly receives the word] and is baptized shall be saved, but he who does not believe shall be condemned" (16:6). A similar exhortation to accept the apostolic preaching and to be baptized occurs at the end of St. Matthew's Gospel, in a context echoing the baptismal ceremony. In these references the distinction between preaching and the baptismal form vanishes, as though the full force of the divine word, built up through centuries of prophetic preaching, is finally funneled down to the baptized through the conduit of the sacramental form.

To speak of Baptism at once recalls St. Paul's celebrated passage in Romans 6:1-11. St. Paul does not refer separately to the sacramental form. In fact, his ideas derive mostly from the sacramental matter of water in which the proselyte is immersed. However, the apostle's constant stress upon salvation through faith rather than through external works and upon the reception of faith through the word of God justifies our use of the passage here. Overlooking the many difficulties of this section, we concentrate upon the power of Baptism to make us, as St. Paul wrote, "live together with Christ" because we "were buried with him by means of Baptism into [his] death" (Rom 6:8-4).

Efficacy of God's Word

At this point, we ask, relative to the sacrament of Baptism, does the word or form *merely symbolize* death to sin and life to God? Does St. Paul intend to say: This is *as if* we were buried in Christ's death and *as if* we were raised to a new life, because as a matter of fact all this is no more than a make-believe ceremony? . . . The power of Baptism depends not so much upon the one who administers, nor even upon the one who receives it, . . . but upon the Lord in whose name the word is spoken.

For the sake of accuracy, it should be admitted that the baptismal ceremony does indeed *symbolize* death and resurrection. The word spoken at the ceremony, *baptizo*, etymologically means to be drenched or plunged into water, and St. Paul develops the symbolical idea of being buried with Christ. To this extent, then, Von Allmen is incorrect when he declares that it "is not an image nor a symbol." What he really intends, however, is to deny that it is nothing more than a symbol or that the symbol is lifeless, like a paper cutout. The word of the Lord, pronounced at Baptism, has in itself an intrinsic power to unite the believer with Christ, so that with Christ he experiences the full effects of the Passion-Resurrection. Through the efficacy of God's word, the redemptive mystery of the Passion-Resurrection is renewed, just as the redemptive mystery of the Pasch was actively and actually relived by the Israelite worshiper through the word pronounced in a liturgical assembly.[6]

We pass now from Baptism to another sacrament, the Eucharist. Its sacramental form is variously given in the New Testament. "The Markan narrative," Vincent Taylor remarks, "commends itself as one of the oldest, if not the most ancient." [7] With St. Matthew's, it is the shortest: "This is my body . . . This is my blood of the new covenant" (Mk 14:22-24). In an article in the *Nouvelle Revue Theologique*, Dupont states that the grammatical argument for the real presence, based on the word *is* ("This *is* my body") is not at all conclusive. Both in Hebrew and in Aramaic, the conjunctive particle *is* would most probably not have been used by our Lord. It is absent in a similar construction in Ezechiel: "This is Jerusalem" (*zo't yerusalaim*). Ezechiel's words are correctly translated in the Chicago Bible: "This is a symbol of the fate of Jerusalem." Dupont says that according to the Semitic mode of expression, present throughout the Bible, the most natural meaning of the Eucharistic form will be: "This symbolizes or represents my body."

"Symbolism of the rite," however, Dupont concluded, "does not exclude its realism." [8] Like the prophetic message of Ezechiel, God's word is efficacious and all-powerful, containing a dynamic element to achieve exactly what it says. Once spoken, it cannot be taken back, no more than God can change His mind or reverse His plans. To stop at symbolism, refusing to take the next step of recognizing the real presence of Jesus in the Eucharist, is setting one's face against the biblical doctrine of the word. The strongest apologetic argument for the real presence rests not with the force of the conjunctive particle *is* ("This *is* my body") nor with a polemic against Eucharistic symbolism, but rather with the divine power of the Word of God.

Faith is required to take the next step and pass beyond the frontiers of apologetics. Reason can recognize a constant biblical tradition on the power of the divine word, but only by faith can anyone confess that the word of God is truly operative here in this particular case. Reason can certainly prepare for the theological position: "I believe that Jesus is present," but the word of God never penetrates beyond the threshold of the mind unless faith first swings open the doors. This mysterious fact of an all-powerful word, thundering its message, yet remaining unheard by someone without faith, is expressed by the Psalmist:

> The heavens declare the glory of God,
> and the firmament proclaims his handiwork.
> Day pours out the word to day,
> and night to night imparts knowledge;
> Yet not a word, nor a discourse,
> nor a voice can be heard (Ps 18:2-4).

The biblical doctrine of the word thus clarifies the object of our faith. It also greatly enriches that faith, because it lifts the ceremonial of the sacraments above the level of dead symbolism onto a plain of life and fulfillment. Symbolism is present both in the form (the words) and in the matter, but as we read in the Epistle to the Hebrews, this symbolism possesses "vital energy." [9]

Because the symbolism of the sacramental *matter* is also important, let us consider a final major point. In doing so, we will call attention to certain Old Testament ceremonies related to the Holy Eucharist.

Sacramental Matter and Old Testament Rites

A study of the sacraments of the Old Testament and the New Testament involves us in the problem of *mediation*. . . . The Bible never analyzed the reason *why*, but simply recorded the *fact* that particular ceremonies were employed to ensure union with God. The whole matter is further confused by other factors: First, the sacred authors never kept a clear distinction between the different agents for mediation, like the Word of God, the royalty, the priesthood, and wisdom; Second, God and the things of God were surrounded with so much mystery that the Hebrews would not dare to rationalize upon them; And last, the Israelites were not disposed to define and explain. . . . Our present division of the sacramental rite into form and matter is based, as noted already, on Christian theology, not on biblical theology; but we do hope to enrich our scholastic theology by recourse to Scripture.

More quickly than for sacramental matter do we accept the value of the word of God, the sacramental form, for transmitting divine favor. There is something spiritual about a word; in it we sense a very close contact with a spiritual God. The Israelites, however, never envisaged a spiritualized word; to them the word must always be enveloped in material elements for its full expression. This biblical practice of not separating matter and form has many important implications for sacramental theology. For us who do separate the two, the biblical notion reminds us that the sacramental matter contains much the same power as the sacramental form.

We will first consider such material elements of the Old Testament sacrifices as these: the imposition of hands; the slaughter of animals; the burning of sacrificial objects; the sprinkling of blood; the sacred banquet. From our study of these actions, two salient truths will emerge: Emphasis is to be placed not upon death and destruction but upon life and vitality; Material objects are not a substitute for the worshiper but are, symbolically, the worshiper himself.

The ceremony of *imposition of hands* is very ancient in Israel. Moses authorized Joshua, the nation's military leader, by imposing hands upon him (Nm 27:18). The people placed their hands upon the Levites at the time of their consecration (Nm 8:10). The offerer extended his hands over the object to be sacrificed (Lv 1:4; 3:2;

and so on). From Leviticus we learn that the imposition of hands occurred in all kinds of sacrifices, not only in sin or guilt offerings, but also in peace offerings which were followed by a sacred banquet, or in holocausts in which the victim was entirely burned. From a comparative study of these different rites we can conclude that the essential purpose was not substitution but union. The Levites did not substitute for the Israelites, thus freeing the other tribes from the service of God; the Levites represented the nation before God and outwardly expressed the interior spirit of every Hebrew. The imposition of hands, even before a sin offering, never indicated that the victim was loaded with the sins of the offerer and died in his place. Physical death never atoned for sin. In fact, sacrifices were not offered for serious faults, committed by anyone "who sins defiantly" (Nm 15:30). Sin-offerings were generally intended only to repair ceremonial or inadvertent faults against God or one's neighbor.[10]

It is more than an academic distinction to claim that the rite of imposition of hands symbolized not substitution but union; the distinction has profound implications for the sacrifice of Jesus on Calvary and in the Mass. Jesus did not die in our place, neither did He, as our *substitute*, take our sins upon Himself and suffer their evil effects. The punishment for grave sin is not bodily death but hell, and despite Christ's temporal death for us, we must still die. The imposition of hands over Israelite sacrifices established a union between offerer and victim; in sacramental theology it indicates union between Jesus and ourselves. We die with Christ, just as He took all our weakness and lowliness upon Himself. We are Christ, and Christ is lacking His full stature without us.

After the imposition of hands, the animal was slaughtered. This act of killing never featured prominently in worship. It was, in fact, almost *a-liturgical*, a preparatory act before the public ceremony. In the sacrifice of the covenant (Ex 24:5) the slaughtering was done not by Moses but by "certain young men." In other cases the animals were slaughtered by the layman-offerer, while only the priests proceeded with other ceremonial rites (cf. Lv 1:5; 3:2). Death was not the central thought of sacrifice. The word sacrifice (*zebah*) referred originally to eating a sacred meal. Leviticus considered even the farmer's slaughter of animals a "sacrifice," not because of the killing but because of the flow of blood. Throughout the Old Testament blood symbolized life, and life was considered God's special property.

The Blood Ritual

In this connection, it can be said that a mistake is made if our thoughts about Calvary or the Mass center almost exclusively around death and destruction. The horrible details of Our Lord's violent death, as endured on the wood of the cross and as symbolized in the double consecration of the Mass, express primarily the loving obedience of Our Lord and the infinite mercy of the Father. "God so loved the world. . . ." At the moment of His death, Jesus was most fully and vitally alive, and nowhere as upon the cross did Jesus manifest the *kebod Yahweh*, the glorious presence of God (Jn 12:28; 17:1-5). "When you have lifted up the Son of Man, then you will know that *I am*" (Jn 8:28)—the mysterious divine name, "I am who am" (Ex 3:14).

After the preliminary act of slaughtering the victim, there occurred the *blood ritual*. Unlike the body of an animal or the first-fruits of the field, blood was never offered to God. It was sprinkled upon an object representing God, like the sides (Lv 1:5) or the horns of the altar (Lv 16:18), the veil between the Holy Place and the Holy of Holies (Lv 4:6), or the mercy-seat (*kipporet*) above the ark (Lv 16:14f). In the sacrifice of the covenant, blood was sprinkled also upon the people (Ex 24:8). During the ordination of priests (Lv 8:23f), blood was placed upon various parts of their body, thereby consecrating them to the service of God. At the sacrifice of the Paschal lamb, blood was splashed upon the door posts, consecrating to God the inhabitants within the home.

The key for interpreting the blood ritual is Leviticus 17:10f: "It is the blood, as the seat of life, that makes atonement." This is how the Confraternity version translates the verse. The Hebrew might also be rendered: "Blood atones, insofar as it is life." Deuteronomy says succinctly: "Blood is life" (12:23). The sight of blood, even for us today, is awesome and fearful. For the Hebrews blood meant not only life, but the presence of God, the Giver and the Keeper of life. The touch of blood consecrated to God, united with God, put one in immediate contact with God. The flow of blood between altar and worshiper symbolized a flow of divine life between God and His people. Again, the central idea appears to be not death and substitution, but life and union.

We would be afraid to make the application to the Precious Blood of Our Lord, if the Epistle to the Hebrews had not done so for us:

"For if the blood of goats and bulls and the sprinkled ashes of a heifer sanctify the unclean . . . how much more will the blood of Christ, who through the Holy Spirit offered himself unblemished unto God, cleanse your conscience from dead works to serve the living God?" (Heb 9:13f). The Blood of Jesus is sprinkled upon us during each Holy Mass. This is a beautiful thought, but it is also a fearful one because of how that Blood was shed. The Blood of Jesus cleanses, not by washing away sin—again, only a contrite heart can do that—but by establishing union with God. The positive element of life, not the negative act of death, is uppermost in the Blood ritual.

Either before or after the Blood ritual there occurred the burning of the victim upon the altar. In the case of holocausts, the entire body was burned. When other sacrifices were offered, only a part was burned: namely, the fatty parts closest to the entrails, since the entrails were considered the center of life. The rest was eaten either by the priests, or by the people, in a sacrificial banquet. What was burned upon the altar was considered a gift to God. It was the gift of one's own life. The priest assured the worshiper that God accepted the gift, if it was offered with the right disposition. . . .

The sacrificial banquet was looked upon by Israel's neighbors as a mystical union with the gods. Israel adopted the rite to express her own joyful companionship with Yahweh.

Throughout this treatment on Old Testament sacrifice, emphasis has been directed toward life and union with God. The Old Testament will greatly enrich our understanding of St. Paul's teaching "with Christ" and apply this doctrine to the sacraments. The death which we endure with Christ in the Mass is not death but life in its most dynamic aspect. The grain of wheat falls into the ground and dies, in order that it may live (cf. Jn 12:24f). Holy Communion is *our* sacrificial banquet, able to unite us with the *living* Body and Blood of Our Lord, precisely because it comes from the altar of sacrifice. Upon that altar, in the moment of sacrificial death, *life* has been manifested in its most intense degree.

The Old Testament notion of sacrifice colored the thinking of Jesus and the apostles. The New Testament presentation of the sacrifice of Calvary or of the Mass cannot be properly understood outside this scriptural background. We must turn to the Old Testament for a full appreciation of the Precious Blood of Jesus, the imposition of hands in the Mass, the sacrificial banquet of Holy Communion. A similar study could be made of the liturgical use of oil, water, incense, confession of sins, and so forth, in Old Testament times. This investigation would enrich the theology of the sacraments.

Conclusion

. . . [Learning] the sacraments from Scripture requires that we become aware of the sacramental power of all creation to sanctify man and make him happy. In the garden of paradise God spoke to man and his wife in the cool evening wind. Man on his part must return to God through the world in which he lives. In the Mosaic covenant, God made a special use of elements like fire, water, bread, and animals. They were to be sacramental mediators. Their use in sacrifice symbolized not death and substitution, but life and union, union between man and sacramental matter, and by means of the latter, union of man with God. The most familiar feature of human life, and therefore the most common means of contact with God and man, is the spoken word. God comes to man in a most special way through the word. In the sacramental form, the Old Testament tradition on the word of God reaches it fullest expression. These elements of human life are employed by the liturgy to enable man to relive the great redemptive acts of God.

God, therefore, who came to us in the Word made flesh, continues to unite us with the redemptive mystery of the Word made flesh, through sacramental form and matter. The form is the Word; the matter is the way in which the Word becomes flesh and part of our life.

References

[1] *Theological Studies*, 17 (1956), 151-66. Cf. O. Cullmann, *Early Christian Worship* (Studies in Biblical Theology, No. 10; Naperville: Allenson, 1953), who examines the sacramental significance of St. John's Gospel.

[2] Cf. P. Palmer, "The Purpose of Anointing the Sick," *Theological Studies*, 19 (1958), 344-409; C. Davis, "The Sacrament of the Sick," *Clergy Review*, 43 (1958), 727-45; P. de Letter, "The Meaning of Extreme Unction," *Theology Digest*, 4 (1956), 185-88.

[3] By these statements we do not imply that the Israelites were pantheists. From the very beginning God transcends this earth and all its weakness. Nor did they consider themselves just high-grade apes. Somehow they knew that man was far superior to animals, but they placed this distinction not in man's spiritual soul but in the special love of God for man. Greek philosophical

thought has touched the Bible only in the Book of Wisdom and possibly in Ecclesiastes.

[4] Cf. Genesis 22:1; 24:66; 3 Kings 11:41.

[5] *An Outline of Old Testament Theology* (Oxford: Blackwell, 1958), p. 239. Vriezen refers to Genesis 12:1ff; 16:10ff; 25:23; 37:5ff.

[6] It is usually denied that the Old Testament sacraments achieved their effect *ex opere operato*. In view of the intrinsic power of the Word of God in Old Testament theology, this opinion may require re-thinking.

[7] *The Gospel According to St. Mark* (London: The Macmillan Company, 1953), p. 543.

[8] J. Dupont, "Ceci est mon corps, Ceci est mon sang," *Nouvelle Revue Théologique*, 30 (1958), 1037.

[9] Hebrews 4:12—*energes* is the Greek word, usually translated "efficient."

[10] E. F. Siegman, "Blood in the Old Testament," *Proceedings of the First Precious Blood Study Week* (Rensselaer, Ind.: St. Joseph College, 1959), p. 46, does not take such a restricted view, but he does admit that "Pentateuchal legislation speaks of expiatory sacrifices mainly with respect to ritual failings."

IV. NEW TESTAMENT STUDIES

"When we were enemies we were reconciled to God by the death of His Son; now having been reconciled shall we be saved by His life. . . ." (Rom 5:10)

DAVID M. STANLEY, S.J.

Christian Revelation as Historical Process

The likely reader of this dynamic article will find a discussion of questions such as these: What are some significant features of recent New Testament studies? What does it mean to say that revelation is not only historical but also a process? Why is the earthly ministry of Jesus only a "stage" in Christian revelation? What new insights were revealed to the apostles in the miracle of Pentecost? Why was the martyrdom of St. Stephen significant for the developing Church? What advantages did Antioch have over Jerusalem as a center for the early Christians? What was Paul's contribution to this development? Why did Paul put more emphasis on Abraham than on Moses? What is the relation of Paul to Jesus in the foundation of the Church?

Father Stanley, the author of a previous article, teaches New Testament theology at the State University of Iowa.

. . . The most significant features of "the new approach to Scripture" as it affects Catholic New Testament studies . . . consist in (1) a more discerning appreciation of the *literary* character of the New Testament books, and (2) a deeper insight into *the historical process* which produced this inspired literature. . . . In recent years we have become more aware of the great value and supreme importance of the historical character of the Christian revelation.

Contemporary interest in studying the New Testament is pri-

This paper was delivered at the 1960 Christmas Conference of the Basilian Fathers in Toronto and was first published in *The Basilian Teacher*. It is reproduced here with permission.

marily in *the message*, the doctrinal content, of the books which embody the Christian revelation. The day is past, we may gratefully assert, when the study of the New Testament was taken up almost entirely with chronology, topography, or various antiquarian interests like first-century Palestinian coinage or reconstructions of the Temple. The day is also past, we confidently hope, when the teaching of the New Testament consisted of ingenious, not to say ingenuous, attempts at harmonizing certain seeming contradictions in the four Gospels.

. . . Interest in the New Testament should, before almost every other consideration, lie in . . . [an awareness] . . . of the historical development which *is* the Christian revelation. . . . Christianity is an historical religion in a unique sense. This is, after all, the meaning of the incarnation: that God has personally entered our human family, has deigned, during a definite period of time, to share our human experiences, and, by so doing, has revealed Himself to us *from within history*. For it is our Christian conviction that God did not suspend the course of history, but worked through it, illuminating its meaning from within, so to say, giving us, in Christ, some inkling of His providential plan for the world's salvation.

Nowadays, perhaps more than in the past, New Testament scholarship has turned its attention to the series of events which constitute the Christian *Heilsgeschichte*, and has come to appreciate the importance of viewing it as a unity, which however was necessarily extended in time. The historical frame of reference for the New Testament salvation history lies in the period between the preaching of John the Baptist and the completion of the inspired writings, which now form the New Testament canon. During this time and because of the events belonging to it, recorded in our sacred books, the Church came into being, with her doctrinal, sacramental, hierarchical constitution. This coming-to-be of the Church is to be regarded (and this insight, I believe, is new in our day) as a dynamic, not a static reality, which thus escapes the neat formulation of theological definition. For we are dealing with an existential, evolutionary process, inextricably bound up with time and events which succeeded one another in history.

This view of revelation as historical process was unknown to the medieval theologians, whose theological method we have inherited. As an example of this inadvertence to the existential nature of the founding of the Church, which has had far reaching consequences, we might cite the tendency in modern theology manuals to fix the Church's institution to a single point in time (for example Jesus' death, the descent of the Holy Ghost), that is, *to divorce it from time*. The not always happy result of this point of view has been to limit the New Testament evidence of the fact that Jesus Christ founded the Church to one or two scriptural texts, rather than to discover it, in the larger context of the whole apostolic age, as a phenomenological process or a structural development.

Accordingly, . . . it might not be inappropriate to review . . . the general lines of the historical process from Jesus' public ministry to Paul's missionary experiences, in order to recall that background against which the teaching of Christ and the inspired authors of the Christian dispensation must be studied. For, to a man who has failed to appreciate the implications in the statement that Christianity is an historical religion, much of the modern development in New Testament studies may well prove puzzling, disturbing, or even dangerous.

Jesus' Earthly Ministry

The Gospels show that during His earthly life Jesus restricted His mission to His own countrymen: "My mission is only to the straying sheep of the house of Israel" (Mt 15:24; cf. also Mt 10:5-6). Moreover, He referred to the future salvation of the Gentiles in only the vaguest terms, His utterances on this subject remaining on the same level as the predictions by the Old Testament prophets concerning the pagans' conversion (Mt 8:11). It was only after His Resurrection, it would appear, that Christ gave His disciples definite commands about the universalist nature of the Church's mission (Lk 24:47-48; Ac 1:8; Mt 28:18-20).

It is also significant for the gradual character of Christianity's emergence from Judaism to recall that the Gospels represent Jesus' own ministry as a continuation of the "baptist" movement, inaugurated by John. In Matthew, the same expression is used to summarize both John's and Jesus' message, "Repent: the heavenly Kingdom is at hand" (Mt 3:2; 4:17). The Fourth Gospel states that Jesus began His public life as a disciple of the Baptist (Jn 1:27; 3:26), and that at least five of the apostles had been originally John's followers (Jn 1:35-51).

Finally, it is to be remembered that when, in the Sermon on the

Mount, Jesus announces the spirit of the future Christian Church, He describes it simply as the perfect flowering of Old Testament religion. The Beatitudes canonize two groups of Israelites, who exhibit the dispositions requisite for entry into the Church: the *'anawim*, or poor and oppressed (Mt 5:3-6), and the prophet-protectors of the poor (Mt 5:7-10). Jesus moreover depicts the "new Justice" of Christianity by means of references to the Sinaitic covenant (Mt 5:17-48), and He urges the practice of those "good works," which were characteristic of the Jewish way of life: almsgiving (Mt 6:1-4), prayer (Mt 6:5-13), and fasting (Mt 6:16-18).

Now when we turn to Paul's epistles, we are apparently dealing with a very different conception of the Christian life. "We believe," he states, "that a person is justified by faith, apart from the works of law" (Rom 3:28). He contrasts the old religion of Israel with the new religion by saying that "the letter kills: it is the Spirit which gives life" (2 Cor 3:6b). For Paul, Christianity's superiority to Judaism consists not in the promulgation of a more perfect moral code or of a higher religious ideal, but simply in the fact that Christian living springs from the dynamic indwelling presence of the Spirit of Christ (cf. Rom 8:1ff), who is God's love, "poured forth in our hearts through the gift of the Spirit to us" (Rom 5:5; cf. *Summa Theologica* 1-2, 106,2).

Since, as we are assured by our faith, there can be no opposition between this Pauline teaching and the doctrine of Jesus, we must seek to understand, by an investigation into the historical development of apostolic Christianity, the various influences which shaped Paul's attitude toward the Gospel, which he himself constantly declared he received from Jesus Christ (1 Cor 11:23; 15:3; 2 Cor 11:4; Rom 14:14; 1 Thes 4:2; 4:15).

The three most formative influences upon Paul's theological viewpoint are . . . the miraculously creative happenings of the first Pentecost, the figure of Stephen the proto-martyr, and Paul's apostolic experiences as missionary to the pagans of the Hellenistic world.

The Miracle of Pentecost

The effects of the coming of the Holy Spirit upon the little group of Jesus' disciples in Jerusalem were of a structural and doctrinal character. While Luke suggests, in the Acts of the Apostles, that, prior to Pentecost, these faithful adherents of Jesus were conscious to some extent of their identity as a social unit (Ac 1:14-15) under the leadership of Peter and the apostles (Ac 1:13), they appear to have retained a materialistic or earthly view of God's Kingdom (Ac 1:6). Moreover, there is no evidence that they proclaimed the "good news" of the Christian Gospel or practised the Christian sacraments.

The Pentecostal experience taught them, first of all, that they had been constituted by the creative force of the Spirit's presence, the *qahal* or congregation of the "new Israel." It also opened their minds to the momentous revelation of Christ's divinity and the personality of the Holy Spirit.

Recognition of their status as the "new Israel" made the disciples aware that "the last days," foretold by the prophets, had actually become a reality, that they were assisting at the consummation of Israel's religious history. As a result they inaugurated the apostolic preaching and began the work of proselytizing their Jewish compatriots. They started to practise Christian Baptism for the first time, as well as the "imposition of hands," to initiate their converts into the Christian community and to share with them the graces they themselves had obtained from the Spirit.

Their realization that the Spirit, whom they knew from the Old Testament to be divine, was a Person, distinct from the Father and the Son, is indicated by one of the most astonishing features of their new Christian faith. I refer to the conviction that the messianic age had begun, not by the return of the parousiac Christ, but by the descent of the Holy Ghost. It is the coming of the Spirit which has (as Joel foretold) ushered in "the last days." This hitherto unknown divine Person has created the community of the "new Israel," the Church.

Since, moreover, they realized that the Spirit had been sent by the ascended Christ, as He had promised (Ac 1:8), they knew that Jesus Himself had "taken His seat at God's right hand." That is to say, they became aware for the first time of Christ's divinity. This belief they now express in a number of ways. They assert, in terms of Psalm 110, Jesus' *sessio ad dexteram Patris,* which means that He participates in the divine government of the universe, a prerogative uniquely attributed to Yahweh in the Old Testament. They state that God had, at Jesus' exaltation conferred the divine name *Kyrios* upon Him. *Kyrios,* in the Greek translation of the Old Testament, had been used to translate the sacred tetragram Yahweh. Since, in the Semitic view, the name of any person or thing is not equivocal, as with us, but expresses the full reality of that to which it is applied, Jesus' bearing of the divine Name meant that He was God. The apostolic testimony to the fact that Jesus had been appointed "by Yahweh, judge of living and dead" (Ac 10:42) represents still another expression of their Christian belief in Christ's divinity.

The early chapters of Acts gives us many precious details which show the undeniably Christian character of the Jerusalem community: they possess the Christian sacraments as well as the essential Christian dogmas. At the same time, they continue to frequent the Temple and participate in Jewish sacrificial worship (Ac 2:46). They are scrupulously observant of the dietary laws of Judaism as well as the regulations forbidding social association with Gentiles, as the episodes connected with Peter's conversion of Cornelius at Caesarea show (Ac 10:1ff). They appear to be merely a fervent sect within Judaism, as may be seen by the fact that at this period they possess no name which would indicate their new religion's distinctiveness vis-à-vis Old Testament religion and Old Testament morality. In a word, the "visible" character of the Church is still to be manifested to the world.

The Significance of Stephen

The idyllic and somewhat anomalous existence enjoyed by the Church during her first years came to an end, as we learn in Chap. 6 of Acts, thanks to a somewhat trivial incident: a disagreement between two groups in the young Christian community, the Hellenists and the Hebrews, about the distribution of alms from the common fund. To settle it, the apostles appointed seven deacons, of whom the most outstanding personality was Stephen. He was a Hellenist, and consequently a Greek-speaking Jewish Christian, whose origins were in the Diaspora, more cosmopolitan and adaptable than the "Hebrews," Aramaic-speaking Jewish Christians of Palestinian provenance. Stephen was, in addition, a man of considerable theological acumen, endowed by nature and grace with the vision to see the essential incompatibility between Judaism and Christianity and the inevitability of a break between the two.

One gathers from the long discourse attributed to Stephen in Acts that he possessed considerable eloquence and the creative genius to construct what is probably the first complete synthesis of Christian biblical theology. He had obviously reread the Old Testament in the light of his Christian faith. Since, as we shall see, Barnabas and Paul, as leaders in the church of Antioch, appear to be the direct heirs of Stephen's attitudes, it will help to define those attitudes clearly.

In his *apologia pro vita sua*, Stephen unequivocally declares that the Mosaic code and cult are of merely relative value in God's plan for the salvation of the world. The fundamental error of Judaism, Stephen perceived, was to regard these institutions as absolutes: she clung blindly to them as God's final word in revealed religion. The first of the Christian martyrs implied that his Jewish contemporaries were guilty of a kind of idolatry, confusing Judaism with God Himself, who was thus reduced to the rank of an idol. The recalcitrance of the Jews led to their rejection of God's definitive work of redemption in the death and Resurrection of Jesus Christ. Like their ancestors, who had persecuted the prophets, they did not realize that this very perversity had been employed by divine Wisdom in the carrying out of the plan of God's providence. They failed to read the writing on the wall, so clear to the eye of Christian faith, which announced the "fullness of time," when a single "Holy Land," with its unique "Holy Place," was to be abandoned for the world-wide Christian mission.

It is not by accident that Luke's account of Stephen's trial and death is reminiscent of the trial and death of Jesus. Stephen had been penetrated more deeply perhaps than many of his fellow Christians by the spirit of Christ. He saw what his Jewish Christian brethren had apparently failed to see thus far, namely that by God's will the type of peaceful coexistence between Judaism and Christianity, which had seemed so natural and so appealing, was destined to disappear forever. The lamp of the Gospel could not remain hidden beneath the bushel measure of Judaism: the new wine of Christianity was already bursting the old wineskin of the Mosaic religion. In short, Stephen's most important contribution was to assert the necessarily visible character of the Church.

He was also to teach a second lesson. By accepting to die before the triumphant return of Christ at his parousia, which the first Christians naturally expected to happen very soon, Stephen drew attention to the meaning of the present period of history, between the first and second comings of the Lord Jesus. It was "the time of the Church," during which she was destined to spread throughout the world, bringing all men to the knowledge of the truths of her faith.

The Founding of the Church of Antioch

The death of Stephen gave rise to a persecution in Jerusalem of the Hellenist branch of the apostolic Community. Some of these Hellenists took refuge in Syrian Antioch, where they took the unprecedented step of preaching the Gospels to pagans (Ac 11:20). They met with such success that in a short time a Christian community of probably predominantly non-Jewish origin sprang to life. Thus, it was at Antioch that the name Christian was first applied to the disciples, who appeared as a group distinct not only from the pagans but also from the Jews (Ac 11:26).

Under the leadership of Joseph Barnabas, whom the mother church of Jerusalem had dispatched to Antioch to investigate this novel experiment in the organization of a Christian community, the new church grew rapidly. Barnabas soon summoned Saul or Paul to work with him in Antioch, and they worked together for over a year in this fully integrated community of Jewish and Gentile Christians, where the risen Christ's command "to make disciples of all the nations" was being carried out for the first time in history.

For at Antioch, the distinctive nature of the Church as an autonomous religious society was far more prominent than it had ever been in Jerusalem. The absence of the influence of the Temple upon Christian living here was perhaps the most obvious cause of this phenomenon. At Antioch, it was easier to forget the deep-rooted discrimination in worship and in social intercourse, which, in Jerusalem, would have separated Jewish from Gentile Christians. There was no "wall of separation" like that in the Temple, dividing the Jews from the Gentiles at public worship. The most significant result of Antioch's distance from the Temple, however, was undoubtedly the central position which the Eucharist now assumed as the liturgical focus of the community's cultic life. In Jerusalem, they had celebrated "the breaking of the Bread" in the privacy of their own homes (Ac 2:26), while "the liturgy" for these Christians still meant the gorgeous ritual of Judaism carried out in the Temple. It is worthy of note that Luke first applies the term *leitourgein* (to perform the liturgy) to the "breaking of the Bread" in describing an Antiochian Eucharist (Ac 13:2).

The Holy Ghost's greatest gift to this new-patterned Christian community was the Christian missionary spirit in its fullest, most catholic sense. In Jerusalem, the disciples were inclined to await upon the holy mountain of Sion (cf. Is 2:2-3) the spontaneous approach of the pagans. Antioch, at the express command of the Spirit (Ac 13:1ff), was the first community to send apostles, Barnabas and Saul, to preach the Christian *kerygma* to the pagans of Asia Minor.

If the Antiochian church was inferior to that of Jerusalem, inasmuch as the latter had the apostles as hierarchical heads of her congregation, still Antioch had "prophets" like Barnabas and Saul to govern her. Indeed, the genuine character of the Christian spirit at Antioch was shortly demonstrated by that church's generous response to a request from Jerusalem for funds to aid her needy Jewish Christians (Ac 11:27-30). Thus in their practice of the "new commandment" of fraternal love, the Antiochians displayed the hallmark of true followers of their Founder (Jn 13:35).

It remained only for the mother church of Jerusalem to recognize the principle of Gentile Christian liberty with regard to circumcision and the observance of the other Mosaic institutions. When she did this, about the year 49, under the direction of Peter and the apostolic college, the way was open for Christian expansion throughout Asia Minor, Europe, and indeed the whole world.

Before we turn to the missionary experiences of Paul to see how this program was realized, I should like to draw your attention to the fact, of which Luke appears to have been quite aware, that in this whole series of events, the sacred history (and consequently the era of Christian revelation), begun with Jesus' earthly career and climaxed by His death and Resurrection, was being continued. That Luke was conscious of the fact that the history of the formative years of the apostolic Church formed an integral part of Christian *Heilsgeschichte* may be deduced from his use of the same literary form, the gospel-form, in writing Acts, which he had employed in his Gospel. Since the Church's growth in "self-consciousness" of her own distinctive "personality," of her own particular mission in the world, was a gradual process, involving, amongst other factors, the events we have just reviewed, we discover new grounds for affirming the truth that Christianity is an historical religion. We obtain perhaps a clearer insight into the statement that the Church was not founded in a moment of time, but that her coming-to-be was actually extended in time, throughout the privileged period of history we call the apostolic age.

Paul and the Greeks

Paul's missionary experiences also belong to the New Testament *Heilsgeschichte*. To illustrate the manner in which the history of his career formed part of the Christian revelation, I should like to show briefly how it answered two problems about the nature of the Church with which apostolic Christianity was preoccupied: the meaning of the period of time between the two comings of Christ, and the Gentiles' inheritance of the promise made to Abraham, father of the Chosen people.

Paul, like the other members of the primitive Church, appears to have taken it for granted that the parousia would occur in the relatively near future, during his own life-time. At least, this attitude is reflected in the earlier Pauline epistles, to Thessalonica and to Philippi.

In the early days in Jerusalem, Peter had stated that the Lord's return was contingent upon the conversion of Israel (Ac 3:20-21); and the relatively large number of Jews who became Christians in Palestine during the first years after Pentecost undoubtedly gave rise to the over-sanguine hope that Israel, as a whole, would enter the Church in the not too far off future.

Certain events in Paul's evangelical career during the forties and fifties of the first century, however, led him to realize that this longed for day was still hidden in the distant future. The Book of Acts attests to the almost unanimous opposition to Christianity on the part of Diaspora Jewry. Moreover, he had to deal repeatedly, at Corinth and in Galatia, with attempts by some convert Jews to impose the observance of the Mosaic Law upon the Gentile Christians. Finally, a personal experience in the form of a mysterious threat to his own life at Ephesus (2 Cor 1:8) made him face the serious probability of his own death before Christ's parousia.

At any rate, we find that by the spring of 58, Paul has introduced into Peter's view of Church history a new element, which implies that he has begun to look upon the second Coming as a hope indefinitely deferred. In his letter to the Romans, he states that, by her rejection of the Gospel, Judaism has, for the time being, yielded place in the Kingdom to the pagans, and her collective conversion will occur only "when the full number of the Gentiles has come in" (Rom 11:25-26).

As this view becomes clearer to Paul, we find him turning his attention to the mission of the Church during the time intercalated between the two comings of the Son of God. He concentrates in his later letters upon the nature of the Church as "the Body of Christ," upon a theology of the Christian apostolate, and upon a reformulation of Christian truths, designed to meet the needs of the inquiring Greek mind.

The second question with which Paul had to deal, how could Christians of pagan origin, and hence without racial ties with Abraham, inherit God's promise to Abraham's seed, was of paramount interest in the apostolic Church. Indeed, because of this, it would appear Jewish Christians naturally assumed that the Gentiles must enter the Church via Judaism. Moreover, while in late Old Testament literature Abraham is rarely mentioned, allusions to him in the New Testament are surpassed only by those to Moses (72 as opposed to 80 times), the most frequently cited Old Testament figure.

Now when we view this fact in the light of another, namely, that most books of the New Testament were written for communities of pagan, not Jewish origin, we may well ask how it was that those who could claim no racial relationship with Abraham should display such interest in him? Paul gives us one answer to this question in his letter to the Galatians, where he provides a theological basis for his Gentile converts' freedom from assuming the burdens of the Mosaic Law. The Law of Moses, he asserts boldly, was an intrusion into the history of salvation, which consists of only two essential moments: God's promise to Abraham and its fulfillment in Christ. It is then the patronage of Abraham, rather than that of Moses, which all Christians, Jew or Greek, should invoke.

Paul solves the problem of the Gentile Christian's relationship with Abraham by establishing that the true conception of that patriarch's paternity lies in its completely supernatural character. Abraham is "father of many nations," first of all, because of God's quite gratuitous choice of him. God gave him His infallible promise without Abraham's performing any "good works" and before he received circumcision. All Abraham "did" was to make an act of trusting faith in God's promise to him, in the face of several natural impossibilities.

As a matter of fact, Paul shows [that] mere carnal descent from Abraham was, in Old Testament history, without significance, as the rejection of Ismael and of Esau proves. The supernatural character of this whole economy is, of course, superlatively demonstrated by the fact that God fulfilled the promise to Abraham by sending His own incarnate Son (Gal 3:15-29).

Accordingly, only those with the true faith found in Abraham are to be considered genuine sons of Abraham (Gal 3:9,14,18,22; Rom 4:11-13,16). It is in virtue of our identification with Christ, Abraham's "seed" in the only true sense, that we Gentiles, through God's gracious favor, inherit Abraham's promise.

Conclusion

When we keep in mind this whole historical process from Jesus' public life to Paul's missionary experiences, there can be no doubt that it was Christ who founded the Church. He gave the blueprint for it, as Matthew in his Gospel clearly shows, by the teaching and the events of His public life: He laid its foundations by His redemptive death and Resurrection; He directed its construction after His Ascension by sending the Holy Spirit to create, out of the first disciples, the first Christian community. But it is not less true that Christ carried the work of founding the Church into the apostolic age through the mediation of men—apostles like Paul of Tarsus. Through Paul's theological reflection and the vicissitudes of his missionary career, Christ continued the revelation of the true nature and mission of His Church, which gradually became clearer in these formative years of the *Urkirche*, the primitive Church, and which were recorded under divine inspiration in the New Testament scriptures containing the canon or norm of Christian belief and Christian practice.

Paul's doctrine cannot be in contradiction with the teaching of Jesus, for, as Paul himself tells the Corinthians, he "also possessed the mind of Christ" (1 Cor 2:16). What we find in Paul is the exploitation of the potentialities latent in the message of Jesus, proclaimed during His public life. It is, however, an exploitation enriched by further revelation given, I believe for the most part, through an historical process, which is the *Heilsgeschichte* of the apostolic age. To be understood completely, the New Testament revelation must be viewed as an existential movement, inaugurated by "all that Jesus began to do and to teach" (Ac 1:1) and brought to term by that divinely guided interplay of human personalities and human events, incarnating, so to say, the efficacious direction of the ascended Christ and of His Spirit, which the New Testament authors have been inspired to present as the history of the primitive Christian Church.

MYLES M. BOURKE

The Gospels as Theologically Interpreted History

The meditative reader will find in this illuminating article a discussion of questions such as these: Why is it true that a denial of sacred history would be a denial of the Christian faith? What are some differences between the Gospels and scientific history that all schools of thought would concede? How can the precise literary form of the Gospels be used to explain variations in details? Is it possible ever to have true history that does not also interpret the events? What theological ideas influenced the writers of the Gospels to interpret the meaning of the events they describe? What is the contribution to this question by the form critics Debelius and Bultmann? How much of their theory can a Catholic legitimately employ? To what extent must he disagree? What are some of the theories on the meaning of Peter's confession as St. Matthew's Gospel gives it: "Thou art the Christ, the Son of the Living God"? Is this a statement of messiahship? Of divinity? Are they the words Peter actually spoke at Caesarea Philippi? How do scholars explain the differences in the lists of Beatitudes as given by Matthew and Luke? How does the modern view of the Gospels as theologically interpreted history show the interdependence of Bible and Church?

Monsignor Bourke is professor of New Testament and Dean of Studies at St. Joseph's Seminary, Dunwoodie, Yonkers, New York.

Like Judaism, Christianity is a religion for which history is of the utmost importance. It is founded on the belief that God has

Originally delivered as part of a paper to the New York region of the Society of Catholic College Teachers, this article in its present revised form was first published in the Spring 1964 issue of *Thought*. It is reproduced here with permission.

acted in human history, and that by His acts salvation has been brought to men. It is impossible, then, for the Christian to be indifferent to the reality of those acts which are believed to constitute the divine intervention. A religion which is concerned only with "timeless truths," which do not depend on God's acting in history, would be in no way affected if it were shown that such acts had never taken place; for the Christian, on the contrary, to deny the sacred history is to deny his faith. Consequently, the historical reliability of the Gospels is a matter of importance for him, and a discussion of the question is especially pertinent in these times when the charge has been made that the Gospel interpretation of many contemporary Catholic scholars is lessening and even destroying the historical value of those priceless documents.[1]

Let us concede at the outset that the type of history, the "literary genus," which those scholars believe the Gospels represent is not the same as that represented by scientific historiography, in which the historian arranges the facts pertinent to his subject in proper order of time and place, and in which his purpose is to produce as faithful a picture of "what really happened" as his materials allow. But can anyone read the Gospels, particularly can anyone compare the Gospels with each other, and fail to see that the evangelists did not have those concerns? Apart from a certain broad outline, the Synoptic Gospels are almost indifferent to the time and place of the events which they narrate, and the synoptic outline gives the reader an impression of the chronology and topography of Jesus' ministry quite different from that which he gets from the Gospel of Saint John. And the instances in which the Gospels differ in their record of the same event or saying are so numerous that one cannot think that exact reproduction of the past was a prime consideration of the authors.

Yet up to a point, even the most "conservative" proponents of the historicity of the Gospels will admit all that. What, then, are the major differences between these adherents of the older views and the majority of Catholic exegetes? We cannot speak of all of them; one important difference which we shall not discuss, at least directly, is the way in which either group conceives of the relation between our canonical Gospels and the authors to whom tradition assigns them.[2] The two points which we have chosen for consideration here are the ones which are principally responsible for the uneasiness felt by some about the direction which the "new Scripture" is taking. First, its proponents believe that since the literary genus to which the Gospels belong is *theologically interpreted history*, the factual data (whether events or sayings) which had been related by the eyewitnesses of the events and the hearers of the words may have been modified and added to in the course of their transmission and in their being committed to writing by the evangelists, in order that their deep significance and their application to the Church might be brought out. Secondly, these exegetes find it quite natural that when a story of an event has been passed down by oral tradition, the event may have been recounted in such ways that differences which defy convincing harmonization have been introduced into the various accounts; they also find no difficulty in supposing that the evangelists, or those who dealt with the traditional material before the evangelists, may have combined into a unit elements of the tradition which originally referred to disparate incidents. Consequently, they believe that some of the events of the Gospels did not take place in the way in which we now find them recorded.[3]

It is surely correct to call such an approach to the Gospels "new," if by that we mean that it is different from the one taken for centuries by scholars both within and outside the Catholic Church. But the new approach has as its goal something ancient, namely the same understanding of the Gospels as that which the Christians of the first century had. There is good reason to think that modern biblical scholarship has come far toward achieving that goal.

The Gospels as Theologically Interpreted History

It is now generally admitted that there is no history in which the historian does not interpret the facts which he records. At a very minimum, his selection of the facts which he considers worth recording and his omission of others involve a value judgment which is itself an interpretation. According to the nineteenth-century ideal, an ideal associated principally with the name of Leopold von Ranke, the historian was a collector and recorder of facts which he scrupulously refrained from interpreting, thus showing himself completely impartial. A more recent judgment is that such an ideal is impossible: ". . . the theory that an historian could be impartial seems to us today one of manifest buckram. We wonder that anyone troubled to destroy it. . . . Not only do we repudiate the ideal of Ranke that history should be colorless, new, and impartial. We do not even suggest that it is desirable." [4] The now prevalent concept of history has been well expressed by C. H. Dodd who writes: "We might indeed say that an historical 'event' is an occurrence *plus* the interest and meaning which the occurrence possessed for the people involved in it, and by which the record is determined." [5] And T. A. Roberts who objects to Dodd's definition on other grounds admits that "there can be no objection to the Gospels as historical documents because they blend fact and interpretation." [6] Interpreting facts does not mean falsifying them; it does mean, of course, that the historian is presenting his interpretation as the one which gives them their true meaning.

In the case of the Gospels, the facts were interpreted in the light of the belief that in Jesus the decisive intervention of God in history had taken place, that the Final Age, the *eschaton*, had arrived, that Jesus of Nazareth was the Messiah of Israel and the Son of God. The confession "Jesus is Lord," expression of the Easter faith of the early Christians, is the classical summary of the belief which casts light upon all the memories which the apostles and the other eyewitnesses had of what they had seen and heard during the public life of their Master. It was by a community which shared the faith of those who had seen the risen Lord that our Gospels were written in the form in which we know them.

The Gospels are, in fact, a development of the apostolic preaching, the kerygma: [7] a development which interprets Jesus' ministry in the light of the central truth of that preaching, namely that through Jesus salvation has been given to men. Christ's public ministry was one of the points of the preaching (cf. Ac 10:38-39a), but so far as that kerygma can be reconstructed from the discourses of the first part of Acts (1:1-15,35) the ministry was given relatively little importance. That is understandable since the preaching was addressed to those who had not yet accepted Christ, and its purpose was their conversion. Consequently, emphasis was laid on the great central themes of the salvation history: Jesus' death, Resurrection, exaltation, His sending the Spirit, His glorious return. The Gospels, on the contrary, were written for those who were believers, and they bring into prominence the meaning for man's salvation of Jesus' ministry. That does not necessarily mean that the traditional data concerning the ministry were modified in the gospel record under the influence of the Easter faith. Each text in which such modification can be suspected must be examined carefully before a decision is reached.

But if examination bears out the suspicion, it would be foolish to deny such modification because of an aprioristic conviction that it would have been impossible.[8]

There are other influences, related to the paschal faith, which must be allowed as possible sources of modification. The life-giving words of Jesus were seen as addressed not merely to those who first heard them, but to all who had come to believe in Him after He had risen from the dead. In many instances, nothing had to be changed to make them pertinent to Christians of whatever generation; in others, they originally had a meaning which was directly applicable only to those to whom they had been spoken during Jesus' public life. It would not be impossible that the early Christians, or the evangelists, conscious of possessing the Holy Spirit who would lead them into all truth (Jn 16:13), might, under the influence of the Spirit, have introduced changes into those words, or have added to them, in order to apply them to their own situation.[9] The life of the Savior, and particularly the redemptive act, was seen as the fulfillment of the Old Testament, foreshadowed and prepared for by the events of the sacred history of Israel, the words of the prophets, and the inspired prayers of the ancient people of God. It can hardly be thought that this interpretation was a creation of the Christian community; it seems rather that it goes back to Jesus Himself. But it is not surprising that in the Gospel record, and especially in the Passion accounts, there are some details which seem to have been composed in order to emphasize the Old Testament fulfillment.[10] Again, whether that was actually done is a question which can be answered only after a careful examination of the texts.

Form Criticism

Here it will be appropriate to make some mention of form criticism (*Formgeschichte*), which has made important contributions to our understanding of the Synoptic Gospels, even though much of the work of its proponents, especially that of Rudolf Bultmann, has been destructive of the historical value of the Gospels and is marked by presuppositions which are unacceptable. Form criticism was a product of German scholarship; the works in which it was proposed appeared in 1919 and the early 1920's. The two most important are Martin Dibelius' *Die Formgeschichte des Evangeliums*,[11] and Bultmann's *Die Geschichte der synoptischen Tradition*.[12]

The position of the form critics is, in the first place, that the chronological and topographical framework of the Synoptics is almost entirely artificial. They point out, further, that those Gospels are not compositions of three individuals who can be called authors in the now accepted sense of that term; they are, rather, compilations of little units which were originally independent, which had originated in and circulated in the oral tradition of the Christian community and had developed according to the laws of popular literature. Only the Passion account seems to have been, from the beginning, a continuous narrative.[13] The two most obvious classifications of the Gospel material are the sayings and the narratives. In the latter, two types can be discerned, which Dibelius called "Paradigms" and *Novellen*, respectively. The paradigms are accounts which lead up to some memorable statement of Jesus (for example, the account of the disciples' plucking the ears of grain on the Sabbath—Mk 2:23-28). The *Novellen* are accounts which normally tell of a miracle of Jesus. Bultmann calls the latter "miracle stories" and the former "apophthegms," and since the statement of Jesus is the important point in the apophthegms, he classifies them under the sayings-material rather than under the narratives.

The rest of the narrative material is difficult to classify according to form. Dibelius includes the majority of it under the designation "legend." Since we are inclined to equate "legendary" with "fictitious," it must be emphasized that that is not the meaning of Dibelius' terminology. For him, "legend" is a neutral term so far as the historical value of a narrative is concerned: "The legend-form as such furnishes no decisive argument against the historicity of the hero or of an event—nor, on the other hand, does it give any guarantee that the account corresponds to reality." [14] He compares the Gospel legends to the medieval legends of the saints, pious stories about the life and death of a holy person. The Passion account is an aetiological cult legend, the purpose of which is to so present the condemnation and execution of Jesus that the hearer or reader may see in them the expression of God's will.[15] Personal legends, which tell of the holiness, wisdom, or piety of their chief character are relatively few in the Gospels; the clearest example of one about Jesus is Luke's account of Him in the temple at the age of twelve (Lk 2:41-50). Finally, the Christ-myth, according to which Jesus is the divine Son of God who came into the world from heaven, is clearly present in the accounts of Jesus' baptism, temptations, and transfiguration; it has influenced some of the *Novellen* such as Mark 6:47-52 and some of the sayings such as Matthew 11:25-30.

For Bultmann, the narrative material exclusive of the miracle stories is "legend and historical narrative" (*Geschichtserzählung*). The legend may have an historical basis, but it shows no particular interest in the historical as such; it has a religious and edifying rather than an historical character.[16] For practical purposes, the distinction between legend and historical narrative is as good as nonexistent: "a separation of legend and historical narrative seems impossible . . . [because] . . . historical narrative is so completely dominated by legend that it can only be treated together with the treatment of legend." [17] In their final form, the Gospels show the considerable influence which the Christ-myth exercised; this is especially true of Mark among the Synoptics and of John.[18]

It is not our purpose here to attempt a criticism of this system.[19] Let it suffice to say that there is no doubt that in trying to trace the various elements of the Gospels to their "situation in life" (*Sitz im Leben*), that is, the circumstances in the early Christian communities which led to the formation of the material, both Dibelius and Bultmann assigned an unwarranted role to the creative power of the community and arrived at excessively negative judgments about the historical value of the gospel record. In that respect, Bultmann was the more radical of the two. Little place was allowed for the activity of those who had been eyewitnesses of the events; supposedly, those who were in a position to give information about Jesus' words and deeds had little or no interest in doing so. But the form critics give no satisfactory basis for that extraordinary hypothesis.

On the credit side, however, it must be said that the methods employed by the form critics can be useful tools in the hands of the Catholic scholar, provided they are used with discrimination,[20] and that the form critics have arrived at some conclusions about the Gospels which deserve acceptance.

It is clear, in the first place, that what they maintain about the chronological framework of the Gospels is in large part true. Probably there are few careful readers of the Gospels who had not recognized, before they ever heard of form criticism, that in the majority of cases it is impossible to determine the time-order of the particular events of Jesus' ministry. But some scholars still hesitate to apply that principle consistently. Faced with the fact that the Johannine account of Jesus' cleansing of the temple (Jn 2:13-22) puts it at the beginning of the ministry, while the Synoptics (Mk 11:15-18 and parallels) put it at the end, they take what T. W. Manson has called "the desperate solution of two cleansings," [21] a solution which . . . by duplicating the event, lessens its significance.

Secondly, there are instances in which the same event is related differently in different Gospels. Some of these accounts vary only by insignificant differences of detail. An example of that would be Mark 10:46-52 and parallels. What judgment should one pass upon the fact that according to Mark's account Jesus cures one blind man, named Bartimaeus, when leaving Jericho; in Matthew, He cures two blind men when leaving; in Luke, He cures one blind man when approaching the city? No other than that the differences are simply the consequence of oral transmission of the same story by different groups. There is surely no reason to try to reconcile them by improbable harmonizations, a technique which was often used by Catholic scholars in the past, and can still be found in so comparatively recent a work as Giuseppe Riccioti's *Life of Christ* (this in spite of the avowed intention of the author to write "a critical work"), and in the even later *Life of Christ* by Andres Fernandez. The accounts of the cure of the centurion's servant in Matthew 8:5-13 and Luke 7:1-10 may be taken as another case where oral tradition has produced two different versions of the same story. And it is as least probable that the Johannine account of the cure of the royal official's son (Jn 5:46-53) is simply another version of that story.

In cases such as these, the differences are not particularly important. But if we compare the Marcan and Matthaean accounts of the disciples with the Lucan (Mk 1:16-20; Mt 4:18-22; Lk 5:1-11), we find that the difference goes far beyond some insignificant variants; in Luke, a miraculous catch of fish is connected with the call. One cannot avoid remarking the similarity between that element of the Lucan story and the post-Resurrection miracle in John 21:1-14. Did Luke himself put into his vocation account the miracle narrated in the Johannine tradition? Or had that already been done before the evangelist began his work on the material which he had received? Does the Lucan version of the call of the disciples depend on the Johannine tradition at all? These are difficult questions and, for our purposes, we need not attempt to answer them. It is sufficient to note that in Luke's Gospel there is a very different version of the call of the disciples from that found in Matthew and Mark. Unlike Bultmann, we do not question the historicity of the miracle, but we may well doubt that its association in Luke with the call of the disciples gives us an historically exact picture of what happened on that occasion.

Peter's Confession; the Beatitudes

We shall now consider two important passages in which it seems that the original data were deliberately modified: the confession of Peter in Matthew 16:16 and the Matthean and Lucan versions of the Beatitudes (Mt 5:3-21; Lk 6:20-23).

In these instances, it seems probable that the modifications were made by the evangelists themselves, rather than in the course of the transmission of the data. One of the weaknesses of form criticism was that it attributed too little to the initiative of the evangelists and reduced them practically to mere compilers of pre-existing material. Within the past decade or so, a needful reaction to that viewpoint has set in: *Redaktionsgeschichte* ("history of redaction"), which is concerned with the theological preoccupations of the evangelists and the influence of those preoccupations upon the way in which they dealt with their material. As R. H. Fuller expresses it: "Recent study of the Gospels has tended toward a greater appreciation of the evangelists as creative theologians in their own right; each offers his distinctive interpretation of the traditions with which he worked. . . . If we are to study the work of the evangelists themselves, we must pay very close attention to their editorial redactions—the connecting links they forge between the pericopes, their arrangement of the pericopes, the alterations which they make to their sources where we have them." [22] Yet *Formgeschichte* and *Redaktionsgeschichte* are complementary rather than fundamentally opposed; Bultmann himself has acknowledged the value and legitimacy of the latter.[23]

In treating Matthew 16:16, I should like to present the interpretation of Father Pierre Benoit of the Dominican *École Biblique* in Jerusalem, a scholar who is recognized as one of the leading scripturists of our day. Benoit dealt with the text in an article on the divinity of Jesus in the Synoptic Gospels which appeared in 1953.[24] He developed there a view which he had already expressed in a footnote in his translation of Matthew in the *Bible de Jérusalem.*[25] The following year, Father David M. Stanley took up Benoit's exegesis and added certain considerations which make it, I think, even more convincing.[26]

Peter's confession, "Thou art the Christ, the Son of the living God," is taken by most Catholic exegetes as a confession to the divinity of Jesus. They see in this affirmation that He is "the Son of the living God" a statement of belief that He is Son of God in the fullest meaning of the term; the text, therefore, contains much more than a confession that Jesus is the Messiah, "the Christ." [27] Admittedly, the title "Son of God" does not, of itself, provide any argument for that position. There are Old Testament texts which show that angels (Jb 1:6), the nation Israel (Ex 4:22f.), the people of Israel (Dt 14:1), the Davidic king (2 Sam 7:14), and the just man (Wis 2:18) were called the son(s) of God. The fact that the king was considered the son of God would make the title peculiarly applicable to the Messiah-King. Strangely enough, it is at least doubtful that it ever was applied to Him either in the Old Testament or in the Jewish apocryphal literature; but there is some evidence that the title was used with only messianic meaning by the Christians, as, for example, in the accounts of Jesus' baptism where the words spoken by the voice from heaven (Mat 3:17; Mk 1:11; Lk 3:22) re-echo, in part, Psalm 2:7.[28] Is Matthew 16:16 a similar case? A comparison of the Matthean version of Peter's confession with the Marcan (Mk 8:27-30) and the Lucan (Lk 9:18-22) suggests that it is not. In the latter two, Peter expresses belief simply in Jesus as Messiah. But there are two significant differences in Matthew: first, the use of the title, "the Son of the living God"; second, and more important since that title *might* be merely a messianic one, the difference in the question which Jesus puts to the disciples. In Mark and Luke He asks: "Who do men (or "the crowds") say that I am?" In Matthew, "Who do men say that the *Son of Man* is?" Most probably, "Son of Man" here is an allusion to the vision of Daniel 7:13f. where one "like a Son of Man" advances to the "Venerable One" (God) and receives from Him "dominion and glory and kingly power," a universal and everlasting kingdom. This Son of Man is certainly a more exalted figure than the traditional Messiah of Israel. In identifying Himself with this heavenly, pre-existing being in His response to the high priest at his trial (Mk 14:61f. and parallels), in answer to the question whether He was the Messiah, the Son of the Blessed One (God), Jesus indicated that He was more than the Messiah whom Israel was expecting.[29] He asserted His heavenly origin and, for Benoit, His divinity: "In assimilating Himself to 'the Son of Man' of Daniel, He (Jesus) gave the title 'Son of God' a meaning which was not metaphorical but proper and transcendent . . ." [30] That union of titles, found in the trial scene, is also present in Matthew's account of Peter's confession, and if Benoit's opinion about the union is right, "Son of God" has the same meaning of divinity in the fullest sense in Matthew 16:16 as in the texts dealing with the trial.

I think that we may pass over an examination of the reason which Benoit gives for taking the title as a strictly divine one in these texts. As we have already mentioned, his interpretation of the title is the same as that held by the majority of Catholic exegetes, even though they may not have arrived at it by the same argument as he has. And it is the interpretation and the consequences of it for our understanding of the formation of the Matthean account of Peter's confession which are of primary importance.

If Matthew 16:16 contains a confession to Jesus' divinity, how is it possible that the Synoptic parallels have nothing of the sort? The suggestion that Matthew's version represents what Peter really said at Caesarea Philippi and that Mark and Luke omitted "the Son of the living God" is entirely improbable. It is, besides, most difficult to think that Peter or any of the disciples had come to explicit belief in Jesus' divinity during His public life. Benoit points out that the too-human conceptions which they had of even the messianic role of Jesus, their lack of understanding, for which Jesus often reproached them, and their attitude and conduct at the time of the Passion make it impossible to think that they clearly perceived His divinity before the Resurrection. Of all these indications the plainest, I think, is Peter's rebuke of Jesus after the first prediction of the Passion (Mt 16:22; Mk 8:32), a prediction which in all the Synoptics follows the account of Peter's confession. Consequently, however sure it may be that Matthew 16:16 contains a confession to Jesus' divinity, it seems certain that one cannot suppose that such a confession was made at Caesarea Philippi. Benoit suggests that it was the author of Greek Matthew (that is, the author of our canonical Gospel of Matthew), a Gospel which is certainly later than that of Mark, who added "the Son of the living God" in the light of the fully developed Paschal faith. But the belief which is expressed was not a *creation* of the Christian community. The situation was rather, that through the Resurrection and the sending of the Holy Spirit the disciples came to an understanding of what had been implied in the way in which Jesus had spoken of Himself in relation to the Father (for example, Mt 11:27; Mk 13:32), a way which was necessarily obscure but sufficient for laying the foundations of that faith which would gradually come to fullness after the Resurrection.

For Benoit, then, if we wish to know what Peter said at Caesarea Philippi we must go to the accounts of Mark and Luke. Matthew's account is a clear case of theological interpretation of the original data and it cannot, therefore, be taken as a record of what actually happened. A similar view is proposed by other Catholic exegetes. Joseph Schmid says that the words "the Son of the living God" are an addition which raises the confession above the level of Jewish messianism (on which it remains in Mark) to that of the early Christian kerygma.[31] In his important article on Matthew 16:13-23, Anton Vögtle states that "the proclamation of the early Church's belief in Christ was more important to the evangelist than the long since surpassed, inadequate messianic confession of Caesarea Philippi . . . by means of the confession to Christ which has been specified and elevated by the addition 'the Son of the living God,' he (the evangelist) allows Simon to express who Jesus, the Son of Man, is."[32]

David Stanley's observations on the evolution of the disciples' faith in Jesus are an important complement to Benoit's study, since they deal more fully with what is implied by the evangelist's procedure. His placing a statement of fully developed post-Resurrection faith back into the public ministry indicates the continuity and homogeneity of the progress of the disciples' belief. From the beginning they had adhered totally to the person of Jesus. But at first they saw in Him only their beloved Master; then, they knew Him as the Messiah of Israel; finally, in the light of the Paschal experience and the coming of the Spirit, they recognized that He was truly divine, the Son of God. In the course of this development there were privileged moments. The event at Caesarea Philippi was one of those, and its importance is shown by Matthew's interpreting Peter's confession to Jesus' Messiahship as a confession also to His divinity, although the latter was a truth which Peter and the other disciples grasped consciously only at the end of the process which had begun when they gave themselves totally to Jesus.

Let us now consider the second example of deliberate modification which we have chosen, in this case a modification of the words of Jesus, the Beatitudes. Here I should like to present the view of Dom Jacques Dupont, a Belgian monk whose scriptural work has won for him a place in the first rank of modern Catholic scholarship. His study of the Beatitudes appeared first in 1954;[33] a second, thoroughly revised and much expanded edition is now in process, and the first volume of it was published in 1958.[34]

The problem presented by a comparison of the Matthean and Lucan versions of the Beatitudes is well known. Matthew has nine (Mt 5:3-12), Luke four (Lk 6:20-23). Besides that, there are significant differences in those Beatitudes which are common to both; for example, in Matthew 5:3 the "poor in spirit" are declared blessed, but in Luke 6:20 simply the "poor"; in Matthew 5:6 the Beatitude speaks of those who "hunger and thirst after justice," whereas in Luke 6:21 the reference is to "you who are hungry now." Moreover, Luke's Beatitudes are followed by a series of "woes" (Lk 6:24-26) which predict misfortune for those who are in the states opposite to those mentioned in the Beatitudes, and there is no parallel in Matthew to these "woes."

The conclusions which Dupont has reached after a minute analysis of the texts are presented by him as tentative and of varying degrees of probability. To suggest that they are certain would be to go far beyond the claims of their author. Yet the method by which he conducts his study is the one which the majority of his colleagues agree is the only valid one. Max Zerwick, S.J., professor at the Pontifical Biblical Institute, has called it "the method which Catholic exegesis must necessarily use in the study of the Gospels." [35] It presupposes that at least in theory three levels of meaning can be distinguished in any Gospel text which records the words of Jesus: (1) the meaning which the words had when Jesus spoke them; (2) their meaning in the apostolic tradition, that is, when they were being passed down both in oral tradition and in writing before the final composition of the Gospels; (3) the meaning given them by the inspired evangelists.[36] Dupont points out that this distinction is a theoretical one, for it is not impossible that in certain instances various levels of meaning may coincide. And in fact he believes that in the form in which Matthew (that is, the author of Greek Matthew) and Luke received the Beatitudes, their meaning was the same as that which they had when Jesus spoke them: "This form which the Beatitudes had received before they were redacted by the evangelists depends on the apostolic tradition . . .

but it does not seem that it can be distinguished from a primitive form which corresponds to the intentions of the Master and to the situations of His public ministry."[37] And again, the text which was the basis on which the evangelists worked "can very well represent the initial form of the teaching of Jesus."[38] It is a different matter, however, when we come to the meaning of the Beatitudes in the versions of Matthew and Luke. For Dupont, neither version retains the original meaning of those Beatitudes (the four common ones) which, in substance, go back to Jesus Himself. Besides this, each of the two versions differs in meaning from the other.

The similarities between the four Beatitudes common to both versions are such that one may conclude that they have been derived from a common source, a document written in Greek. By eliminating those elements which seem to be due to the literary activity of the evangelists, one can arrive at the form which the Beatitudes had in that basic document, and it was probably the following:

> Blessed are the poor, for theirs is the kingdom of heaven.
>
> Blessed are the afflicted, for they shall be comforted.
>
> Blessed are those who hunger (and thirst), for they shall be satisfied.
>
> Blessed will you be when men hate you and exclude you and insult you and utter a bad name against you (that is, defame you) because of the Son of Man. Rejoice and be glad, for your reward in heaven is great; for it was in that way that they persecuted the prophets, your predecessors.

In determining the meaning of these Beatitudes in the basic document, Dupont makes a distinction between the first three and the fourth. The former are related to the prophecies of Isaia 49:8-13; 55:1; 57:14-20; 61:1-3, in which the benefits of the messianic kingdom are promised to the poor, the afflicted, those who hunger and thirst. By announcing the good fortune, the blessedness, of those who are in that lowly situation in which they count for nothing so far as purely human judgment is concerned, Jesus proclaims that in His person and mission the promised kingdom has come (or is on the point of being inaugurated). "If the poor are blessed, it is because Jesus claims for Himself the specific task which marks the Messiah whom Isaia prophesied. That task is defined in relation to the disinherited of this world. In announcing to them that it is going to be accomplished, in fact that it is already beginning to be accomplished, Jesus presents Himself as the Messiah of the poor who is described in the oracles of the great prophet." [39] The beginning of Jesus' ministry is the time which suits perfectly this joyous proclamation of the coming of the kingdom.

The fourth Beatitude is quite different. It speaks of the recompense which those who have suffered persecution for Jesus, the Son of Man, will receive at the time of the Last Judgment. The attitude which they have taken in regard to Jesus the Messiah has been the cause of their suffering and it will be the reason for their reward. "If one is blessed in suffering for Jesus, it is because Jesus is the Messiah, the Son of Man, He who will preside at the Last Judgment. The christological import of the Beatitude is inseparable from its eschatological significance." [40] The situation in Jesus' ministry which suits this Beatitude is the last period, when the hostility of His adversaries was apparent and growing. It was then that He foretold that His disciples would have to bear the same kind of persecution as He, and encouraged them by the thought of the reward which they would receive from His own hands.

It is clear, particularly in the case of the first three of these common Beatitudes, that their original meaning could have pertinence only at the time of Jesus' ministry and at the time of the apostolic preaching to those who did not yet believe. A proclamation of the coming of the kingdom would have nothing but historical interest for those who recognized that it had come, and that they were members of it. Yet the precious words of Jesus were there, susceptible of new meaning which would make them applicable to Christian communities of the post-Resurrection time. And under the inspiration of the Holy Spirit, Matthew and Luke reinterpreted them, but each did so in a different way. By his additions to the original Beatitudes [poor *in spirit;* hunger and thirst *after justice* (Mt 5:3,6), and by his incorporation of new ones (5:7,8,9)], Matthew has given a moral tone to what was originally a joyous proclamation of the kingdom. In his version, the Beatitudes represent the ideal of perfection, the justice which is demanded of those who are in the kingdom, and they promise reward to those who strive to fulfill that demand. This justice is the principal theme of the Matthean Sermon on the Mount (5:20; 6:1). The Beatitudes are a fitting prologue to the sermon and together with it constitute a perfect unit.

Luke has reinterpreted the Beatitudes in a quite different manner.

Leaving the original text of the basic document much as he found it, he has added the corresponding "woes," which quite clearly refer to social status. Consequently, since those to whom the woes refer are contrasted with those who are declared blessed, the meaning of the Beatitudes is changed. They now declare that the poor and afflicted of this world are blessed because they do not live for this world, and their fortunes will be reversed in the life after death.

The situation-in-life which is revealed by Luke's version is that of the early Church, composed in major part of the poor. Naturally, it is not poverty *as such* which is their guarantee of happiness and reward in heaven; right moral dispositions are presupposed. But emphasis is not laid on those dispositions, as it is in Matthew's version. And Dupont thinks it probable that the "woes" were not only added to the Beatitudes by Luke, but composed by him under the inspiration of the Spirit, in order to give the Beatitudes the meaning which they have in his version.

Although both evangelists have modified the original meaning, they have done so by drawing out virtualities contained in the Beatitudes as Jesus pronounced them, in order to make them pertinent to the Church of their time. In doing this, they were entirely faithful to the teaching of Jesus, for the meaning found in each version corresponds to teaching which the Lord Himself had given—not, indeed, when he spoke the Beatitudes, but at other times during His ministry. The moral perfection demanded in Matthew's version was surely the demand of Jesus as the Sermon on the Mount attests; the contrasting fate of the poor and the rich in the next life, taught in Luke's version, with the high estimate of the value of actual poverty and the awareness of the spiritual danger of riches that that teaching involves—all that is a faithful echo of Jesus' doctrine as we find it in the parable of Dives and Lazarus (Lk 16:19-31) and in that of the rich fool (Lk 12:16-21). By making the Beatitudes a vehicle for conveying to the early Church a message which was as pertinent to it as a proclamation of the coming of the Kingdom would have been anachronistic, the evangelists showed their awareness that the words of Jesus were indeed words of *life*.

The few examples which we have touched on may be fairly taken as representative of the type of Gospel interpretation now prevalent among Catholic scripturists. Far from weakening the historical value of the sacred books, it has disposed of many a pseudo-problem and given insights into texts whose richness had previously hardly been suspected. The early Christians passed down narratives and sayings which they had received from the eyewitnesses of Jesus' ministry, yet they realized that they themselves had a better understanding of what the Lord had said and done than it was possible to have at the time that the deeds were done and the words spoken. The evangelists, who put the traditional material into final form, each in his distinctive manner, were, particularly, men guided by the Spirit in their interpretation of the sacred history. It was the intention of those who contributed to the formation of the Gospels that the readers should know the full meaning of what Jesus had said and done, that they should see that the heavenly Lord of the Church was none other than the historical Jesus of Nazareth and that there was true continuity between His earthly ministry and His present guidance of the Church. In so far as the community or the evangelists deliberately modified the original data, they did so the better to carry out that intention. And the fact that what the eyewitnesses recounted, what the community retold, what the evangelists wrote, was recounted, retold, and written down by men of the Church for the Church—this fact points to the central role of ecclesiastical tradition in the formation of the Gospels and shows how foreign to primitive Christian thought is any imagined opposition between Bible and Church.

References

[1] Cf. J. A. Fitzmyer's excellent survey, "A Recent Roman Scriptural Controversy," *Theological Studies*, 22 (1961), 426-44.

[2] Cf. F. McCool, "Revival of Synoptic Source Criticism," *Theological Studies*, 17 (1956), 459-93, esp. 484-86; V. T. O'Keefe, "Towards Understanding the Gospels," *CBQ*, 21 (1959), 171-89, especially 173-76.

[3] Cf. R. E. Brown, "Incidents that are Units in the Synoptic Gospels but Dispersed in St. John," *CBQ*, 23 (1961), 143-60.

[4] H. W. V. Temperley, "Research and Modern History," quoted in A. Richardson, *Christian Apologetics* (London, 1960), p. 94, n.1. Cf. also M. C. D'Arcy, *The Meaning and Matter of History* (New York, 1950), esp. pp. 15-62.

[5] C. H. Dodd, *History and the Gospel* (London, 1938), p. 27.

[6] T. A. Roberts, "Some Presuppositions of Gospel Historical Criticism," *Studia Evangelica*, ed. K. Aland, *et al.* (Berlin, 1959), p. 69.

[7] Cf. C. H. Dodd, *The Apostolic Preaching and Its Developments* (London, 1936).

[8] C. P. Ceroke's "Is Mk. 2:10 a Saying of Jesus?" *CBQ*, 22 (1960), 366-90 is an example of the type of examination we mean. As a result of his thoroughly scientific study, Ceroke concludes that the question posed in the title

must be answered in the negative: "Son of Man in Mk. 2:10 envisions Jesus, not in His earthly public ministry, but as resurrected and ascended. As Head of the messianic community, He exercises the function of the forgiveness of sins on earth" (387).

[9] For an interesting study in support of the view that the *interpretation* of the parable of the Sower (Mt 13:19-23 and parallels) is an example of an addition made to the words of Jesus, "a traditional interpretation which was in accord with the intentions of the Lord and yet pointed His message so that it applied to the condition of their [the evangelists'] own, very different age," cf. F. J. McCool, "The Preacher and the Historical Witness of the Gospels," *Theological Studies*, 21 (1960), 517-43.

[10] A classic example of this is Matthew's account of Jesus' entrance into Jerusalem (21:1-11) according to which two animals, an ass and a colt, are brought to Jesus who settles himself upon *them* (!). In the Synoptic parallels and in John 12:12-19 there is mention only of one animal. In Zecharia 9:9, which Matthew sees fulfilled in Jesus' entry, an ass and a colt are spoken of, but that is clearly a case of poetic parallelism. In order to emphasize the fulfillment, Matthew holds to the *letter* of the Old Testament prophecy and speaks of two animals.

[11] Martin Dibelius, *Die Formgeschichte des Evangeliums*, 3rd. ed. (Tubigen, 1959). All our references are to the second edition (1933), of which the third is an [almost] exact reproduction with some minor exceptions.

[12] Rudolf Bultmann, *Die Geschichte der synoptischen Tradition*, 4th. ed. (Gottingen, 1958); cf. English translation by J. Marsh, *The History of the Synoptic Tradition* (Oxford: Blackwell, 1963).

[13] Dibelius, *op. cit.*, 178.

[14] *Ibid.*, 106.

[15] *Ibid.*, 101ff.

[16] *Op. cit.*, 260.

[17] *Ibid.*, 261.

[18] *Ibid.*, 334.

[19] For a good evaluation see A. Wikenhauser, *New Testament Introduction*, tr. J. Cunningham (New York: Herder and Herder, Inc., 1958), pp. 253-77.

[20] Cf. R. Aubert, *La Théologie Catholique au milieu du XX Siècle* (Paris, 1954) who says (18f.): "Some Catholic exegetes do not hesitate to make their own a number of the conclusions of the *Formgeschichtliche Schule*. . . . Monsignor Cerfaux has not hesitated to use [this method], which at first seemed destined to pulverize the historical worth of the Gospels, and in so doing has transformed it into a very fruitful instrument for penetrating the first Christian catechesis, permitting one to find there certain primitive aspects as well as certain hitherto neglected nuances."

[21] T. W. Manson, *Studies in the Gospels and Epistles* (Manchester, 1962), p. 118.

[22] R. H. Fuller, *The New Testament in Current Study* (New York, 1962), p. 72.

[23] Cf. *Die Erforschung der synoptischen Evangelien*, 4th ed. (Berlin, 1961), p. 53.

[24] Pierre Benoit, "La divinté de Jésus dans les évangiles synoptiques," *Lumière et Vie*, 9 (1953), 43-74. This was reprinted in *Exégèse et Théologie*, I, 117-42 and our references are to that as more accessible.

[25] Benoit, *L'Évangile selon Saint Matthieu*, 1st. ed. (Paris, 1950), p. 103: "To the confession of Jesus' Messiahship, reported by Mark and Luke, Matthew adds the formal profession of his divine origin."

[26] David M. Stanley, "Études matthéennes: La Confession de Pierre à Césarée," *Sciences Ecclésiastiques*, 6 (1954), 51-61.

[27] For an indication of some who think that in this text "Son of God" has only a messianic meaning, cf. D. J. Saunders, "The Confession of Peter," *Theological Studies*, 10, (1949), 522.

[28] This seems to be the case also in the closely related Temptation accounts; cf. Benoit, *Exégèse et Théologie*, I, 129.

[29] It is widely accepted that Jesus' designation of Himself as "Son of Man" is derived from Daniel 7. There is disagreement whether, in addition to that, the late-Jewish book of Enoch also influenced Jesus in His choice of the title. In Enoch, as in the Gospels, the term is applied to an individual, whereas in Daniel the collective meaning is prominent. If one explains Jesus' use of the title solely in terms of Daniel 7, it is difficult to see it in the notion of "heavenly origin" on which Benoit lays much stress. It is not said in Daniel that the "Son of Man" is of heavenly *origin*, whereas He is clearly so in Enoch.

[30] *Op. cit.*, 141.

[31] Joseph Schmid, *Das Evangelium nach Matthaus*, p. 247. One might point out that the character of the excellent and much praised series to which Schmid's commentary belongs is such that one cannot say that his view is a hypothesis which a professional exegete might present for the consideration of fellow specialists, but which has no place in works intended for the formation of theological students or for the instruction of educated laymen.

[32] Anton Vögtle, "Messiasbekenntnis und Petrusverheissung," 2. Teil, *Biblische Zeitschrift*, 2 (1958), 96.

[33] Dom Jacques Dupont, *Les Béatitudes: Le problème littéraire, Le message doctrinal* (Bruges-Louvain, 1954).

[34] Dupont, *Les Béatitudes: Le problème littéraire* (Bruges-Louvain, 1958).

[35] Cf. Max Zerwick's review of the first edition in *Verbum Domini*, 33 (1955), 299.

[36] *Op. cit.*, 2d ed., 10-16; cf. also R. Schnackenburg, *La Théologie du Nouveau Testament* (Bruges, 1961), p. 47; cf. Engl. transl. by D. Askew, *New Testament Theology Today* (New York: Herder and Herder, Inc., 1963).

[37] *Op. cit.*, 15.

[38] *Ibid.*, 16.

[39] *Op. cit.*, 1st ed., 176.

[40] *Ibid.*, 136.

DAVID M. STANLEY, S.J.

The Divinity of Christ in New Testament Hymns

The nonprofessional reader will discover in this well-illustrated article a discussion of questions such as these: What pagan testimony do we have of the Christian practice of singing hymns to Christ as God? Why is this important? What evidence does the New Testament give that such hymns were commonly sung among the earliest Christians? When would these hymns be sung? Can we trace the gradual development of the apostles' belief in the divinity of Christ? What are some examples of New Testament hymns and what theological doctrines do they emphasize? How do these hymns reflect the naïve and concrete language used by the first Christians to express their belief that Christ is God?

Father Stanley, also the author of two previous articles, teaches New Testament theology at the State University of Iowa.

In the year 112 of our era, Caius Plinius Caecilius made a report to the Emperor Trajan on his success in Asia Minor at stamping out Christianity. In his letter, he refers to two different types of Christian reunion, which had a liturgical character. "They (the Christians) insisted, however, that their whole crime or error came to this: they had the custom of meeting on a certain fixed day, before daybreak, to sing a hymn, alternately among themselves, to Christ as God; and to bind themselves solemnly by oath, not with any criminal intent, but to avoid all fraud, theft, adultery, unfaithfulness to their promises, or denial of 'the deposit,' if summoned

This article was first published in the *Proceedings of the Fourth Annual Convention of the Society of Catholic College Teachers of Sacred Doctrine* and is reproduced here with permission.

to do so. After dispatching this business, it was their habit to disband, reassembling once more to take food, which is, however, of an ordinary and innocent kind . . ." (Pliny, *Letters*, Book 10,96).

The precise nature of these two religious services, held on "a certain fixed day," which means undoubtedly Sunday, has been the subject of much discussion among scholars. However, it appears probable that the first was a ceremony at which Baptism was administered, the second, the Eucharistic liturgy, the Lord's Supper, the Mass, celebrated in the late afternoon or evening. It is the reference by Pliny to a hymn sung by the community during the baptismal liturgy which interests us principally: *carmenque Christo quasi deo dicere secum invicem.* That such hymn-singing should be mentioned at all shows its importance in the minds of these early Christians who made the deposition before the imperial official. The detailed description of this act of worship is also significant: it was a hymn sung to Christ "as God," a hymn whose principal theme was the divinity of Christ; it was a hymn, sung by the whole community *secum invicem*, that is, sung by two or more groups alternately. These data are of considerable interest to us, since they show that at the beginning of the second century of the Christian era the Christian communities of Asia Minor were still faithful to a tradition of hymnody which we find attested by New Testament writers, notably St. Paul.

There is a passage in Acts, based on one of the earliest sources at Luke's disposal, which probably refers to the use of hymns at public worship in the Palestinian communities of the first years of the Church. "Breaking the Bread at home, they partook of the Food with transports of joy and utter simplicity of mind, while they sang God's praises" (Ac 2:46-47). One of the directives, given by Paul to the Corinthian Church, makes it clear that the singing of hymns, composed, it may well be, on the spur of the moment under the influence of the Holy Spirit, was a regular feature of Christian liturgical reunions. "When you convene, each of you has a hymn, or some teaching, or a revelation, or an ecstatic utterance, or some interpretation" (1 Cor 14:26).

It is the Captivity epistles, however, which provide us with the most specific references to the Christian cultic use of hymns, and it is instructive to note that the same details, already noted in the passage from Pliny, recur. There are two passages from these Pauline letters which deserve citation.

In Colossians 3:16, we read: "May the Word of Christ dwell within you, rich in wisdom, as you instruct yourselves by means of songs, hymns, inspired canticle, and sing gratefully with all your heart to God." Paul probably does not intend to make a distinction between various categories of sacred songs used in the Christian liturgy. What is more important, however, is the twofold purpose he assigns to this public recital of hymns. They are sung as an offering of cultic prayer to God, and they are a means used by the community to instruct herself in Christian doctrine. Thus . . . these songs were, in every sense of the term, "community cultic hymns." They originated within the community, and, unlike the later hymns composed by the Gnostics, remained anonymous. They were community property, and undoubtedly were continually reworded or re-adapted to varying liturgical needs. Most important of all, they were looked on as the "Word of Christ," since they were the voice of the community, the *alter Christus*, the "Body of Christ" mentioned in the verse preceding our citation. "You have also been called in one Body to (the peace of Christ): hence express your gratitude" (Col 1:15b). Thus the voice of the Body of Christ is this *Logos tou Christou*, or "Word of Christ" expressed in liturgical hymns.

Our second passage is found in Ephesians 5:18-19: "Stop getting drunk on wine, which only leads to licentiousness. Seek instead to be filled with the Spirit, by reciting songs, hymns, inspired canticles, by singing to the Lord and chanting his praises with all your heart, giving thanks always for everything in the Person of our Lord Jesus Christ to God the Father." The text is clearly a parallel to that just quoted from Colossians; but there are two variations in the present passage which throw more light on these primitive Christian hymns. Where the hymns are said to be sung "to God" in Colossians, here there is question of "singing to the Lord," that is, to the risen Christ as a divine Person. The Ephesians text mentions the Holy Spirit explicitly, and explains the meaning of the term "spiritual" applied to the hymns by both passages. They are "spiritual" or "inspired," not merely because of their religious character, but principally because, through the liturgical recitation of such hymns, the community becomes "filled with the Spirit," who, as this letter stated earlier (Eph 4:4), brings about the unity of the "one Body."

Both texts speak of the reciprocal instruction or mutual edification of the community as a primary function of this cultic chant, a point of contact between these Pauline statements and Pliny's remark that the hymn "to Christ as God" was executed *secum invicem*, "alternating with one another."

What was the nature of this ancient Christian hymnology, and can we find any examples of it preserved in writing? I believe we can. Moreover, I feel we can discover, in the inspired writings of the New Testament itself, examples of hymns sung "to Christ as God," which may be traced back to the earliest period of the Church's life.

But first, it might be helpful to state what we understand by a New Testament hymn. It might be defined as a New Testament passage, of rhythmic character, expressing some phase of the Christian mystery, composed most probably for use in the public or liturgical worship of the primitive Church. To be more specific on this last point, the fragments of such hymns as are recoverable from the New Testament writings were probably sung, or solemnly recited, as credal formulae during the Baptismal or Eucharistic liturgies. Indeed, it is altogether likely, as the passages in Paul and Pliny assert, that in earliest Christian times the Church was accustomed to express her beliefs, notably that in Christ's divinity, by means of hymns. According to Balthasar Fischer, this use of hymns in the apostolic liturgy preceded the use of the psalter as a liturgical chant book. The Old Testament Book of Psalms "appears only to have become a book of liturgical chant at the moment when the youthful Church, turning her back upon hymns that had been seriously compromised by Gnostic abuses, redirected her attention to the Bible" (in the late second, or early third centuries).[1] Dom Henri Leclercq concurs with this opinion and rejects the curious notion of Frederick Ozanam, who insisted that for the first three centuries of her existence, the Church "rejected the imagination, and, in her guidance of her people, spoke to them in prose and only in prose."[2]

There is another point which calls for some clarification before we attempt to study some examples of early Christian hymnology; and that is the meaning of the phrase, "the divinity of Christ," as it is expressed in many parts of the New Testament. We all know, of course, what we mean today by the phrase: the central Christian belief that Jesus Christ is Son of God, or that the Second Person of the Trinity has assumed a human nature. This same belief was held by the Christians of the apostolic age, but their expression of it differed notably from our own, at least in the earliest formulations of this dogma which have survived. It is important to realize that the most archaic forms of this truth, which were proclaimed in the apostolic kerygma or preaching, followed the psychological process by which the first disciples became aware of Christ's divinity. And even for a considerable period after this dogma became an integral part of the Christian doctrinal treasure, the way in which this revelation had been imparted to the apostles left its mark on their expression of the mystery of Jesus Christ.

As an illustration of what I mean, let us take a sample of the early preaching, attributed to Peter in Acts 2:22-36. "Fellow Israelites, pay attention to the following facts. Jesus the Nazarene was a man accredited to you by God by means of miracles, prodigies, and signs, which God performed through him among you, as you yourselves are aware. In accordance with God's fixed purpose and foreknowledge, you did away with him after handing him over by having him crucified at the hands of evil men. God, however, raised him, annihilating death's horrors, since it was impossible that he should remain under death's power. [Here reference is made to Ps 15, which is shown to be inapplicable to David himself, but David's prophecy of the Resurrection of Christ. The sermon continues as follows.] This man Jesus God raised—all of us are witnesses of that. Thus having been exalted to God's right hand and receiving from his Father the promise of the Holy Spirit, he has poured out this which you are observing and hearing. [After citing Ps 110:1, the preacher continues.] Therefore let the whole house of Israel know for sure that God has made him both Lord and Messiah, this Jesus whom you yourselves crucified."

The context in which this speech is set by Luke is to be noted. The occasion is that of the first Pentecost, and Peter is attempting to explain to the pilgrimage crowd the meaning of the phenomenon of "tongues" which they have witnessed. He describes their newly found faith in Christ's divinity as a result of the outpouring of the Holy Spirit. The preacher begins by referring to Jesus as "a man," and concludes by asserting the divine prerogatives which are His as the result of His exaltation to God's right hand. Jesus has been accorded a share *ex aequo* by the Father in the divine governance of the universe. He has been made "*Kyrios*," or given God's own Name, which is an apodictic, if somewhat primitive way of stating that His divinity has been revealed to His disciples. If such an unsophisticated mode of expression may seem to us naïve, theologically speaking, its very lack of theological refinement attests to its authenticity.

It may not be out of place here to recall briefly the very gradual manner in which the first disciples became aware of their Master's divinity, and to sketch the various ways in which they first expressed, with the aid of biblical symbolism, their initial insights into this central belief of Christianity.

The schema of the kerygma or apostolic preaching, which we find also reflected in the written Gospel, begins with the message of John the Baptist. In other words, John's preaching was considered, by the apostolic age, as initiating the revelation of the mystery of Jesus. In essence, it consists in the twofold proclamation that "the Kingdom of heaven is at hand" (Mt 3:2), and "a mightier one than I is following me" (Mk 1:7). According to the tradition preserved in the Fourth Gospel, John passed on some of his own disciples to Jesus (Jn 1:35ff.). It does not seem, however, that they at once recognized in Jesus the messianic figure announced by John. The fact that they left John to follow Jesus indicates that they felt Him to be a greater rabbi than the Baptist. The Fourth Gospel suggests that they were attracted to Jesus by some mysterious and winning quality in His personality (Jn 1:38-39). The Synoptic Gospels, unfortunately, fail to indicate the psychological reactions of these men to the new teacher.

As they lived with Him, listening to His doctrine and witnessing His miracles, they came gradually to look upon Him as a prophet, indeed, one greater than the Old Testament prophets. At one privileged moment in the public life, which the Gospel tradition has linked with Caesarean Philippi, Peter, and through his mouth, the whole apostolic group, expressed the truth, divinely revealed, that Jesus is the Messiah.

Yet, despite such a precious grace, their conception of Jesus as the Christ remained colored by contemporary Jewish dreams of an earthly "restoration" of Israel's hegemony in the political world, and their undoubted devotion to Him was in the main an all too human loyalty. It was therefore necessary that their belief in Jesus as Jewish Messiah had to undergo a complete eclipse during the terrible events of His sufferings and death. Luke perhaps of all the evangelists brings this fact out most strikingly: "We for our part were indeed hoping that He was the man who was going to redeem Israel" (Lk 24:21). The sad truth was, however, that, until they found faith in Jesus' Resurrection a few hours later, these disciples no longer believed in Him as Messiah. Only through the instructions of their risen Lord did they begin to acquire a true conception of the spiritual nature of Jesus' mission and of the purpose of His Passion as revealed by "the Scriptures" (Lk 24:44-46). This new-found Paschal faith reached its apogee through the gift of the Holy Spirit, associated by Acts with the miracle of Pentecost. It is He who led them "into the whole truth" (Jn 16:13), that is, revealed to them Christ's divinity. Since Jesus sent the Spirit upon them, He was, they knew, enthroned at God's right hand, had been given a share in God's uniquely divine Function as Lord of the universe. As a fragment of an earlier credal formula preserved by Paul in Romans puts it, He had been "constituted Son of God in power by Resurrection from death" (Rom 1:4). The apostles also learned that their divine Master would return again at the end of human history, in order, by a glorious second Coming, to complete the task of subjecting the universe to His divine sovereignty.

Once the Spirit had put them in possession of the whole revelation concerning Jesus Christ, the disciples had to reflect upon the significance of these supernatural facts and attempt to express, in human language, the mystery of Christ's divinity. First of all, this truth clothed His earthly career, His sufferings and death, with an entirely new significance. Son of God in His glorified and heavenly state, He had been Son of God during His mortal life upon earth, although unrecognized by men. Moreover, before He entered on this earthly career, He had been pre-existent Son of God from all eternity. Ultimately, with John's Gospel, this theological thinking-out of the mystery of Jesus reached its climax in the realization of the redemptive character of the Incarnation, a truth, by the way, which never seems to have operated consciously in the mind of Paul.

How did the apostolic Church attempt to express the various facets of this completely new revelation? We can, I believe, perceive three patterns in the writings of the New Testament which were followed by the earliest Christologies. The revelation of Jesus' divinity was expressed, in the first place, as His elevation or enthronement at God's right hand. Second, it appears quite clearly in the descriptions of Jesus' work as redeemer which are based upon the Deutero-Isaian theme of the suffering and glorified Servant of Yahweh. Finally, it is portrayed by means of the conception, found first in the book of Daniel, of the Son of Man, which is developed by Paul into the theology of the second or last Adam.

It is these three symbols which are constantly employed in the Christological hymns of the New Testament. Occasionally, two or even three of these themes will be found in combination, as we shall have occasion to remark in our study of two of these hymns, to which the remainder of this paper will be devoted.

The first hymn we wish to consider is found in one of Paul's most simple and personal letters, that to the Philippian Church (Phil 2:5-11). This song, undoubtedly familiar to his addressees from its use in the Eucharistic liturgy as celebrated at Philippi, celebrates Christ's work as redeemer, and is inspired mainly by the fourth Servant song (Is 52:13-53, 12). What reasons have we for regarding it as a hymn? Perhaps the most persuasive argument that it is a citation of some carefully constructed summary of Christ's redemptive work, already familiar to the Philippian Christians, is the marked contrast there is between these few lines and the rest of the epistle, which . . . is not dogmatic in character and does not attempt to explain any problem of faith. Given the utter simplicity of this personal note, written by Paul to the community of his predilection, it seems difficult to explain the presence of such a densely theological passage as the one in question, except as a quotation from some source very familiar to Paul's readers. The rhythm, parallel structure, and presence of certain words or phrases indicative of the hymn-form employed in early Christianity make it most probable that we are here dealing with a hymn. Msgr. Lucien Cerfaux has already pointed out the indications in the style and vocabulary of the pericope which justify the conclusion that the hymn was composed for liturgical use: Christ is designated here simply as "Jesus," after the manner of the primitive Palestinian community; He is called Servant (of God), as in the earliest liturgical prayers that have survived (cf. Ac 4:24-30); and the final doxology also belongs to the liturgical style.[3] One final question: Is Paul himself the author of the hymn? I venture to suggest that he is not, but that he has merely quoted a liturgical hymn, in use at Philippi, but probably originating in Palestinian

Christian circles. My reason for this is that nowhere else in all Paul's letters do we find such an elaborate exposition of the redemption in terms of the Deutero-Isaian Servant motif. While we know that in the most ancient Palestinian churches this theme was very popular as a vehicle to express Christ's work as Savior, Paul does not seem to have employed it. On the contrary, in several places in his letters, he himself becomes the Servant of God; and the theme provides a basis for Paul's very original theology of the Christian apostolate.[4]

If all these conjectures be correct (and they are for the most part commonly admitted today by scholars inside and outside the Church), then we have in this hymn a most precious and very ancient monument to the faith of the primitive Palestinian community in the divinity of Christ.

Before discussing the hymn in detail, it will be useful to quote it in full, in a translation which is my own.

> Who, while He kept His character as God,
> Did not consider His divine equality
> Something to be proudly paraded.
>
> No, He despoiled Himself,
> By taking on the Servant's character,
> Becoming similar to mortal men.
>
> And looking outwardly like any other man,
> He carried self-abasement, through obedience,
> Right up to death, yes, death by the Cross.
>
> Therefore did God in turn immeasurably exalt Him.
> And graciously bestow on Him the Name,
> Outweighing every other name;
>
> That everyone, at Jesus' Name,
> Should bow adoring: those in heaven,
> On earth, in the infernal regions,
>
> And every tongue take up the cry,
> "Jesus is Lord,"
> Thus glorifying God His Father.

While most of the poem, as we have said, is inspired by the conception of Christ as Servant of Yahweh, the first stanza depicts Him as pre-existent Son, and, with remarkable theological exactitude, contrasts the Son's retention of "His character as God," which was His from all eternity, with His assumption in time of "the Servant's character," referred to in the second verse. Still the whole theological pattern of the hymn is a simple one, almost naïve in some respects. When the Son might rightly have claimed the divine honors, which were His due eternally, He chose instead, in order to carry out His mission of redemption in this world, the lowly way of humiliation and suffering. Thus, in reward for His sublime obedience, which included even the acceptance of a criminal's death, the Son won His divine honors and the adoration of the whole universe. The archaic nature of this Christology is perhaps best seen in the notion that the "becoming similar to mortal men" is part of the Son's self-abasement or despoiling of Himself. In the later Incarnation-theology, characteristic of a more Hellenized Christianity, which makes its appearance with the Fourth Gospel and second Epistle of Peter, the adoption of human nature by the Son is considered as an ennobling or divinization of mankind upon whom He confers the possibility of the divine adoptive sonship.

The repetition of the word *morphe*, "form," here translated as "character," which is employed in stanzas one and two, has enabled the author to present an admirably concrete description of the hypostatic union. *Morphe* denotes the way in which a thing presents its outward appearance in virtue of what it really is in itself. When it is a question of the divine *morphe* or character, the word retains only the sense of reality, since God is, by biblical definition, the Unseen. When employed to describe the human nature of the incarnate Son as "the Servant's character," *morphe* underscores the reality of the Son's humanity while reminding us that such a kenosis has interfered in no way with "His character as God." In my interpretation of the last line of the opening stanza, I have followed Msgr. Cerfaux, and have departed from both the Challoner-Rheims' "robbery" and the Confraternity's "a thing to be clung to." Cerfaux refers to the interpretation which Clement of Rome seems to have favored: "The sceptre of God's greatness, the Lord Jesus Christ, did not come with a boastful or arrogant display, although He could have, but in humility . . ." (1 Clem 16:2). Consequently, the *harpagmos* is taken to mean, not *res rapta* or *res rapienda*, but something which, though rightfully possessed, is not made the object of ostentatious display.[5]

The second and third stanzas describe Christ's role as the Suffering Servant, whose life on earth had been characterized by obedience to the will of God, which He had crowned with the sacrifice of Himself. "When He was oppressed, He humbled Himself, and opened not His mouth, like a sheep that is led to the slaughter, or a lamb that is dumb before its shearers" (Is 53:7).

To reward the fidelity of His Servant, Yahweh had promised to exalt Him in the sight of kings and nations (Is 52:13-15), to prolong His life, and give Him the spoils of the mighty (Is 53:10-12). The reality of this prophecy's fulfillment in Jesus' exaltation surpasses all human thought or imagination. Accordingly, the last half of the hymn is devoted to describing it as an exaltation "beyond all limit."

In the first place, it is described as the bestowal upon Jesus "of the Name outweighing every other name." What is this new Name conferred by God upon His exalted Servant? It is the divine title, *Kyrios*, as we learn from the acclamation cited in the last stanza of the hymn: "Jesus is *Kyrios*." In the Greek Bible, the Septuagintal translation of the Old Testament, the *Kyrios* was constantly used for the sacred tetragram, Yahweh, the personal name for God which the Hebrews scrupled to pronounce.

To appreciate the significance, in biblical language, of God's giving Jesus the divine Name *Kyrios*, we must recall that for the Semite a name was not equivocal, as it is in Western thought. It expressed the nature or character of the person or thing to which it was attached. Hence a change of name, in the case of a person who receives a new office or calling, is considered natural, if not indeed necessary, by the Hebrew. There come to mind significant changes of name in the case of Abraham (Gn 17:5), Jacob or Israel (Gn 32:28), Simon or Peter (Mt 16,18). With regard to the divine names, Yahweh and its Greek counterpart *Kyrios*, they were considered to be particularly expressive of God's transcendence and unique prerogatives. If Christ received the divine Name, then, it could only be possible because He was really God. In other words, to speak, as our hymn does, of God's gift of His own Name to Jesus is a characteristically Semitic way of signifying the revelation of Jesus' divinity, through His exaltation, to His own disciples.

It is of interest to note that the hymn describes the conferring of the Name *Kyrios* upon Jesus *as a grace*, the Greek verb *charizomai*, translated as "graciously bestow," having that signification. Such artless expression is evidence for the great antiquity of the poem. I believe that it reflects the sense of wonder which the revelation of Christ's divinity undoubtedly caused in the minds of the first disciples. It is a valuable reminder to an age like ours, so accustomed to regard Jesus as a divine Person, what a complete revolution this dogma caused in the religion of a group of Jews, whose Old Testament monotheism had given them no inkling of the Trinitarian mystery.

The second way in which our hymn highlights the divinity of Christ is its imaginative description of a kind of cosmic liturgy in which all the creatures inhabiting the Hebraic three-story universe participate. This conception is probably inspired by another passage in Deutero-Isaia (Is 45:22-24): "Turn to me and be saved, all ends of the earth. For I am God, and there is no other: by myself I have sworn . . . that to me every knee shall bow, every tongue shall swear, saying, 'Only in the Lord are righteousness and strength.' " Our poem represents the universe of creatures united to adore the God-Man and to offer the doxology, *Jesous Kyrios*, "Jesus is Lord," the simplest form of the Christian credo, which is found elsewhere in Paul's writings (cf. 1 Cor 12:3; Rom 10:9). This acclamation, and indeed the whole hymn in honor of Christ as Servant of God, is equivalently, as the last verse states, an act of praise to God the Father, author of Christ's work of salvation and revealer to men of His Son's divinity.

The second hymn we should like to discuss is that found in 1 Timothy 3:16, which expresses the doctrine of the hypostatic union by means of the enthronement theme. This symbolism, which occurs constantly in the apostolic preaching, was derived from the Psalms. In the Pentecostal speech of Peter, to which we have already referred, it is based upon Psalm 110:1: "An oracle of the Lord to my Lord: 'Sit at my right hand, till I make your enemies your foot-stool.' " In the version of the kerygma attributed to Paul (Ac 13:33), the enthronement motif appears as a borrowing from Psalm 2:7: "Let me tell of the decree of the Lord: He said to me, 'You are my son; today have I begotten you,' " Paul interprets this act of God as fulfilled in the resurrection of Christ. A third psalm, which celebrates the dignity of "the Son of Man," was also employed in this connection: "You have made Him but little lower than God, and you crown Him with glory and honor. You make Him ruler over the works of your hands: you have put all things under His feet" (Ps 8:5-6). Hebrews 2:8-9 uses this idea in a striking description of the God-Man.

Modern commentators incline to the view that the hymn-fragment cited by Paul in Ephesians 5:14 is part of the same liturgical canticle quoted in 1 Timothy 3:16. Accordingly, we shall combine the two passages in our translation.

> Wake up, you sleeper,
> And arise from death,
> And Christ will light you up . . . (Eph 5:14)
> Who was revealed through his humanity,
> was justified by the Spirit,
> was beheld by angels,
> was proclaimed amongst nations,
> was believed in throughout the world,
> was taken up in glory. (1 Tim 3:16)

The three lines which appear in Ephesians are clearly from a hymn used in the baptismal liturgy. In Pauline theology, Baptism is conceived as a rising from the death of sin with the risen Christ (cf. Rom 6:3-14). It is also described in New Testament writings as an illumination, on the analogy of the creation of light (Col 1:12-14; Heb 6:4-6; Jn 9:1-41), as it is in the passage just preceding our citation in Ephesians 5:8. In terms of the divinity of the risen Christ, these verses are of interest since they point up two aspects of His role in Christian salvation: He is the source of the new supernatural life of grace and the source of the specifically Christian illumination, the infused virtue of faith.

One further point connected with this hymn-fragment in Ephesians 5:14 deserves mention here, since it appears to confirm what was said earlier about the Pauline view of liturgical hymns as the "Word of Christ," inspired by the Holy Spirit. I mean the fact that this citation is introduced by the words, "That is why He (or it) says . . ." Who or what is subject of the verb "says"? This has been a point of debate since patristic times: is it God, or Christ, or the Holy Spirit? Does the citation come from a written document or an oral source? Many commentators, following Hippolytus and Origen, have tried to find the passage in the Old Testament. Others following Epiphanius have thought of the apocryphal literature. Clement of Alexandria suggested it was a *logion* of Christ's, while Jerome held that the introductory phrase was equivalent to "The Lord says." Several modern authors as well as several Fathers of the Church suggest that the subject is the Holy Spirit who, according to the pericope found in this same chapter which we have already cited (Eph 5:18-19), inspired the liturgical hymns of the Church. This explanation seems to be the most satisfactory.

The section of the hymn quoted in 1 Timothy 3:16 is an elaborate presentation of the enthronement theme and consists of three pairs of verses arranged antithetically. This triple structure appears to have been modeled upon the threefold rite involved in the coronation of ancient Near Eastern monarchs, as we know it to have been practised in Egypt and in Mesopotamia. The ceremonial consisted of (1) the *elevation* of the new monarch to the divine dignity, (2) his *presentation* to the gods of the national pantheon, and (3) his *enthronement*, or accession to supreme power in the state.

We have another example of this same manner of presenting the revelation of the divinity of Christ in the opening chapter of the Epistle to the Hebrews. There, however, instead of a hymn-form, the author employs a series of Old Testament citations, which aptly illustrate the three steps in Jesus' glorification. I quote the passage in a translation, adapted from the French of Père C. Spicq.

In Hebrews 1:5-6a, Christ is proclaimed Son of God by the Father Himself (Ps 2:7; 2 Sm 7:14 being the citations):

"For to what angel did God ever say, 'You are my Son. I have today become your Father'?—Or again, 'I will become His Father, and He shall become my Son'?"

The second step consists in the Father's presentation of Christ to the angels (who here, as in the Old Testament, replace the pantheon of ancient mythologies) for their adoration and submission. This is described in Hebrews 1:6-7 by means of citations from Psalm 97:7 and Psalm 104:4:

"Again, when He brings His firstborn Son into the world, He says, 'And let all God's angels bow before Him'. In speaking of the angels He says, 'He who makes His messengers spirits and His ministers a flame of fire.'"

The enthronement of the Son is presented by means of citations from Psalm 45:7-8 and Psalm 102:26-28 (Heb 1:8-12), a final contrast with the angels being added from Psalm 110:1:

"But of the Son He says, 'Your throne, O God, is forever and ever,' and 'The sceptre of justice is the sceptre of His royalty. You have loved right and hated wrong-doing. That is why He has anointed You, O God, with the oil of gladness in preference to Your associates.' And, 'You, Lord, in the beginning founded the earth, and the sky is the work of Your hands. They will perish, but You continue. And they will all wear out like a coat, and You will fold them up like a mantle, and change them as one changes his coat. As for You, You remain the same, Your years will have no end.' But to what angel did He ever say, 'Sit at my right hand, until I make your enemies a footstool for your feet?' "

In our hymn, Jesus' "elevation" is depicted in function of His death and Resurrection:

> "Who was revealed through His humanity,
> was justified by the Spirit."

Through the mediation of His sacred humanity, Jesus' divinity has been revealed to men particularly in the Passion and His death on the Cross. The Gospels, in varying degrees, insist on this truth. Thus for Mark, whose theme is the Mystery of Jesus, the final revelation comes through Jesus' death, as he indicates to the reader through the exclamation of the centurion, "It is clear this man was God's Son" (Mk 15:40). In the Fourth Gospel, Jesus' exaltation begins with His "elevation" on the Cross: the Passion reveals that "glory" of Jesus, a term which, by analogy with the Old Testament *kabod Yahweh*, means the revelation of His divinity. It was in His Resurrection that Jesus was "justified by the Spirit." The phrase may seem strange, until we recall Jesus' remark in the Fourth Gospel that the Paraclete is to convince the world "of justice, namely that I am returning to the Father" (Jn 16:10). In other words, His justification by the Spirit involves His return to God.

In the second pair of verses, we have Christ's presentation in heaven to the angels, on earth to all men throughout the world by the apostolic preaching:

> "was beheld by angels,
> was proclaimed amongst nations."

In terms of the salvation history, it is the events connected with Pentecost which appear to be commemorated here, namely, Christ's *sessio ad dexteram Patris*, contemplated by the angels and His proclamation by the apostles to "men of every nation under heaven" (Ac 2:5).

Finally, Christ's enthronement, that is to say, the revelation of His divinity, is the subject of the last pair of lines:

> "was believed in throughout the world,
> was taken up in glory."

This revelation is described first in terms of the universal acceptance of the Christian faith by Gentiles as well as by Jews, and then in terms of His glorious entry into heaven. This event terminates the first phase of Christian salvation history and looks forward to Christ's glorious second Coming at the parousia. It also inaugurates the time of salvation through the Church, guardian of divine truth, to whom the revelation of Christ's divinity was committed as a precious heritage.

. . . This hymn expresses the Christian mystery, "the mystery of religion" as the introductory line calls it, in a form probably professed in the early Hellenistic Christian communities. It has not the Palestinian flavor of the hymn in Philippians 2:5-11 with its Hebraic theology of "the Name." Its universalist references to the Gospel's proclamation "among nations" and to the spread of Christian faith "throughout the world," as well as its non-biblical portrayal of Christ's enthronement are precious indications of the way that the "new wine" of the belief in Christ's divinity was bursting the "old wineskins" of Jewish thought-forms in the Greek-speaking centers of the apostolic age.

In these two hymns, then, we have a monument to the most ancient Christian faith, expressed with admirable precision and striking theological acumen, dating very probably from the middle of the first century of our era. Indeed, when we consider that Philippians was likely written by Paul in the mid-fifties and when we realize he is citing a hymn already familiar to that Church, I venture to suggest that the passage in Philippians 2:5-11 may well have been composed in Palestine or Syrian Antioch in the early forties. The hymn in 1 Timothy is probably somewhat later, since it seems to have originated in some Gentile Christian community (could it be Ephesus, whither Paul addresses this note to Timothy?) and presupposes that the Church is rapidly becoming, if it has not already become, predominantly non-Jewish in membership and outlook.

It is hardly necessary, I believe, to point out . . . the superlative value of this most ancient testimony to the divinity of Christ. . . .

And in this connection also, I believe that the liturgical character of these hymns can be utilized to give the American Catholic . . . in the twentieth century a deeper sense of solidarity with his Christian brothers in the faith two thousand years ago. Removed from him by their language, their civilization, by the very newness of a faith which seems so ancient to him, they are nonetheless united to him most closely in the worship of Jesus Christ, God's only Son, by the efficacious breath of that Holy Spirit who inspires Him, as He once inspired them, to express "the Word of Christ" in the liturgy of Baptism and of the Holy Eucharist.

References

[1] Balthasar Fischer, "Le Christ dans les psaumes," *La Maison-Dieu*, n. 27 (1951), 88.

[2] H. Leclercq, *art.* "Hymnes," *Dictionnaire d'archéologie chétienne et de liturgie*, Vol. 12, cols. 2826-2928.

[3] L. Cerfaux, *Le Christ dans la théologie de saint Paul* (Paris, 1951), pp. 283-98.

[4] D. M. Stanley, "The Theme of the Servant of Yahweh in Primitive Christian Soteriology, and its Transposition by St. Paul," *CBQ*, 16 (1954), 412ff.

[5] Cf. Cerfaux, *op. cit.*, 289f.

BARNABAS M. AHERN, C.P.

The New Testament Idea of the Church

The observant reader will find in this profound article a discussion of questions such as these: What agreement is there between Catholic and non-Catholic scholars on the roots of the Church in the New Testament? Did the apostles see any need for a break with Judaism immediately after Pentecost? Did they see themselves as distinctive from the Jews in any way? Who were the Hellenist Christians and what was their contribution to the development of the Church? How can Paul's disagreement with St. Peter be explained? Was Paul loyal to tradition? Was his creativity and originality legitimate? How does Paul bear witness to the sacramental life of the early Church? What is meant by the realism of Paul's teaching on the body of Christ? Is Paul an effective witness to the element of authority in the primitive Church? How does Paul compare with other New Testament authors as a witness to the nature of the Church? How is the Church, as described in the New Testament, related to the plan and intention of Jesus?

Father Ahern of the Passionist Fathers teaches Sacred Scripture at the Passionist Seminary in Louisville, Kentucky. He is a distinguished expert and consultant to the American Bishops at the Second Vatican Council and the author of *New Horizons: Studies in Biblical Theology*.

Biblical scholars today are coming to see that the Church has deep roots in the soil of the New Testament. To many this may seem like the discovery of a truism. It is rather a significant advance on the fire-tried level of scholarship.

Originally entitled "The Concept of the Church in Biblical Thought," this article was first published in the *Proceedings of the Society of Catholic College Teachers of Sacred Doctrine Seventh Annual Convention*. It is reproduced here with permission.

It was a previous fashion in some circles to treat the Church as a foundling fathered by an ingenious primitive community and laid on the doorstep of an unsuspecting Christ. For Adolph Harnack the Gospel was set four-square within the highly personal framework of God the Father, His Providence, man's sonship, and the infinite worth of the human soul. There was little room even for Christ in a Gospel like that—much less for the Church. For Albert Schweitzer Jesus' message centered in the imminent breakthrough of the heavenly kingdom by a divine coup d'état. So, too, most other liberal scholars in the first quarter of the present century found it difficult to ascribe to Jesus of Galilee any idea of founding a church.

Today, however, a change is notable. . . . This is due in great part to the influence of the German Form-Criticism school. Scholars like Rudolph Bultmann and Martin Dibelius have so emphasized the creative power of the primitive community that unwittingly they have made it difficult to accept their parallel thesis on the Church's spontaneous origin. An *anonymous* source for such a dynamic group as the early Christian community constitutes a vexing problem.

The disciples of Bultmann, therefore, are coming to see why their master has always shown signs of embarrassment when asked to explain the community itself. The primitive Church is a total anomaly unless one accepts its pristine claim to intimate dependence on the person and ministry of Jesus. It is not surprising, then, that . . . recent [trends] . . . show the pendulum swinging back to center.

This return is inevitable. The Church looms so large and clear in the apostolic writings that it provides its own best proof of foundations which are solid and deep.[1] . . . This is the confidence which our Catholics today must possess. They must share in the conviction that the image of the Church is so clear and consistent in the apostolic writings that this very image offers perennial proof of deep roots in the earthly life of Jesus.

A Caution

This does not mean that we are to search the Scripture for anachronisms. The Church is not monolithic; it is living. It has grown from a seedling to a world-wide organization, with a viability which requires adjustment to changing times and places. In the beginning it was a family where everyone knew everyone else, where Peter was a brother among brothers, and where those who had lived with Jesus and spoken with the risen Lord enjoyed prestige and authority everywhere. To seek identity between our local bishops and the *episcopoi* of Acts is to seek an anachronism. To look for what is *Roman* in Peter and to try to square Pope John XXIII with the lean fisherman of Galilee—this is like trying to fit the Roman office of the Passionist Generalate into the little hut where St. Paul of the Cross founded the Congregation in the eighteenth century.

It is not our purpose to search the apostolic writings for anachronisms which we shall never find there. What we are looking for are the basic elements of the Church's organization, the rationale of its disciplinary activity, and the richly eminent source of its divine life and teaching.

The Messianic Community of Pentecost

Let us start at the beginning. Something happened at Pentecost —just as something happened at Sinai—to bring a new people into being. Looking back years later St. Luke illumines the full significance of the event by developing in a highly literary form all the involvements of the coming of the Spirit. His midrashic description of the "tongues of fire," his rich use of the Old Testament prophecies in the Petrine discourse—all this emphasized the truth that on Pentecost itself the followers of Jesus knew clearly that they had received from Him God's own Spirit. The risen Savior, therefore, was truly the messianic Son of God (cf. Ac 13:33) and they His messianic community.

This faith of Pentecost needs no proof. Though the opening chapters of Acts owe much to the insights of Luke and to his power of evoking impressions through a literary use of rabbinical and scriptural themes, this section shows also a consistent fidelity to the spirit and contents of its source material. Whatever may have been the penetrating power of his own developed theology Luke often presents the thoughts of Peter and Stephen just as they thought them in that first burst of Pentecostal light.

There is a tell-tale tang of primitive Christian thinking in Peter's words when, with full conviction, he announced the ringing challenge: "Let all the house of Israel know most assuredly that God *has made* both Lord and Christ, this Jesus whom you crucified" (Ac 2:36). Later Pauline theology with its more careful precision would give an adoptionist color to this formulary. St. Luke, however, lets it stand. This same spirit of originality flavors St. Stephen's discourse in Acts 7. For this witness to the faith, the *risen* Christ is everything while His Passion and death are crucial problems calling for apology.[2] The substance of the sermon, therefore, comes from the first days of Christianity, from a level which was not yet enlightened by Paul's profound insight into the real efficacy of Christ's death.

One truth especially emerges from these first pages of Acts. The followers of Jesus believed that the "last days" promised by the prophets had come. He whom they had seen risen from the dead had Himself given them the Spirit of God. He, therefore, was the Messiah, and they were the messianic community.

Their life flowed along smoothly in the channels of Jewry because they looked on themselves as its perfect fulfillment. They felt no sharp cleavage with their own people, since they were simply enjoying the privileges planned for all in Israel who would believe. When after the Resurrection they chose Matthias to fill out the number of the twelve apostles, they had in mind that judgment over the twelve tribes which the "last days" would bring. Now that this time had come they recognized themselves as the perfect Israel (Ac 3:24ff). Their sense of having arrived filled these first days with halcyon peace and overflowing joy which left a deep impression on their fellow Jews (Ac 2:46-47).

Their belief that Jesus had risen from the dead as the messianic Son of God was bound to bring clashes especially with the Saducees (Ac 4:1-22; 5-17ff.). Jesus as dead Messiah, however, did not create the same problem as Jesus the living reformer. Whatever tensions existed were not sufficient to cause a full rift; conflicts could be smoothed over in the same way in which Pharisees and Saducees agreed to disagree over resurrection and life after death and the number of inspired books. We can speak, therefore, of a true continuity between Jewry and the primitive community. Just as Jesus had found place in the life of His people, so the followers of Jesus sensed no compelling reason in the Pentecostal experience to break with their background. They had simply entered upon the age for which Israel had always yearned.

The Particularism of the Messianic Community

There was, however, something dynamically new among Jesus' followers. Their prestige was the appeal of vital youth. All around them was the shadow of aging hope; they, however, possessed the glorious substance of hope and the newness of life which only the Messiah could give. Jewry was powerless with the weakness of flesh; the community was strong with the vigor of the Spirit. Many elements of their life, therefore, made them different from their fellow Jews.

First of all, their preaching (the kerygma) set them apart. Their one message to all men was the startling truth that the crucified Jesus had risen from the dead and had bestowed the messianic gift par excellence, the Holy Spirit (cf. Ac 2:29-36; 3:12-16). This made Him truly Messiah and Lord, the only source of salvation for all men (cf. Ac 4:8-12; 5:29-32). For those who accepted this truth there was always further instruction drawn not from Jewry but from Jesus. This was known as the "teaching (didache) of the apostles" (Ac 2:42).[3]

This brings to light a second distinctive characteristic of the new community. It was no longer the doctors of the Law or the Jewish leaders who taught and directed this group but rather the followers of Jesus who were in a special way the qualified "witnesses of His Resurrection" (Ac 1:22; 5:32). The Twelve were now the acknowledged leaders, the chosen chiefs who spoke for the community and suffered for it and proclaimed intransigently all that it stood for.

The distinctiveness of the community was emphasized by a third special mark, its rite of initiation and its central mystery, "the breaking of bread." Even a circumcised Jew could not belong to this new group unless he professed faith in Jesus as the messianic Son of God and accepted the baptism which resembled the rite of heathen admission into the fold of Israel (Ac 2:38). Continuance in the community meant frequent sacramental contact with the Messiah Lord through the "bread" which He had provided. This was the one mystery which the community kept for itself as its special treasure and as the foretaste of the Lord's imminent return (the parousia). For though the followers of Christ prayed in the temple, they "broke bread" in their own homes (Ac 2:42,46). While awaiting the glorious return of the Messiah Lord they found strength and joy in the Bread which was Himself. This was what held them together; sharing in the Body of Christ they became themselves that Body which is the Church (cf. 1 Cor 10:16-17).

For the primitive community Christ was all in all. The belief of all centered in Him (cf. Rom 10:9-10); their leaders were men chosen by Him; their very worship meant a sharing in the mystery of His Body and Blood. Now they awaited anxiously the days of refreshment, the parousia, when their judge and king would return to them in glory that they might rejoice with Him forever (Ac 3:20). How much they had yet to learn of God's plan.

Universalism and Missionary Apostolate

The next move was precipitated by the Hellenist Christians. As Oscar Cullmann[4] has shown, these Greek-speaking Jews had always irritated the homelanders by their disdain for the physical elements of Israel's worship. Living in the Diaspora they had found God away from the temple and had worshiped Him with a spiritual devotedness which spurned the smell of blood and burning flesh. In coming to know Jesus these Hellenists found the way of spiritual worship wide open to them in the "Temple not made by hands." When Stephen the Hellenist, therefore, spoke of Jesus, his hearers had ears only for that irritating sentence which echoed the old anti-Temple polemic: "Solomon built Him a house; yet not in houses made by hands does the Most High dwell" (Ac 7:47-48).

That sentence was the signal for persecution. If the Jews could tolerate within their own fold men who followed Jesus as the Messiah, they could not stomach fellow Jews who cast aspersion on the most sacred element of Jewish worship. And so "a great persecution broke out on that day against the Church in Jerusalem" (Ac 8:1). Yet not against all the Church. Prosecution left the Galilean apostles untouched. Only Stephen the Hellenist was martyred, and only the Hellenist Christians were driven from their Jerusalem home.

This was a stroke of Providence. By it the Church was forced to seek a home on earth outside of Jewry. The messianic community was to become in fact what it was in nature—the community of the world.

Philip the Hellenist went to Samaria and preached Christ there (Ac 8:4-6). It was a likely place of refuge, for the Samaritans shared the Hellenist opposition to the Jerusalem Temple (Jn 4:20). Other Hellenist Jews went to Antioch where for the first time they extended their apostolate to full-blooded Greeks (Ac 11:19-20). This new move away from Jewry served to emphasize the stress which had been present from the beginning. Christ was all in all for the new community: "They preached the Lord Jesus" (Ac 11:20). People sensed the emphasis. They took from it their cue in giving a name to this new group which had arisen in their midst. If Jesus were the Christ, the Messiah, they were Christians, the messianic community: "It was in Antioch that the disciples were first called 'Christians'" (Ac 11:26).

Word, Sacrament, Authority in the Community

The Church of Christ was expanding. For "Church of Christ" it truly was. Israel of old was called the *Qahal* (LXX—*ekklesia*) because it was the assembly of God's chosen people.[5] For the same reason the new Israel was also the Church of God (*ekklesia tou theou*) and even more the Church of Christ, for He was its very life.[6]

As it expanded this Church remained true to itself, taking direction from its leaders, drawing life from its word and sacrament. The story of Philip in Samaria is typical. "He went down to the city of Samaria and preached the Christ to them" (Ac 8:5) . . . . "And when they believed Philip as he preached the kingdom of God and the name of Jesus Christ, they were baptized, both men and women" (Ac 8:12). The preaching of the word and the acceptance of the sacrament are both essential in the life of the new community.

Quite as important, however, is the seal of approval from the only ones who could give approval and a full share in the riches of the community's life: "Now when the apostles in Jerusalem heard that Samaria had received the word of God, they sent to them Peter and John. . . . Then they laid their hands on them and they received the Holy Spirit" (Ac 8:14,17).

It is noteworthy how large Peter looms in this whole picture of expanding Christianity as Luke presents it in Acts. He seems to move always in first place as spokesman and representative of the community (Ac 1:15ff.; 2:14-36; 3:1-11; 4:8ff.; 5:3-11; and so forth). There is, however, no blatant note in his claim to authority. He lives and works in a family where everyone knows and loves everyone else. In such surroundings he could fulfill perfectly the behest of Jesus that he who is first should be as he who serves: "Now when the apostles in Jerusalem heard that Samaria had received the word of God, *they sent* to them *Peter* and John" (Ac 8:14).

Paul as Witness to the Church

One Jew was clear-sighted enough to see what it all meant. The new Israel threatened the old; the Christ-Lord of Christianity introduced a raucous note into the *Shema*' faith of Jewry. The soul of Paul, therefore, seethed with the bitterness of Voltaire; *Ecrasez l'infame* became the burning passion of his life. He would stamp out this blasphemy; if need be, he would drown it in the blood of his fellow Jews.

All this, however, was only the darkness before dawn. On the way to Damascus sunlight burst upon him in a blaze of glory and he heard the stunning words, "Saul, Saul, why dost thou persecute me?" (Ac 9:4). In the twinkling of an eye Paul the hater of Christ became a Christian. The persecutor of the Church became its theologian.

Scholars like Lucien Cerfaux . . . have written long, penetrating analyses of his doctrine on the Church. It would be endless to rehearse their meticulous erudition. We desire instead to center attention on Paul's contribution not as a theologian but as a *witness.* When he entered the Church, it was already in existence and fully self-conscious. In his epistles, therefore, we touch the flesh and blood Church of the first generation Christians. These earliest writings of the apostolic period bear glowing testimony to the life of the Church just as Paul found it, just as he knew it must remain.[7]

Paul, Witness to the Unchanging Word

There is no doubt that this man was a rugged individualist, the keen-sighted theologian of the early Church. In his Epistles to the Galatians he is at his unique best, boasting flagrantly that his are the penetrating insights and the God-given message of liberty. The other apostles seem merely to plod along in a pedestrian way: "What they once were matters not to me—God accepts not the person of man" (Gal 2:6). Indeed, "When Cephas came to Antioch, I withstood him to his face, because he was deserving of blame" (Gal

2:11). Restricting their view to texts like these, Baur and Strauss created the image of a Paul who opposes his Gospel to the limited teaching of Peter and the Jewish element in the early Church.

Long ago, however, the Tübingen view of Paul has been discounted as myopic. It was based on Galatians and overlooked the other epistles. And even in Galatians it read only Chap. 2 and conveniently forgot that there was also Chap. 1.

There is no doubt that Paul was always conscious of his God-given authority; he is "an apostle sent not from men nor by man but by Jesus Christ and God the Father" (Gal 1:1). This confidence rings in the salutation of all his letters. In making this claim, however, Paul has only one purpose—to validate his right to preach the Gospel of Christ.

He considered it his first duty to deliver to others the kerygma which had been in the Church from the beginning. Like all the apostles he presented everywhere the saving truths which Matthew had jotted down in Aramaic as an official record of Peter's preaching in Jerusalem (cf. 2 Tim 2:8). Paul could say to all his converts what he wrote to the Corinthians, "I delivered to you first of all what I myself *received*" (1 Cor 15:3).

He knew well that every preacher would try to present the Church's teaching in the most attractive and compelling way he could. Paul himself theologized to his heart's content. He used the juridical and cultic thought patterns of Jewry; he gave full rein to his knowledge of Stoic diatribe and utilized its antitheses in presenting the Christian message. He insisted, however, that these elucidations were valid only insofar as they presented the authentic Christian message. The preacher might build with gold, silver, precious stones, wood, hay, straw; but the essential factor consisted always in the foundation of the Church's saving message (cf. 1 Cor 3:11-12).

This teaching of the Church must be safeguarded at any cost. When men showed too much concern with the bric-a-brac of human philosophizing Paul went out of his way to center attention on the fundamental teaching itself. The Corinthians loved a display of "wisdom"; they listened delightfully to the brilliant phrases of Apollo and to his finely spun Alexandrian allegories. Paul sensed danger. Men might come to prefer the tangible beauty of human words to the ineffable power of God's deeds. Paul, therefore, deliberately avoided the brilliance of "wisdom" to present the simple truths which Peter and James and John had recounted on the morrow of Pentecost: "And I, brethren, when I came to you, did not come with pretentious speech or wisdom, announcing unto you the witness of Christ. For I determined not to know anything among you, except Jesus Christ and Him crucified" (1 Cor 2:1-2).

In every epistle Paul shows his reliance on the traditional teaching which is everywhere the same.[8] Writing to people like the Romans and Colossians whom he has never seen the apostle takes it for granted that they are thoroughly familiar with the truths which he himself is preaching. How often he bases his own doctrinal developments on this presumed knowledge: "Do you not know?" "Have you not heard?" "Do you not remember?" Writing to the Romans Paul takes it for granted that their primitive credal formulary (Rom 1:3-4) contains the same faith which he himself would express with greater theological exactness (cf. Rom 9:5; Phil 2:5-11). Writing to the Colossians who had been evangelized not by himself but by Epaphras, he simply presumes that they know the Church teaching from which he himself draws the contents of his instructions (cf. Col 1:5-7; 2:6-7).

This reliance on the traditional teaching made Paul suspicious of new customs (cf. 1 Cor 11:16) and intransigently hostile to distortions of the primitive Gospel. He was speaking of false teachers when he wrote: "If anyone destroys the temple of God, him will God destroy; for holy is the temple of God, and this temple you are" (1 Cor 3:17).

This witness to the unchanging teaching of the Church is the first factor one must reckon with if he wishes to share Paul's mind on the Church. He who is looked upon as the most creative of the apostles, the artisan of Christian theology, places his chief glory in being "approved by God to be entrusted with the Gospel" (1 Thes 2:4). In the traditional teaching which is always and everywhere the same Paul sees a dynamic power to save (Rom 1:16-17). Through the Church message the risen Christ was able to enter the heart of every man to save and to sanctify.

Paul therefore could write to the Thessalonians in the first letter of his long correspondence: "We give thanks to God without ceasing, because when you heard and received from us the word of God, you welcomed it not as the word of men but, as it truly is, the word of God, who works in you who believed" (1 Thes 2:13). So long as the message was presented accurately and integrally Christ could do His work. When, therefore, the imprisoned Paul learned that others were busy preaching the Gospel in order to curry favor with the new converts, he cried out, "What of it? Provided only that in every way, whether for sincere or insincere motives, Christ is being proclaimed; in this I rejoice, yes, and I shall rejoice" (Phil 1:18).

His mind is crystal clear. Christian life comes from a Gospel message which is fixed and credal and dynamically powerful. For Paul faith is not the fideism of blind surrender to an unknown God as it would be in the systems of Rudolph Bultmann and Paul Tillich. Paul's faith instead is dependent on the spoken word and reaches God truly through surrender to its conceptual element. For the Gospel is a mirror held up to the heart of God that it may reflect His thoughts into the heart of man (cf. 2 Cor 3:18). As an apostle, therefore, Paul considered it his prime duty to witness and to transmit, not to create: "Let a man so account us, as servants of Christ and stewards of the mysteries of God. Now here it is required in stewards that a man be found trustworthy" (1 Cor 4:1-2).

Paul, Witness to Sacramental Life

The apostle's concept of sacramentality is a second factor which one must keep in mind in order to share his understanding of the Church. Scholars of the Lausanne school have suggested that for Paul salvation consisted in a mere psychological assent to the salvific deed of Calvary proclaimed by the Gospel. In that event God's intervention at Calvary would have no greater efficacy than His divine intervention on Sinai; and once more man would be left to himself and to his own devices.

Paul's teaching, on the other hand, presupposes that the believer is really and effectively united to the risen Christ as body-person to body-person (*soma* to *soma*) in the sacramental rites of baptism and the Eucharist. For Paul, Christ did not speak in a metaphor when, on the way to Damascus, he complained, "Saul, Saul, why are you persecuting *me*?" [9]

The first time that Paul clearly asserts the realism of sacramental life in the Church is when he chooses to challenge an ugly problem on the level of its own realism. Christians of Corinth had fallen back into fornication, into commingling of body with body not merely as a physical experience but as a full personal interchange of thought and affection. Paul opposes the sin by appealing to another bond which the Christian has already contracted, the well-known bond between his person and the person of the glorified Christ which is as real as the union between a man and a harlot: "Do you not know that your bodies are members of Christ? Shall I then take the members of Christ and make them members of a harlot?" (1 Cor 6:15).

In both cases the full person is involved in a real way. For Paul the Hebrew, the word "body" does not have the same meaning as in our twentieth-century Western vocabulary.[10] Instead of denoting the physical part of the body-soul composite (as with us), the word "body" in Paul's vocabulary signifies the whole reality of man as an animated and personalized body living a fully human life. When, therefore, he speaks of the Christian's union with Christ his thought is very realistic. He sees all Christians as completing and extending one and the same person and life, Christ Himself.

This first allusion to the Body of Christ is incidental, the emergent of a given context. Yet it has a validity all its own because it expresses so aptly the realism of the Christian's union with Christ as Paul sees it and as he, or his disciple, will express it later in the consummate synthesis of his thought in Ephesians 5:25-32 where he likens the union of Christ and His Church to the bond between a devoted husband and wife. No union could be more intimate, because no dependence could be more complete.[11] All that the Christian has as a Christian he receives in the total surrender of his body-person to the body-person of Christ: "You are in Christ Jesus, who has become for us God-given wisdom, and justice, and sanctification, and redemption" (1 Cor 1:30-31).

This union begins at baptism, as Paul indicates in Galatians 3:27-28. Though shifting his thought pattern he maintains the dynamic realism of the Christian experience: "All you who have been baptized into Christ have put on Christ." The analogy is drawn from the action of putting on a garment; but, as G. Duncan points out, "In Scripture it denotes that the wearer becomes in a subtle way identified with what he puts on."[12] The present text shows how intimate is the identification it evokes. For Paul goes on to affirm that in the psycho-somatic rite of baptism the body-person (*soma*) of the Christian is so totally surrendered to Christ that whatever is merely "flesh" disappears, so that "There is neither Jew nor Greek; there is neither slave nor freeman; there is neither male nor female. For you are all one person (masculine) in Christ Jesus."

Paul therefore teaches clearly that Christian life involves a real and personal union between the individual Christian and the glorified Christ,[13] a union in which the Christian depends so completely upon Christ that He alone functions as the directive spiritual force: "He who cleaves to the Lord is one spirit with Him" (1 Cor 6:17).

This same realism prevails when Paul comes to speak of Christians as a collectivity in his discussion of the Eucharist. Once more the point of departure for his memorable statement is a particular problem, the danger of syncretism arising from sharing in the banquets of pagan worship. The apostle declares that such conduct is incompatible with the celebration of the Christian supper which joins the Christian to Christ: "The bread that we break, is it not the partaking of the Body of the Lord?" (1 Cor 10:16).

As proof of the real presence of Christ in the Eucharist, Paul appeals to a fact which carried a barbed thrust to the disunited Corinthians. He recalls the truth which was recognized from the beginning: the remarkable fellowship (*koinonia*) of Christians with one another has its total cause in the fellowship (*koinonia*) of each individual with Christ in the breaking of the bread: "Because the bread is one, we though many are one body, we who partake of the one bread" (1 Cor 10:17). In this text the "one body" is still the individual body-person of the risen Christ. The many are one body because the "one bread" makes each one concorporeal with Christ.

In the realism of Paul's thought, both baptism and the Eucharist enable Christ to become "all in all," the one source and only center of Christian life. Dr. Rawlinson, therefore, is on firm ground when he emphasizes the importance of the Eucharist as a prime element in shaping Paul's doctrine on the Church as the body of Christ.[14]

For Paul, then, the Church was not merely a society founded by Christ to endure forever as the best way of saving men. It was far more the enduring sacrament of Christ's abiding presence among men, the real and permanent means He has chosen to fulfill His promise, "Behold, I am with you all days, even unto the consummation of the world" (Mt 28:20).

The apostle constantly witnesses to this reality and permanence of Christ's presence in and through the Church. He likens the Church to a temple where God dwells and where His son gives Him ceaseless praise (1 Cor 3:16-17; 2 Cor 6:16). He affirms that Christ cherishes the Church just as a devoted husband loves and cherishes his wife (Eph 5:28-32). He is most expressive, however, when he speaks of the Church as the "body of Christ" (1 Cor 12:12-27; Rom 12:4-5; Col 1:24; 2:19; and so forth).

For Paul, Christ is "all in all." Whether he speaks of the individual Christian, the local congregation, or the whole Church, Paul sees all as belonging to the body of Christ, as completing and extending the person and life of the risen Christ Himself. For the Savior living gloriously in heaven is Himself the Body-Person, the one central figure with whom all Christians are intimately united and on whom they totally depend.[15] In Paul's classic phrase they are "in Christ Jesus,"—precisely because He is in them, as the total source of all spiritual life in the Church. "Here (in the Church) is no more Gentile and Jew, no more circumcised and uncircumcised; no one is barbarian, or Scythian, no one is slave or freeman; there is nothing but Christ in any of us" (Col 3:11).

Paul, Witness to Authority in the Church

The apostle's doctrine on the Church as the body of Christ gives special force to his teaching on authority. It is difficult to understand why Anders Nygren has spoken only of Paul's doctrine on the word and on the sacrament in his excellent monograph, *Christ and His Church.* The truth is that from the very beginning of his epistolary correspondence Paul shows a vital awareness of the function of authority in the Church.

He glories in his apostleship and boasts of his power because he knows well that the apostle is a *shaliah*—one sent by Christ with the fullness of His authority: "On behalf of Christ, therefore, we are acting as ambassadors, God, as it were, making appeal through us" (2 Cor 5:20). This consciousness of bearing the authority of Christ was with Paul always and everywhere. He acted with complete liberty and aplomb whether he enjoined commands on those who were present or leveled threats against those who were absent. This confidence never failed him for he looked on himself always as the representative of Christ: "I have already warned, when present, and now in my absence I warn again those who sinned before, and all the rest, that, if I come again, I will not spare. Do you seek a proof of the Christ who speaks in me, who is not weak in your regard, nay, is powerful in you? . . . We also shall live with Him through the power of God in your regard" (2 Cor 13:2-4).

Paul recognized this same authority in other leaders of the Church. For it is clear in his epistles that others ruled the local churches during the absence of their father and founder. As in Judaism itself, elders (*presbyteroi*) were chosen to direct the conduct of the community. Besides this group—and probably selected from among them—certain administrators (*episcopoi*) were empowered to watch over the needs of the community and to preside at its liturgical assemblies. From the very beginning Paul enjoined obedience to these men of authority (1 Thes 5:12-13). The fact that they discharged their duties in the Church, the body of Christ, made the exercise of their authority a function of Christ Himself (cf. 1 Cor 12:27-28; Rom 12:4,8).

As time went on, Paul would share more and more of his own power with subaltern officers, men like Titus and Timothy. What belonged to the apostles eminently, the unique power of theirs which shaded all lesser authority, became more and more the possession of the local overseers. Yet even in the period of the Pastoral Epistles the local authorities had not yet received the full power of the monarchical Bishop in St. Ignatius' letters. This would become necessary only when death brought an end to Paul's over-all regency.

There is also, of course, the crucial question of Peter's authority. What did Paul think of it? He has never answered this question, simply because he writes out of a living tradition where Peter's role was taken for granted. His casual remarks, however, shed an aura of light about Peter as someone special in the ruling body of the Church.

After his conversion Paul paid a courtesy visit to Jerusalem—to see Peter (Gal 1:18). Later in his apostolate at Antioch he was greatly disturbed when Cephas, of all people, placed a principle in jeopardy by discrimination against the Gentiles (Gal 2:11-14). At Corinth Paul has to accept the fact that one of the dissenting groups centered its loyalty on Peter, as though he had as much right to that loyalty as Paul and Apollo, the founders of the Corinthian church (1 Cor 1:12). For Paul, as for the others, Peter stands in a category of his own: "Have we not the right to take about with us a woman, as do the other apostles, and the brethren of the Lord, and Cephas?" (1 Cor 9:15; cf. 15:5).

Paul's letters, therefore, reflect authentically what the rest of the

Church thought about Peter. If he has left no formal proof of Peter's authority, it is because . . . this truth was a universally accepted part of the Church's life.

Witness of Other Apostolic Writings

This long discussion of Paul's witness to the existence and nature of the Church finds its warrant in the uniqueness of his testimony. First, his epistles stand as the earliest extant record of everyday life in the Christian community (between 50 and 67 A.D.). Second, they come from a man who first knew Christianity as an unbeliever and a persecutor and who forfeited many privileges to accept its claim (cf. Phil 3:3-8). Third, the Church life he describes was being lived in persecuted communities who, like Paul himself, would have had everything to gain by reverting to earlier religious loyalties. Fourth, Paul's value as a witness is all the more significant since it is so easy to distinguish it from his role as an original and creative thinker. His testimony, therefore, is not only a faithful transcript of life and practice in the Church but also a guarantee of its historical claim. A man of Paul's character and background would have been the last one in the world to "create" Christianity.

Other apostolic writings come from a later period; but their witness to the constituent elements of Church life matches the pattern of Paul's testimony. The Johannine writings, for instance, though coming from the traditions of Asia Minor, are in perfect agreement with Paul's portrait of the Church. In them we find the same tenacious emphasis on the unchanging word (1 Jn 1:3; 2:27; 2 Jn 8-11) and on the true authority of those who watch over the Church: "He who knows God listens to us; he who is not of God does not listen to us" (1 Jn 4:6). The whole Johannine Gospel is a witness to the sacramental sources of the Church's life.

Another independent witness may be found in the Greek Gospel of Matthew. Coming from the latter part of the first century this Gospel presents a delineation of the Church as its distinctive cachet. It emphasizes the role and authority of the Petrine office even at a time when Peter was himself already dead (Mt 16:17-20), the power of the Church leaders (Mt 18:15-18), the presence of Christ in the liturgical assembly (Mt 18:19-20), the unchanging firmness of the Church's word (Mt 7:24-27). Moreover, "by transposing a saying of Jesus regarding the Mystery of the Kingdom (cf. Mk 4:11), Matthew shows his awareness that the Church in his day already possessed a body of doctrines that had been entrusted to the apostolic magisterium: 'to you the knowledge of the mysteries of the heavenly Kingdom has been confided' " (13:11).[16]

Relation of the Church to Jesus

Acts, Paul, John, Matthew—all the apostolic writings witness to the Word, the Sacrament, and Authority as constituent elements in the life of the Church. What connection does it all have with the Jesus of history? Some find it difficult to read the thought of the Church back into the mind of Jesus; the really impossible thing is to read it out of His mind. For if the Church did not come from Jesus, we are faced with the anomaly of an effect without a cause.

It is true, all that we know of Jesus comes from the Church of the first century, from writers who already believed in Him as the Risen Savior and the Messianic Son of God. These records and memories, however, come from men who not only believed in Him but had also lived with Him. They were well qualified to judge whether the kerygma of the apostles misrepresented the facts of history. If, therefore, they became members of the Church and accepted its teaching and sacraments and leaders, it is only because they were convinced that the structure of the Church rested four-square on the foundation which the apostles affirmed was of Jesus' own making.[17]

During His lifetime He had presented Himself in the role of Daniel's Son of Man (Dn 7) and of Isaia's Suffering Servant (Is 53). He was, therefore—in the light of this composite picture—a corporate personality, a Son of Man who embodies the "saints of God" (cf. Dn 7:13-14 with Dn 7:25-27), a Suffering Servant who gives His life "for the many" (Is 53:11-12). His death and glorification involved all; His fate would have weighty meaning in the lives of others. In the days of His earthly life, therefore, He took care to provide for the world-family which would come into being through the power of His Resurrection.

If He had not actually made such preparations, the Jews of Jerusalem (who were eyewitnesses of His life) would have been the first to reject the apostles' false claims. They had everything to lose and nothing to gain in accepting a merely fabricated Pentecostal message. This first generation of Jewish Christians, therefore, offers an irrefragable argument for the intimate bond between the Church of Pentecost and the Jesus of history.

It is only His choice and preparation that can explain why these first Christians turned from the learned doctors of the Law whom they had always venerated to accept the religious leadership of ignorant Galilean fishermen whose very background disqualified them from all doctrinal or religious authority.

It is only the teaching of Jesus, illumined and corroborated by His Resurrection, that can explain why men accepted a Word which not only altered the cardinal tenet of the *Shema'* but also cut through the maze of respected rabbinical doctrine to deep underlying principles (*ap arches*) which only the Creator of the Law could lay bare.

It is only the institution of Jesus that can explain why Jews who gloried in circumcision could come to restrict salvation to a rite which resembled the baptism previously required only of heathen converts to Judaism. It is also only an act of Jesus that can explain why these same Jews chose the Christian "breaking of bread" as their true and only Passover celebration.

In His lifetime, therefore, Jesus prepared for the future life of His Church by choosing its leaders, by providing it with Sacraments, and by ministering the word which would form the heart of its teaching. Were this not so, the image of the primitive Church which looms so large and clear in the apostolic writings would remain forever an inexplicable anomaly.

References

[1] D. M. Stanley, S.J., "Kingdom to Church: The Structural Development of Apostolic Christianity in the New Testament," *Theological Studies*, 16 (1955), 1-29.

[2] The first preachers always had to take into account the fact that Jewish religious thought knew nothing of a suffering Messiah. The teaching of Isaia 53 on the Suffering Servant had never been popularly applied to the expected Son of David. This ignorance explains the apologetic tone and color of the early propaganda literature treating of the death of Christ.

[3] D. M. Stanley, S.J., "*Didache* as a Constituitive Element of the Gospel-Form," *Catholic Biblical Quarterly*, 17 (1955), 336-48; cf. B. Reicke, "A Synopsis of Early Christian Preaching," *The Root of the Vine: Essays in Biblical Theology*, ed. A. Fridrichsen (New York, 1953), pp. 128-60.

[4] O. Cullmann, "L'opposition contre le temple de Jérusalem," *New Testament Studies*, 5 (1959), 161-62.

[5] In his critical review of J. Kritzinger's thesis, *Qehal Jahweh* (Kampen,

1957), Roland De Vaux, O.P., *Revue Biblique*, 65 (1958), 133, points out that ethnic membership in Israel was of prime importance in belonging to the *Qahal*.

[6] L. Cerfaux, *The Church in the Theology of St. Paul*, tr. G. Webb and A. Walker (New York, 1959), pp. 95-117.

[7] This fact emerges most clearly in those letters which Paul addresses to Churches which he himself had not founded, for example, Romans and Colossians. In dealing with these communities he counts on the same life and doctrine which prevailed in communities founded by himself.

[8] C. H. Dodd, *Gospel and Law* (New York, 1960), pp. 12-24.

[9] B. M. Ahern, C.P., "The Christian's Union with the Body of Christ in Cor, Gal, and Rom," *Catholic Biblical Quarterly*, 23 (1961), 199-209.

[10] J. A. T. Robinson, *The Body: A Study in Pauline Theology* (Chicago, 1952).

[11] With a Semite's love for metonymy, Paul uses the hardy figures of "growing together" (Rom 6:5), "being clothed" (Gal 3:27)—figures which might trap a non-Semitic mind into gross imagery which would nullify the apostle's thought. As the Fathers were to express it, the risen Christ and His followers are "concorporeal" because both live by the one life that is in Christ, namely, both are ruled by the one Holy Spirit. Cf. St. Cyril of Alexandria on 1 Corinthians 12:12 (*PG*, 64:888-89): "We are joined to one another and in our whole being are united with Christ (*cum Christo corporati*), for He has brought us together in perfect union through the one Spirit Who is in us all."

[12] *The Epistle of St. Paul to the Galatians* (*Moffatt NTC;* London, 1934), p. 123.

[13] P. Benoit, O.P., "Corps, Tête et Plérôme dans les épîtres de la Captivité," *Revue Biblique*, 63 (1956), 14, calls this "a prime conviction of Paul's faith and of his theology."

[14] "Corpus Christi," *Mysterium Christi*, ed. G. K. Bell and A. Deissmann (Berlin, 1931), pp. 275-96.

[15] A. Wikenhauser, *Pauline Mysticism: Christ in the Mystical Teaching of St. Paul*, tr. J. Cunningham (New York, 1960), pp. 49-108.

[16] D. M. Stanley, *The Gospel of St. Matthew* (*New Testament Reading Guide;* Collegeville, 1960), p. 9.

[17] F. J. McCool, S.J., "The Preacher and the Historical Witness of the Gospels," *Theological Studies*, 21 (1960), 517-43.

BARNABAS M. AHERN, C.P.

Union with Christ After Death

The perceptive reader will find in this encouraging article a discussion of questions like these: What theories of reward and punishment were current among the Jews of Our Lord's time? What are three characteristics of every biblical doctrine of reward and punishment? What is Christ's teaching on the end-time and of the period in between? Why did the end-time dominate Paul's thought? What specifically Christian note do we find in Paul's teaching on death? What are some concrete expressions Paul uses to indicate the effect of union with Christ in death and in life? What was Paul's attitude toward the experience of death? What is the difference between our modern thinking on death as contrasted with the attitude of the early Christians?

Father Ahern, the author of the previous article, teaches Scripture at the Passionist Seminary in Louisville.

Catholic thought today has registered its own emphasis in eschatology. The popular mind centers attention on the definitive judgment which launches the soul at death upon an eternity of joy or of anguish. In this frame of reference the apocalyptic events of the end-time claim little interest. For most people the general judgment is only consequential and secondary, a mere ratification of the preliminary decision which is far more important.

It may come as a surprise, then, to learn that the Christians of New Testament times did not share this outlook. Their preoccupa-

This article was first published in the *Proceedings of the Sixteenth Annual Convention* of the Catholic Theological Society of America. It is reproduced here with permission.

tion centered in the Parousia, in the apocalyptic return of Christ as Judge and Savior. The interest in the final restoration was so dominant that it tended to withdraw attention from the immediate aftermath of death.

Jewish Background of Early Christian Eschatology

This outlook of the early Church was the emergent of its biblical and Jewish background.[1] Christ and the Judaeo-Christian community made their own the eschatology which Hebrew thought had formulated after the long and intricate processes of its development.[2] Even now it is difficult to trace the devious course which led from the early belief in collective and worldly retribution to the post-Exilic hope of other-worldly reward both for the solidarity and for the individual.[3] The course of development was so complex that the Jews never produced a universally accepted eschatology. We cannot speak of a Jewish *dogma* of retribution even in our Lord's own day.[4] The Saducees, with no belief in reward after death, could and did attain to the highest positions in church and state.[5]

The theology of the Pharisees, however, dominated the scene. These respected leaders taught the doctrine of an apocalyptic end-time and the bodily resurrection of the just as it is enunciated in Daniel 12:1-4, 2 Machabees 7:9, 12:44-45, Henoch 91:10, 92:3-5, 102:6-11, 103:1-4, Psalms of Solomon 3:11-16. . . . Christ accepted this doctrine and made it His own, thus giving certainty to the essential features of final retribution. His synthesis of the highest developments in Old Testament revelation stands as a basic assumption in all New Testament thought.

Prime Elements in Biblical Doctrines of Reward

The essential features of the doctrine of Christ and the Pharisees bring to the fore the three elements which remained constant in Hebrew thought on retribution despite the many changes which preceded its final formulation. For in all stages of its development this doctrine shows three characteristics which are inherent in biblical thought. These dominant elements must be kept in mind if we are to understand the teaching and spirit of our early Christian sources.

First of all, every biblical theory of retribution provides for man as an animated and personalized body and not as a dichotomy of body and soul as in the Greek system.[6] Whether in the early concept of reward and punishment on this earth or in the late development of retribution in an after-life, the *whole* man is always involved. Biblical man lives always as an animated body, and so as a body he must be rewarded. No people ever had so keen a sense of man's psycho-somatic unity as did the Semites.

Secondly, every Hebrew theory of retribution looks primarily to the social group.[7] With historical origins in a close-knit tribal society and with divine origin in a covenant between God and the people, Israel never lost sight of the fact that it must live as a people. Even when the individual emerges in the theology of Jeremia and Ezechiel,[8] the devout Israelite finds his fulfillment and mission in the nation's destiny to glorify God as a corporate personality. A markedly personal note characterizes the post-Exilic piety of the *Anawim*; in their prayer, however, they remain always aware of membership in the *Qehal Yahweh*. This corporate ambient is the very context in which they lived. It is the background of their piety and the support of their confidence.

The Bible, therefore, is alien to the subjectivism and atomistic individualism of our age. The hopes of the individual may be fired with the flame of his own personality; their fulfillment always includes the collectivity. Whether retribution is on this earth or in a world to come, whether reward involves the whole nation or only the just, Hebrew thought always centers in the social group.

Thirdly, every theory of retribution always gives first place to God and His glory. In the beginning men were content to die after a blessed long life on earth and to pass into the namelessness of Sheol,[9] happy in the thought that their people would continue to dwell on the land and to glorify God. When this halcyon confidence was shattered by the nation's infidelity, men had to seek another theory of retribution to safeguard God's glory.[10] His honor was one of the motives which drove Israel from one theory to another until at last it reached the perfect eschatological dream which envisioned endless glory for God through endless praise offered by the risen just.

These three themes dominated the retribution thesis of the Pharisees. The end-time would bring full reward in the presence of God to the resurrected nation and to the righteous individual. The nation of the just would thus glorify God forever. This belief rings through the confession of faith uttered before Antiochus by the

Machabee martyrs (2 Mc 7:9-11,14,23,29). It is true, the 2nd Book of Machabees and the Alexandrian Book of Wisdom, coming from a Greek background, emphasize the spiritual joys of final retribution (cf. Wis 2:22-3:19). This emphasis, however, merely stresses what is most important in man's salvation; it does not negate the Hebrew thesis that the *whole* man must share this reward.[11]

Late Hebrew thought knew also that reward and punishment begin in some way immediately after death. The justice of God and the survival of man required this. In the inter-Testamental literature, therefore, Sheol ceased to be merely an abode of the dead, without distinction in reward and punishment. It became instead a provisory stage where the dead anticipate their future lot. One part of this resting place is called Paradise for there the just enjoy felicity; another part, called Gehenna, is a place of punishment for the wicked.[12]

The late development in Jewish eschatology lacks the clearness and certainty of the Pharisee thesis on retribution at the end-time. The Hebrew mind, with its compelling sense of man's unity, found it difficult to conceive of reward and suffering for a disembodied spirit. Whatever is positive in this picture of man's lot during the interim period seems to borrow shape, tone, and color from the picture of the final drama.

Teaching of Christ on the End-Time

Christ made His own the doctrine of the Pharisees on the end-time, sharpening its focus and stabilizing its certainty through His own teaching and that of His apostles. We turn to the Gospels first; though they are among the latest compositions of the early Christian church, they are true to the teaching and emphases of Jesus Himself.

During His earthly life Christ was engaged in building a bridge between the worlds of the Old and New Covenants. It was His task to herald the fulfillment of Old Testament hopes and to manifest Himself as the *auto-basileia,* the full and perfect embodiment of all that God had promised. Men had to see in Him the eminent source of all salvation and the consummation of age-long expectancies.

He made clear enough that His kingdom would enjoy moments of growth and would suffer moments of waning. He was by no means the "eschatologist" created by . . . Schweitzer and Loisy.

At the same time, however, He did look forward to playing a special role in the eschatological consummation. Contrary to the suggestion of C. H. Dodd,[13] Christ did not limit His vision to a "realized eschatology." The fact is that a true eschatological note recurs in the Gospel record of His teaching.[14]

Teaching of Christ on Death and the Interim Period

Christ spoke also of the immediate aftermath of death, making His own the Pharisee doctrine on the interim period. It is to Luke we are indebted for the memory of these words of Jesus. This is significant. Luke the Greek writing for Greeks takes care to record the doctrine which matches their interest in the fate of man when life on earth comes to an end.

To Luke we owe Christ's parable of Dives and Lazarus (16:19-31). Christ speaks here of reward and punishment after death, painting His picture as the Pharisees did with the colors of final retribution, yet scaling down the perspective to accord with the interim period. The picture was a common one; in renewing it and making it His own, Christ confirmed belief in reward and punishment following immediately upon death.

Luke makes a more important contribution in recording Jesus' word to the thief on the cross: "This day thou shalt be with me in Paradise" (23:43).[15] This promise serves as a flange guiding to our own doctrine on the interim period. Jewish thought had focused attention on a place of bliss described in terms of earthly pleasure—the food of life, living water, shade, rest, light; this they called Paradise. In His messianic proclamation from the Cross ("Today") Jesus effects a transition from the Jewish hope of Paradise to the Christian hope of union with Christ: "You shall be *with me*." This word makes clear that even immediately after death the righteous man enjoys the companionship of the king of the messianic kingdom.[16]

We are indebted to Luke also for the revealing incident of Stephen's death. The account in Acts 7:54-60 makes clear that even though the thought of the Parousia dominated the mind of the early Christian writers, they possessed at the same time a concept of union with Christ at death. As L. Cerfaux points out, it is the Christ of the Parousia whom Stephen beholds.[17] The circumstances of the vision, however, indicate that His presence is meaningful here and now. Christ does not "sit" at the right hand of the Father in the role of Parousia judge. Instead He "stands" in an attitude of expectant welcome. The words which Stephen utters, "Lord, receive my spirit," are the very words which Jesus used to surrender Himself into the bosom of His Father (Lk 23:46). "With these words he (Stephen) fell asleep." [18] The real meaning of this cliché, so frequent in Jewish literature, must be gleaned from the context. There is no question of "awaking" only at the final resurrection. Even at the moment of death Stephen lives in some way "with Christ."

St. Paul's Eschatology

St. Paul has hardly made any real advance beyond these contributions of St. Luke. In his eschatology as in his anthropology he is a Pharisee of the Pharisees; he knew and accepted what was best in Jewish thought. There is great value, however, in studying his contribution. As the theologian of the Church he saw clearly what Christianity had done to sharpen the focus of Old Testament revelation and to illumine it with the light of Christ.[19] Second, his letters are the earliest writings of the New Testament period, not written like the Gospels to reproduce the words and teachings of Jesus but to show the full mind of the Church in Paul's own day. In reading his epistles, therefore, we come to grips with flesh and blood Christianity between 50 and 60 A.D.—its attitudes and interests.

In these letters the Parousia comes frequently to the fore, not only in the beginning of his ministry (it is the whole problem of Thessalonians) but also at its close. In dying Paul looks forward to "that day": "There is laid up for me a crown of justice which the Lord, the just Judge, will give to me in that day; yet not only to me, but also to all those who love His coming" (2 Tim 4:8).[20]

In the captivity epistles his attention to the mystery of Christ leads him to concentrate on anticipated eschatology; through the *arrabon* of the indwelling Spirit (Eph 1:14), the Christian has already begun his future life.[21] If anything, however, this foretaste serves to whet the desire for that day when, through resurrection, the whole man shall be with the Lord.[22]

This prospect of a rich personal experience provides only a partial reason for the magnetism of the Parousia. The last day drew the mind of Paul much more because it represented the salvation of the whole Body of Christ for the glory of the Father. For Paul the Hebrew, salvation had to include the note of solidarity and further the glory of God. For Paul the Christian this meant the Resurrection of the whole Body of Christ for the glory of the Father. "Then comes the end, when He delivers the kingdom to God the Father. . . . And when all things are made subject to Him, then the Son Himself will also be made subject to Him who subjected all things to Him, that God may be all in all" (1 Cor 15:24,28).

St. Paul's Teaching on Death

In Paul's judgment nothing could compare with the final consummation. For up until the Parousia death would reign; and for Paul death is not a mere biological fact but a tyranny, a penalty for man's offense which lay heavy not only upon the living but also in some way even upon the dead.[23] The symbol and effect of sin . . . was a power hostile to God which would continue to blight humanity even until the very end: "The last enemy to be destroyed will be death" (1 Cor 15:26). Paul's lack of interest in the immediate aftermath of death and his yearning for the Parousia make clear that in his judgment even those who have died in the Lord still lack something.

In this regard it is significant that when the Thessalonians mourn their dead (1 Thes 4:13) the apostle does not comfort them with the reminder of a consummation in glory already achieved. He is content simply to point out that the living will have no advantage over the dead at the time of the Parousia (1 Thes 4:14-18). He says nothing more than this to reconcile his readers to the fate of those who have already died. For Paul the Hebrew, death stripping man of his body stood in open hostility to the full consummation of God's glory and man's definitive salvation.

This attitude is fundamentally biblical and Hebrew. Paul's yearning for the Parousia echoes the hope of the author of Daniel for the total messianic victory over sin (Dn 9:24-25). The apostle shares fully the ardent longing of the prophet who looked beyond the "seventy weeks" to the definitive defeat of all evil and the total realization of all good.

The Christian Note in Paul's Teaching

There is, however, another essential element in Paul's teaching, and this is formally Christian. It is this aspect of his doctrine which illumines death with truly Christian light.

Through an act of supreme generosity Christ has made Himself one with the human solidarity which lies under the burden of sin and death (2 Cor 5:21; Rom 8:3). As a man, incorporating in Himself all that is human, He went through death in order to change the whole meaning of death. On Calvary He faced all the horrors of a death which sin had made terrible. He endured the experience dreaded by every man as God's worst punishment, and thus He Himself underwent God's judgment on the fallen human race (Jn 12:31).

It was precisely by this act that Christ took the bitter sting out of death (1 Cor 15:56-57). Because He was God's own Son, death *had* to be for Him the doorway to life, the return to the bosom of His Father. Previously death was the consummation of man's separation from God; in Christ it became the way to God. Previously it was the symbol of sin separating man forever from the living God. In Christ it became the supreme manifestation of loving obedience which promised immediate access to God.

Such a death, the death of God's own Son beloved by the Father and totally devoted to the Father, contained a compelling right to glorious risen life with the Father. "He became obedient unto death, even to death on a cross. *Therefore* God has exalted Him" (Phil 2:8-9). The connective "therefore" marks the consequence not of mere promise but of inherent necessity. Resurrection was contained in the very nature of this death as the life of the flower is contained in the seed.

For Paul nothing could be more definitive than the death-Resurrection of Christ. His *transitus* from life in this world broke the tie which bound Him to *sarx*, the solidarity of earthly existence, with its inherent qualities of weakness, mortality, and distance from God. Death swept Him out beyond everything which bore the blight of life upon earth—the flesh and the law, sin and suffering, earthly weakness and death itself. Through Resurrection He began an entirely new life in which He could give full play to the love and power which is His as messianic Son of God: "We know that Christ once raised from the dead, is never to die again: He is no longer under the dominion of death. For in dying as He died, He died to sin, once for all, and in living as He lives, He lives to God" (Rom 6:9-10).

A Further Christian Note in Paul's Teaching

There is also another factor equally essential to Paul's thought. The death-Resurrection of Christ is of benefit not only to Himself but to all Christians. He died and rose again as a corporate personality, bearing all men in Himself to the Father. The Hebrew conception of corporate personality underlies Paul's whole concept of the role of Christ. Like Adam, Christ embodies and represents all men; He is the new Adam (1 Cor 15:22,45-49; Rom 5:14-19). Through the law of solidarity, therefore, His death and Resurrection are efficacious for all: "We have come to the conclusion that, since one died for all, therefore all died" (2 Cor 5:14). The experience of Christ, like the life in Adam, has power to extend and to renew itself in every man. That is why Paul can write in the name of every Christian: "With Christ I am nailed to the Cross. It is now no longer I that live, but Christ lives in me" (Gal 2:20).

Paul is not speaking of mere external imitation—"As Christ . . . so the Christian." His thought rests not on the level of external concomitance but on the deeper level of organic functioning. He speaks of the experience which he describes as life "in Christ Jesus."

In the Pauline vocabulary this phrase means a real and psychosomatic union between Christ and the Christian. Through baptism the neophyte is so united to the risen body-person of the Savior that he shares the very life of Christ and becomes capable of extending the influence of His personality: "All you who have been baptized into Christ have put on Christ. There is neither Jew nor Greek; there is neither slave nor freeman; there is neither male nor female. For you are all one in Christ Jesus" (Gal 3:27).[24]

This union is both real and dynamic, bringing a vital share in the redemptive mysteries of Christ's own death and Resurrection. What Christ has done in His body in dying on the Cross and in rising from the dead is shared and reproduced in the Christian. The union between them is as exclusive and communicative as that of man and wife. This truth comes to clearest expression in Romans 7:4: "Therefore, my brethren, you have died to the law by becoming identified with the Body of Christ, and accordingly you have found another [husband] in Him who rose from the dead, so that we may bear fruit for God."

The Christian does not merely assent psychologically to the redemptive activity of Christ, as some of the Lausanne scholars would hold. If that were the case, Calvary would be nothing more than another Sinai, and our justice would no longer be the gift of Christ but the wages of our own tedious human effort which always fails. To this latter suggestion Paul would have only one answer—*me genoito!* It repeats the fundamental error of the Judaeo-Christians which Paul strove against throughout his ministry. He himself knows no other way of justice except that which he describes in Philippians 3:8-10: "I count everything dung, for the sake of gaining Christ and finding myself incorporate in Him, with no righteousness of my own, no legal rectitude, but the righteousness which comes from faith in Christ. . . . All I care for is to know Christ, to experience the power of His Resurrection, and to share His sufferings."

All this becomes possible through the gift of the Spirit which the Christian receives when he is united to the body-person of Christ in baptism. For the Spirit renews in the member of Christ the very death which the Savior died on the Cross (death to the flesh and to sin); at the same time He vitalizes the Christian with the very life which Christ Himself now lives in glory.[25] This share is so real that Paul does not hesitate to write: "We were buried with Him by means of baptism into death, in order that, just as Christ has arisen from the dead through the glory of the Father, so we also may walk in newness of life" (Rom 6:4).

Effect of Union with Christ: Death-Life

This sharing in the mysteries of Christ is real, yet not static. All during his days upon earth man must live *en Christo* while at the same time continuing his human life *en sarki*. The criss-cross of these two levels leads inevitably to tension and contradiction. Man is constantly drawn to assume again the "mind of flesh" (Rom 8:5) which represents primarily a denial of man's dependence on God and a proud confidence in what is of mere human effort or origin. To react against this the Christian must often renew his baptismal death to sin and to *sarx* (Rom 6:12ff.; Col 3:5-11).[26]

Life with God, too, must know its constant deepening and increase (Col 3:1-3). If the Christian has "put on" Christ at baptism, he must ever continue to "put Him on" more and more throughout the course of his life upon earth. The mystery of Christ's Resurrection once shared in is to be lived always more intensely. Christian life, therefore, knows a fundamental law of growth—*magis magisque*. The conformity to Christ which gives new shape and new vitality to the whole personality at baptism is to grow constantly until at last it becomes perfect conformity through the Parousia resurrection.[27]

It is unfortunate that Paul's words on bodily resurrection in 1 Corinthians 15 have so often been considered apart from the consistent doctrine of the rest of his epistles. This has led to the mistaken notion that the final change will have in it something quasi-magical. Many indeed think of resurrection only as a physical resuscitation. They have overlooked Paul's words on the bond between resurrection and the indwelling Holy Spirit (Rom 8:11). This Spirit is always at work preparing the Christian for the Parousia by perfecting his likeness to Christ. The glorious moment of bodily resurrection, therefore, is but the last and consummate stage of that conformation to Christ which has been going on all during life.[28]

The Full Pauline Perspective

We are now in a position to estimate the full Pauline perspective on death and the Parousia. As a Jew and as a Christian he could not think of man's perfect salvation except in terms of the full glory of God, the full redemption of the solidarity, the full conformity of all men to Christ through the Parousia resurrection. Obviously, therefore, his best thoughts always rested on the end-time of perfect consummation. Whatever took place before that was simply the development of man's first conformation to Christ through baptism.

Père Feuillet has aptly pointed up what is essential in this perspective:[29]

> Paul is interested above all in two crucial moments of our participation in the risen life of Christ: baptism which inaugurates this sharing and the Parousia which consummates it. Baptism makes us one with Christ in His death and Resurrection; the glorious Parousia places the final seal on our conformity to Him. All that takes place between these two moments does not establish any really new relation to Jesus.

Physical death, therefore, claims no special attention in Paul's letters. In his eyes it does not bring that full life with God which only the *total* man can know. For this resurrection is necessary, the resurrection of the individual and of the people of God. Death, therefore, marks only one more moment in the progressive conformation to Christ which is life's whole purpose.

He conceives of it only in the line of the progressive mortification of *sarx* which began at baptism.[30] Paul envisages all Christian existence as a death realized in principle on Calvary (2 Cor 5:14), commenced in fact for each Christian at baptism (Gal 2:20), continued all through life (Rom 6:12; Col 3:5), and completed by death "in Christ" at the term of one's earthly existence.

Death, therefore, is significant in Paul's mind not because it marks the consummation of entry into a new solidarity (only the Parousia could do that) but because it marks for the Christian the dissolution of the old solidarity of *sarx*. Even this significance, however, must be qualified. The dissolution is only partial; for the solidarity of the *sarx* is bound up with "this age" rather than with this earth. Even those who have died in Christ must still await the "redemption of the body" and the restoration of all things (cf. Rom 8:23).

Paul's First Word on Death—Philippians 1:21-23

We cannot say, however, that Paul was indifferent to the experience of death. He has spoken of it twice, and both times with an awareness that death is a blessing.

In Philippians 1:21-23 the apostle, faced with martyrdom, expresses his longing for death and speaks of it as "a gain." [31] "For to me to live is Christ and to die is gain. But if to live in the flesh is my lot, this means for me fruitful labor, and I do not know which to choose. Indeed I am hard pressed from both sides—desiring to depart and to be with Christ, a lot by far the better; yet to stay on in the flesh is necessary for your sake."

The most obvious remark one can make on these words is to note that were it a question of choice between life and the Parousia, instead of between life and death, Paul would not have experienced his present uncertainty in making a choice.

In the present instance he inclines toward death. His reasons appear in the very words he employs. He sees death as a departure from the world of *sarx* and therefore the last stage in his baptismal death to sin and weakness. This means conversely an intensification of his life "with Christ." [32] From now on he would walk uninterruptedly in that "newness of life" which has been his since baptism (Rom 6:4). Death, therefore, is a true "gain" rendering definitive his baptismal death with Christ and intensifying his baptismal life with Christ.

The fact remains, however, that death is not the Parousia. It affects only Paul and not the solidarity. It brings the dissolution of *sarx* for Paul but not for the world. It lends new intensity to his personal life with Christ; but it does not bring life to the *whole* man. Death, therefore, leaves much to be desired. And so, apart from this single fervent wish in Philippians 1:21-23, Paul centers his attention throughout the rest of the epistle on the Parousia (cf. 1:6; 1:10-11; 2:16; 3:21; 4:5).

Paul's Second Word on Death—2 Corinthians 5:1-10

This same spirit pervades Paul's second word on death—in 2 Corinthians 5:1-10. In this passage, moreover, he makes explicit the perspective which governs all his thinking. He begins with the mention of resurrection (5:1) and ends with the reminder of judgment (5:10). The Parousia is always to the fore in his thought.

He is aware, though, that life has its immediate term in death when man leaves his body "to be at home with the Lord" (5:8). Interpreted in the light of Paul's constant and fervent devotion to Christ, this phrase has overtones of a rich personal companionship, which becomes all the more constant once *sarx* is laid aside.

To lay aside *sarx*, however, means to lay aside the body also. This prospect fills him with dismay (cf. 5:4). He frankly confesses that it takes courage to face this ordeal, for "to be unclothed" ruptures the securities of life as man knows it; death even at its best is an exile (5:8).

Once more Paul has sketched his scale of values. No matter what death may achieve in intensifying life with the Lord it cannot match the full and rich consummation of the Parousia.

Conclusion

It is now clear that early Christian thought laid little emphasis on death and its immediate aftermath; interest centered chiefly in the Parousia. It was the task of later theology to illumine the interim period between death and final consummation. This it did by focusing the light of precise philosophy on the data of revelation to formulate a full thesis on the beatitude of the soul immediately after death.[33]

Unfortunately, the modern mind (product of nineteenth-century subjectivism and individualism) has so concentrated on the "salvation of the soul" at death that it no longer adjusts easily to the complementary perspective of the Parousia.

The vision of the early Church, however, is the very perspective most needed in our day. The salvation of all men and the glorification of the total man through resurrection are divine answers to a communism which glorifies the collectivity and looks upon man above all as an animated body.

The salvation of the body corporate and the renewal of family ties before the Father on the last day provide a living hope which gives moment and meaning to our present ecumenical efforts.

The ultimate glory destined by God for the whole world is one of the best incentives to true Christian humanism. It is in the light of the Parousia that men come to understand best of all their duty to develop the world's resources, to foster men's talents, to lift human life from an inferior to a higher level. This is not merely a matter of social obligation or of civic pride; it is rather the working out of God's plan for the consummation of all things at the Parousia. For what will this final consummation mean except that once more the whole world which God has created will come completely under the control of Christ, Christ completely under His Father, giving into His hands the family and the Kingdom which He Himself has perfected.

References

[1] The Jewish theories of retribution are treated at length in the following studies: R. H. Charles, *A Critical History of the Doctrine of a Future Life in Israel, in Judaism, and in Christianity* (London: Black and Co., 1899); G. F. Moore, *Judaism in the First Centuries of the Christian Era*, II (Cambridge: Harvard Uuiversity Press, 1958), pp. 279-322, 377-95; M. J. Lagrange, *Le Judaisme avant Jésus-Christ* (Paris: Gabalda, 1931), pp. 343-63; E. F. Sutcliffe, *The Old Testament and the Future Life*, 2 ed. (Westminster, Md.: Newman, 1947); A. Gelin, *The Key Concepts of the Old Testament*, tr. G. Lamb (New York: Sheed and Ward, 1955), pp. 70ff.; R. Martin-Achard, *De la mort à la résurrection d'après l'Ancien Testament* (Paris: Delachaux et Niestlé, 1956).

[2] A. Gelin, *Key Concepts*, p. 73, tries to schematize in three stages the development of the Israelite doctrine of retribution: (1) Divine retribution is conceived of as something collective and temporal; (2) as something individual

and temporal; (3) as something individual and other-worldly. He adds significantly, p. 79, "It will be recognized that my schematized presentation of these problems is not, necessarily, rectilinear or strictly chronological."

[3] G. F. Moore, *Judaism,* p. 318, points out that the slow arrival at full doctrine on reward in the after-life really gave Israel an edge over other religions whose notion of the after-life took early origin in the ancient myths.

[4] Besides the notable differences in the doctrine of Pharisees and Saducees, we must also take into account our uncertainty about a Qumrân doctrine of resurrection. Cf. M. Burrows, *More Light on the Dead Sea Scrolls* (New York: Viking, 1958), pp. 343-52, esp. 344-46.

[5] In many of their views the Saducees tended to be conservatives who refused to accept that progress in dogma which flowed logically from the principles of the ancient faith.

[6] J. A. T. Robinson, *The Body: A Study in Pauline Theology* (Chicago: Regnery, 1952), p. 14, draws this precise distinction between the Hellenic and Hebrew concepts: In the Hellenic conception of man "the body is nonessential to the personality: it is something which man possesses, or, rather, is possessed by. 'The Hebrew idea of the personality,' on the other hand, wrote the late Dr. Wheeler Robinson in a sentence which has become famous, 'is an animated body, and not an incarnated soul.' Man does not *have* a body, he *is* a body. He is flesh-animated-by-soul, the whole conceived as a psycho-physical unity."

[7] G. F. Moore, *Judaism,* pp. 311-312; R. Martin-Achard, *De la mort à la résurrection,* pp. 25-27. This same emphasis is observable also in the Qumrân Scrolls; cf. M. Burrows, *More Light on the Dead Sea Scrolls,* pp. 295-96.

[8] Jeremia 31:29-34; 18:11; 25:5; 35:15; Ezechiel 18. When in 587 the era of the covenant seemed to be near its end, Jeremia was led to formulate the idea of the new covenant.

[9] The Israelites, like many primitive people, believed that the dead are found assembled in a vast territory which is reserved for them, in general under the earth. The world of the dead, Sheol of the Hebrews, is comparable to Hades of the Greeks and Arallu of the Assyro-Babylonians. If the Israelites borrowed this idea from their neighbors, this borrowing antedates the entry of the Hebrews into Palestine; cf. E. Dhorme, "Séjour des morts chez les Babyloniens et chez les Hébreux," *Revue Biblique* (1907), pp. 5ff. In late Israel Sheol became a place of both reward and punishment, a provisory resting place where the dead await the final consummation.

[10] The compelling influence of the thought of God's glory is seen most clearly in Deutero-Isaia.

[11] The Alexandrian Book of Wisdom is not a finished treatment of eschatology; Cf. Wisdom, 1:12-14. It must be complemented by other streams of tradition in Israel, for example, Daniel and the apocalyptic writers.

[12] G. F. Moore, *Judaism,* pp. 287-322, surveys the inter-Testamental literature and indicates all occurrences of this theme.

[13] C. H. Dodd, *The Parables of the Kingdom,* (London, 1946).

[14] H. Conzelmann, *Theology of St. Luke,* tr. G. Buswell (London: Faber and Faber, 1960), p. 96, points out that Luke has recast much of the primitive eschatological material to bring out the timeless and ethical application of the doctrine on the hereafter.

[15] G. W. MacRae, S.J., "With Me in Paradise," *Worship,* 35 (1961), 235-40.

[16] This aspect was unknown in Jewish theology of the interim period.

[17] *Christ in the Theology of St. Paul,* tr. G. Webb and A. Walker, (New York: Herder and Herder, Inc., 1959), p. 72.

[18] In ancient times death was spoken of as a sleep. The New Testament also uses this word, but with a different accent.

[19] There is considerable progress in Paul's doctrine, a progress which consists in rendering explicit everything that belief in the final resurrection involves—baptismal resurrection, the rigorous imperative of moral resurrection, and the glorious resurrection at the end. Cf. A. Feuillet, "Le mystère Pascal et la résurrection des chrétiens d'après les Épîtres pauliniennes," *Nouvelle Revue Théologique* (1957), pp. 337-54.

[20] Not only the expression "in that day" but also the word for "coming" (*epiphaneia*) are technical terms denoting the Parousia.

[21] O. Cullman, *Christ and Time,* tr. Floyd V. Filson (Philadelphia: Westminster Press, 1949), p. 72, speaks of the Holy Spirit as "the anticipation of the end in the present."

[22] Cf. Paul's description of the activity of the Spirit in Romans 8:1-17 with the words which immediately follow (8:18-25) wherein he describes man's desire for the Parousia.

[23] Death, as man's destiny, "came by man" (1 Cor 15:21); as a fate, if not as a biological fact (Paul never so distinguishes), it "entered into the world . . . through sin; and . . . passed unto all men, for that all sinned" (Rom 5:12). Cf. S. Lyonnet, "Le péché originel et l'exégèse de Rom 5:12-14," *Recherches de Science Religieuse,* 44 (1956), 63-84.

[24] The doctrine briefly summarized here has been called the "lynch-pin" of Paul's thought; cf. J. A. T. Robinson, *The Body,* p. 48. The theme is developed at length in "The Christian's Union with the Body of Christ in Cor, Gal, and Romans," *Catholic Biblical Quarterly,* 23 (1961), 199-201.

[25] It is the presence and activity of the Holy Spirit which explains the bond between the Body of Christ and the renewal and transformation of the bodies of those who are united to it (cf. Rom 8:11; 2 Cor 5:17). By union with the Body of Christ the Christian receives the powers of the age to come, just as the beneficiaries of the healing miracles of Jesus received His power. This explains why, at the stage of 1 Corinthians (11:29-31), Paul explains sickness and death as resulting from the profanation of the Eucharist. . . .

[26] This directive for Christian life recapitulates the message of the Old Testament, "Cursed be the man who trusts in human beings, who seeks his strength in flesh, whose heart turns away from the Lord" (Jer 17:5).

[27] This bond between baptism and eschatological glory is expressed in Ephesians 5:26-27.

[28] It is interesting to note the concatenation involved in Paul's use of the verb *enduesthai* to describe the Christian's relation to Christ. In Galatians 3:27 he speaks of initial union with Christ by saying that all the baptized "have put on Christ" (*ependusasthe*). In Romans 13:14, Ephesians 4:24, and Colossians 3:10, he employs the same metaphor to urge progress in developing the Christian spirit. Finally, in 2 Corinthians 5:4, he once more uses this verb to show that the resurrection of Christians at the Parousia is but the perfect consummation of the "putting on" of Christ which baptism has inaugurated: "We do not wish to be unclothed, but rather clothed over (*ependusasthai*), that what is mortal may be swallowed up by life."

[29] Père Feuillet, "La demeure celeste et la destinée des chrètiens," *Rech Sc Rel,* 44 (1956), 401-402.

[30] Physical death, therefore, consummates the sacramental death of baptism. Christian tradition in the early centuries was in line with Pauline thought when it spoke of Christian death, at least of martyrdom, as a second baptism, the baptism of blood after that of water; cf. Tertullian, *De Baptismo,* 16

(*PL* 1:1217); Cyprian, *Epist*, 77 (*PL* 4:418); Cyril of Jerusalem, *Catech*, III, 10 (*PG* 33:340); Augustine, *De Civitate Dei*, 13:7 (*PL* 41:381-382).

[31] The language of Paul in this passage shows considerable Greek influence. This does not mean, however, as Père Dupont suggests, *Syn Christo, L'union avec le Christ suivant saint Paul* (Paris: Desclée, 1952), p. 186, that "Hellenism has taught the apostle to conceive of the life of the soul separated from the body." If Paul had grasped that, it would have come to the fore in his following epistles.

[32] Père Dupont, *Syn Christo*, pp. 181-87, recognizes in this phrase the connotation of personal companionship which he would not concede for the same phrase in Thessalonians. One wonders if Paul, the ardent apostle, could have written this phrase at any time without thinking of a deeply personal bond.

[33] Cf. Decree of Benedict XII in the Constitution *Benedictus Deus*. Here he affirms that *mox post mortem* the purified are rewarded with beatific vision.

FRANK B. NORRIS, S.S.

The Christian and the Trinity

The questioning reader will find in this brief, rather personal but very pointed essay a discussion of questions such as these: What has the traditional theological treatise on the Trinity done to make the presentation of this doctrine seem rather dry and impersonal? Why were the Christians of the first three centuries less self-conscious in their expression of this mystery? What was more dynamic about the ancient way of speaking of the three persons? How does Sacred Scripture describe our relation to each of the three persons? What expressions does Scripture prefer when speaking of the Father? of the Son? of the Holy Spirit? How true is it that the Trinity is in some sense *our* mystery?

Father Norris teaches theology at St. Patrick's Seminary in Menlo Park, California. He is the author of *God's Own People*.

The understanding of the Blessed Trinity I had as a child—and, candidly, for some time after I had reached my majority—was something like this. I realized that the inner life of God is essentially a mystery, a reality beyond man's power to comprehend or fathom. For His own good reasons—and again, candidly, I did not see what they were—God had told us something about His inner life, something we can't possibly grasp. Perhaps it was to test our obedience. Perhaps it was to test our humility—to see if we would bow our proud minds and accept the difficult truth. At any rate, whatever

This paper was originally delivered at a study group session at the North American Liturgical Week held in Oklahoma City. It was published in the *Proceedings* by The Liturgical Conference and is reproduced here with permission.

His reasons were, God had told us that while He is one in nature, He is triune in personality. If, then, He had spoken, I had no choice but to believe. The mystery of the Blessed Trinity is something every orthodox Christian must accept, simply and solely because God Himself has spoken. But that is about as far as my appreciation of the doctrine of the Trinity went. I certainly did not see how the mystery entered practically, effectively, daily, into the life of the ordinary Christian. The truth was something one accepted reverently—because it concerned God. It was something one believed humbly—because man's puny mind cannot be expected to understand God. But it was hardly the center of a Christian's life. I can remember, indeed, my puzzled reaction the first time I heard the statement that the Christian life is essentially an entering into the Trinitarian life. I thought the remark somewhat "rare" and exotic, something that applied to mystics, perhaps, but hardly to ordinary Christians. . . .

Perhaps my experience was exceptional. Perhaps I just did not receive the message that the rest of my fellows were getting. Somehow, however, I feel that such was not the case. I dare say that many . . . [others] were "introduced" to the mystery of the Blessed Trinity in much the same way. We were given a brief, precise, and theologically correct statement of the mystery. We were given a static, objective, "impersonal" view of the mystery of God's own nature. And that is about all. I submit that under such conditions it is difficult to conceive of any deep and vital "devotion" to the Blessed Trinity. It is difficult to see how the Christian will think of the mystery of the Trinity as *his* mystery. He will accept it, of course. He will believe it. But it will not mean much in his everyday life as a Christian.

For the first three centuries of the Church's life the situation was altogether different. The appreciation the average Christian had of the mystery of the Godhead was, from one viewpoint, considerably less precise and less clearly formulated than is ours. There was, for example, no uniform terminology employed throughout the Universal Church when speaking of the Trinity. We today have learned from the time we were children to speak of one *nature* and of three *persons*. The terminology is uniformly accepted and used by all Catholics, indeed, by all orthodox Christians. The early Church had no such precise terminology. The Christian of that day knew, indeed, that he was no polytheist. God was one. When he spoke of

"God," he thought first of all of God the Father. Yet he knew, too, that Jesus was God's Son, Himself divine and—most important of all—Himself the proper object of divine worship. He knew that he offered a worship to "the Lord" that indicated His essential equality with the Father. The Holy Spirit, too, was seen as belonging to the "sphere" of the divinity. He was the personal Principle within a Christian which gave him a share in God's own life—and therefore must Himself be divine. For the most part, however, the ordinary Christian was content to let things go at that. He was not theologically self-conscious about formulating his belief concerning the nature of God, considered objectively. Not that there was a total absence of theological speculation concerning the Trinity during those first centuries of Christianity. What speculation there was, however, never assumed great proportions and certainly did not affect the life of the average Christian.

While the early Christian's understanding of the Blessed Trinity from the static viewpoint was imperfect when compared with ours, his appreciation of the mystery was immeasurably richer from another viewpoint. He saw his Christian life as essentially a Trinitarian life. He saw himself as vitally related to each one of the persons of the Trinity. In a word, his view of the mystery was a dynamic one —with the dynamism on the part both of God and of man. It was the very one reflected in the pages of the New Testament.

What is this dynamic view of the mystery of the Godhead familiar to Christians of all conditions in the early Church? Briefly it is this. The Father is seen as the source and origin of all things, as the One who out of love has created us and out of love has made us His sons, who has become *our* Father. The Son is seen as the Bridge, the Mediator between the Father and mankind, as our Way to the Father. The Son has taken us by the hand, as it were, and leads us to the Father. It is because the Son of God became man and our Brother that we have access to the Father, the Invisible God. Divine though He is as Son of God, He is, for us, before all else our Mediator and Way to God. The Holy Spirit, finally, is seen as the supreme Gift of Father and Son to us, as the personal divine Guest within us whom we receive from Christ, who hallows us with Christ's own life, and who, therefore, enables us to call God "our Father." "God has sent the Spirit of His Son into our hearts," St. Paul writes to the Romans, "in virtue of which we cry out Abba! Father!" God the Father is *our* Father because we are joined to Jesus His Son. We are vitally linked to Jesus because He has poured forth His Holy Spirit into our hearts.

Furthermore, because the Spirit is one and indivisible, He is the supernatural bond of fellowship linking Christian to Christian. He is the Soul of the Church. The liturgical doxology common throughout the first three centuries of the Church's life summed up well the early Christian's view of the mystery of the Trinity. "Glory be to the Father through the Son in the Holy Spirit." We can approach and give glory to the Father because we have been made members of His only-begotten Son. And we are living members of the Son because we have been immersed, as it were, all of us, in the living and life-giving Holy Spirit. "Glory be *to* the Father—*through* the Son—*in* the Holy Spirit." St. Paul gives us an insight into his own dynamic view of the Blessed Trinity in the sentence with which he ends his second letter to the Corinthians. To his converts he writes: "The grace of the Lord Jesus Christ, and the love of God, and the fellowship of the Holy Spirit be with you all." Grace—love—fellowship: each noun is significant. The attribution of each noun to a specific person of the Godhead is important.

"The *grace* of the Lord Jesus Christ . . ." It is from the Son Incarnate that we have received "the grace," that is, the gift of divine life restored, of adoptive sonship renewed, of reconciliation to the Father effected. It is the Son who brings us "the grace." He is our Way to God.

"The *love* of God (the Father) . . ." The word for love here—*agape*—means for St. Paul totally outgoing, selfless love. It is particularly attributed to the Father ("God"), who is the beginning and source of all things, whose sole motive for creating us and for making us His sons was love. Before all else God is a Father who *loves* us.

"The *fellowship* of the Holy Spirit . . ." It is the Holy Spirit communicated to each Christian in baptism and confirmation who has broken down the barriers which sin erected between man and man, who has formed us into the one Body of Jesus Christ, through whom we have "fellowship" with one another, with Christ, and with the Father. "The fellowship of the Holy Spirit be with you all."

It should be clear, I think, that the earlier, dynamic view of Trinity is one which can and should be the center of a Christian's life. Seen from the viewpoint of vital relationships, the mystery of the Blessed Trinity *is our mystery*. How the dynamic view of the Godhead was replaced, in practice, by the static view is answered by history. The Arian crisis of the fourth century, which called into question the divinity of Christ, forced Christians to focus their attention upon the absolute equality of the three persons of the divinity. Under the pressure of an inevitable reaction against heresy the ancient dynamic liturgical doxology gave way to the theologically precise but static formula: "Glory be to the Father and to the Son and to the Holy Spirit." It fixed our attention upon an important truth concerning God's nature—one which needed to be asserted in the face of heresy. But it had the unfortunate side effect of pushing into the background of Christians' thinking an equally true and practically more relevant truth about the relationship of the persons of the Blessed Trinity to those who have been given a share in Their inner life.

I submit, in conclusion, that unless we restore—or rather give—to our faithful the dynamic, scriptural understanding of the mystery of the inner life of God, there can be no such thing, in practice, as a living devotion to the mystery of the Blessed Trinity. . . .